The Art of Teaching Philosophy

ALSO AVAILABLE FROM BLOOMSBURY:

Doing Philosophy, by Danielle Lamb, David Mossley,
George MacDonald Ross, and Clare Saunders
Doing Philosophy Comparatively, by Tim Connolly
Teaching Philosophy, edited by Andrea Kenkmann
The Philosophy Skills Book, by Stephen J. Finn

The Art of Teaching Philosophy

Reflective Values and Concrete Practices

Edited by Brynn F. Welch

BLOOMSBURY ACADEMIC
LONDON • NEW YORK • OXFORD • NEW DELHI • SYDNEY

BLOOMSBURY ACADEMIC
Bloomsbury Publishing Plc
50 Bedford Square, London, WC1B 3DP, UK
1385 Broadway, New York, NY 10018, USA
29 Earlsfort Terrace, Dublin 2, Ireland

BLOOMSBURY, BLOOMSBURY ACADEMIC and the Diana logo are
trademarks of Bloomsbury Publishing Plc

First published in Great Britain 2024

Copyright © Brynn F. Welch and Contributors, 2024

Brynn F. Welch has asserted her right under the Copyright, Designs and
Patents Act, 1988, to be identified as Editor of this work.

For legal purposes the Acknowledgments on p. xiv constitute
an extension of this copyright page.

Cover design by Louise Dugdale
Cover images: Top, HolyCrazyLazy © Shutterstock
Bottom, Segeng © Shutterstock

All rights reserved. No part of this publication may be reproduced or
transmitted in any form or by any means, electronic or mechanical,
including photocopying, recording, or any information storage or
retrieval system, without prior permission in writing from the publishers.

Bloomsbury Publishing Plc does not have any control over, or responsibility for,
any third-party websites referred to or in this book. All internet addresses given
in this book were correct at the time of going to press. The author and publisher
regret any inconvenience caused if addresses have changed or sites have
ceased to exist, but can accept no responsibility for any such changes.

A catalogue record for this book is available from the British Library.

A catalog record for this book is available from the Library of Congress.

ISBN: HB: 978-1-3504-0482-3
       PB: 978-1-3504-0481-6
       ePDF: 978-1-3504-0483-0
       eBook: 978-1-3504-0484-7

Typeset by Integra Software Services Pvt. Ltd.
Printed and bound in Great Britain

To find out more about our authors and books visit www.bloomsbury.com
and sign up for our newsletters.

*For my dad and Liz, the two best teachers I've ever had.
I want to be just like you when I grow up.*

Contents

List of Figures xii
List of Tables xiii
Acknowledgments xiv

Introduction Brynn F. Welch 1

Part I The Philosophy Course

1 **De-centering the Professor (Not by Design)** Karen Adkins 13

2 **Freedom Anchoring: Teaching Philosophy as a Dialogic Endeavor** Corey Reed 23

3 **Syllabus Design and World-Making** Rima Basu 41

4 **Deadlines, Learner-Centeredness, and Nonideal Pedagogy** Christopher Blake-Turner 49

5 **Philosophy through Spectacle** Meg Wallace 57

6 **Ethics for Everyday Life: Designing a Core Philosophy Course** K. Lindsey Chambers 69

7 **Less Is More: How and Why to Avoid a Content-Driven Class** Heather Anne Phillips 77

8 The (Un)Political Classroom: How Content and Positionality Intersect to Encourage Students to Be Agents of Change *John R. Torrey* 85

9 A Student's Reflections *Zyaire Hadrian Agee* 91

Part II The Philosophy Classroom

10 Save the 1001 Cats! Lecture as a Performance Art *Jimmy Goodrich* 97

11 Flatten That Hierarchy: Everyone Wins When We All Teach (and Learn) Together *W. John Koolage* 101

12 Trust in the Classroom *Barrett Emerick* 111

13 What to Do When Students Don't Do Course Readings *Alida Liberman* 119

14 When Conversation Goes Wrong: Managing Student Errors *Russell Marcus and Alessandro Moscarítolo Palacio* 129

15 Gender Dynamics in the Philosophy Classroom *Harry Brighouse* 139

16 Cultivating Playfulness for Unlearning in the Philosophy Classroom *Rebecca G. Scott* 145

17 When Crito and Plato Came to Class: Gameful Learning in the Philosophy Classroom *Greta LaFore* 153

18 Not Just for the Kids: Using Children's Literature and P4C Methods in the College Classroom *Karen S. Emmerman* 161

19 Participation as Gratitude Practice *Stephen Bloch-Schulman* 167

20 In Conclusion, I Don't Know: Humility as the Beginning and End of Every Class *Brynn F. Welch* 173

21 A Student's Reflections *Anna E. Ulrey* 183

Part III Exercises and Assessments

22 A Primer for Assessing Dispositional Growth *David W. Concepción* 189

23 Dialogue, Virtue, and Assessment: Teaching for More than Technical Proficiency *Kristopher G. Phillips* 197

24 Student Transformation through Civic Engagement Projects *Monica "Mo" Janzen and Ramona Ilea* 209

25 Discussion, Self-Assessment, and the Discussion Moves Framework *Christopher Blake-Turner* 217

26 Argument Diagramming as a Teaching Tool for Philosophy *Maralee Harrell* 227

27 **A Jigsaw Lesson for Symbolic Logic** *Russell Marcus* 235

28 **Teaching with Puzzles** *David O'Brien* 245

29 **Students Make Pudding** *Stephen Bloch-Schulman* 253

30 **Prisoner's Dilemma and Prisoner's Delight: A Simple Activity That Helps Students See the Complexity of Others** *Joshua DiPaolo* 261

31 **Will the Gendered Division of Labor Be an Issue in Your Generation? An Exercise** *Harry Brighouse* 269

32 **Feminist Critiques of the Original Position** *Susan Kennedy* 273

33 **The Clear and Concise AF Assignment: A Quick and Effective Way to Teach Basic Writing Skills** *Dustin Locke* 281

34 **Emile and Sophie on Tinder: Using Social Media as an Assessment for Philosophy** *Claire Katz* 289

35 **On Writing Fun, Joyful, Open-Ended Exams** *C. Thi Nguyen* 297

36 **It's Not "Stephen's Final" Project** *Stephen Bloch-Schulman* 305

37 **A Student's Reflections** *Micah Williams* 313

Part IV What Comes Next

38 The Why and How of Mentoring in Undergraduate Philosophy Teaching *Emma Prendergast* 323

39 Making Teaching Count *Britta Clark and Gina Schouten* 333

Notes on Contributors 342
Index 351

Figures

5.1 *The Circus Lab* at the University of Kentucky. Photo credit: Ayna Lorenzo 58

20.1 A web showing connections between topics named each week in a Bioethics syllabus and the connections between these topics. © Brynn F. Welch 180

26.1 An argument diagram representing an argument for reducing greenhouse gas emissions. © Maralee Harrell 229

27.1 The three steps of the jigsaw lesson. Each member of each base group attends a work group with a different topic, and then returns to their original base group. © Russell Marcus 236

Tables

20.1 Decision grid: Cochlear implant debate
© Brynn F. Welch 179

24.1 The Organize an Activity experiment
© Monica Janzen and Ramona Ilea 212

24.2 Scaffolding optional experiments
Reproduced with permission 213–214

Acknowledgments

First and foremost, this book would not have been possible without the brilliant contributors who took a leap of faith in responding to a random email not so long ago. Your enthusiasm for teaching is unmatched, and your creativity has been nothing short of inspiring. Reading your work has been one of the highlights of my career as an academic philosopher, and I cannot believe how lucky I am to know and work with you all. Thank you so much for sharing your time and wisdom.

Suzie Nash and Colleen Coalter at Bloomsbury Academic, thank you both for your constant support and guidance. Special thanks to Colleen for thinking through titles while touring elevators. Anna Ulrey, thank you for sharing your time and wisdom, graciously reviewing everything I sent your way. Harry Brighouse, thank you for treating advising as a lifetime gig. Thanks to Josh Filler, the first teacher I started stealing ideas from. It became a habit that resulted in the idea for this book. I have learned so much from the teachers and students at Red Mountain Community School, who have patiently challenged everything I thought I knew about education. Thanks to you all.

I teach about family, so it's only fitting to recognize the emotional labor of those who listened to endless updates on the book's progress. Mom and Dad, thanks for so enthusiastically getting on board with the whole philosophy thing. Lizzy, Charlotte, and Kevin, there are not enough pages in any book to tell you how grateful I am for you. When I started this project, we had no idea how many hours it would consume, how much table space I would occupy, or how many of my "good thing, bad thing" dinner discussions would be about this book. Liz and Charlotte, thank you so much for your help coming up with titles. They were all magnificent, just like you. Kevin, thank you for always believing in me and in this project. I love you all to pieces.

Finally, thanks to my students. I have learned so much about teaching, the classroom, your experience, and what I want the world to be like just from being in the room with you. Please keep pushing us to be better. You deserve it.

Introduction

Brynn F. Welch

An Origin Story

When I was in graduate school, there was one class graduate students taught that was something like a rite of passage. For most of us, it was our first time taking full responsibility for the design and implementation of an entire semester-long undergraduate course. This was our chance to fly solo! Sort of. The class satisfied a university-wide writing requirement, which meant that instructors had clear requirements their course had to include. By the time any of us taught the class, we had worked as a teaching assistant for several faculty usually across a range of courses. We'd be observed at some point during the semester. Additionally, the class was capped at a small number and met more frequently than other classes, so we got to know the students well. In short, there were enough guardrails that it was a relatively safe solo-flying experiment.

    A friend of mine gave me his syllabus so I could think about how I wanted to design my class. At the top, he'd included a quote from Socrates: "We are discussing no small matter, but how we ought to live." Had I ever read this quote? No. Is it still—almost two decades later—at the top of almost every syllabus I use? Absolutely. This is true for two reasons. First, as soon as I saw the quote, I thought it offered a nice way to signal to students that what we're doing here really does matter to them. Second, I reasoned that he was quite a good teacher, he was farther along in the program than I was, and that if it worked for him, I wanted to use it.

    Both experiences—learning to teach by teaching and shamelessly swiping ideas from excellent teachers—have been recurring themes in my professional development. Indeed, I would wager that trial by fire is how most professional philosophers (most academics, really) learn to teach and that most of us rely heavily on advice and tips from those around us. Many if not most of my best "moves" as a teacher are the result of casual hallway chats with other teachers about what works (or doesn't) for them.

Learning to teach often involves practicing, or looking over someone else's syllabus, or simply observing styles we decide we like or don't like. However, teaching training rarely (if ever) requires that we take the time or space to reflect on the values we want to express in our own syllabus design, or in the eventual class itself. Additionally, the profession (and academia in general) offers relatively few opportunities to learn how to teach and plenty of disincentives for prioritizing teaching development during one's career. There are conferences, but travel money is limited, and the structure of the profession generally prioritizes research. There are blogs, but they are diffuse, and one must have a good sense of what one is looking for or check back frequently. There are journals, but these face some of the same challenges blogs face and can at times be something less than accessible for newcomers who just want some ideas for being a better teacher. Even the most well-meaning professors can find themselves without the resources—training, time, funds for travel, etc.—to devote to thoughtful course design and execution. Moreover, even if they did have plenty of resources to devote to their teaching, they might not know how to explain in performance evaluations or job applications why what they did mattered in the way other professional activities matter. In this edited collection, teachers who have devoted significant time and energy to developing their teaching strategies offer their own thoughts on how to teach philosophy well.

This collection explores what it means to teach a philosophy class, from content selection and deadline policies to reflecting on and developing one's own teaching in ways that are effective and manageable. Thoughtful teaching begins before the syllabus is written and continues well beyond the end of the semester, both in terms of mentoring students and in terms of the lasting impact (we hope) the class will have on the students who take it.

What follows is not merely an abstract discussion of theories of pedagogy, nor a recipe book for a philosophy class. It is neither entirely about the values at stake nor simply a collection of sample syllabi and assignments. Instead, the chapters here balance reflective values with concrete practices. The contributor list represents a wide variety of teaching backgrounds, approaches, and styles, as well as a staggering number of award winners.

The unifying theme is that every contributor thinks seriously about what it means to teach well and was graciously willing to share their experience with the philosophy classroom—including from the student perspective—so that others can benefit from it. Reflecting on how lucky I have been to receive so much brilliant teaching advice during quick chats with friends and colleagues when I run into them in a hall somewhere, it seemed only natural to try to expand the hallway. That is the goal of this book: to fill the hall with experts and invite everyone in to chat.

How to Use the Book

This collection is designed with institutional pressures and life constraints in mind so that anyone with a few minutes and some curiosity can learn something new they might consider adopting or modifying in their own teaching. The entire collection may just change what you think is possible in your own classroom in ways that are nothing short of thrilling. Nonetheless, each chapter stands alone as a quick hallway chat. Intended to be "bite-sized" reflections so that readers can maximize the benefit they get from hanging out in the hallway without having to maximize the time they spend there, the chapters are all considerably shorter than standard philosophy articles, including scholarly articles that focus on pedagogy. Have a few minutes and want to think about how you can encourage better discussion participation in class? You can quickly pick up the book—or step into the hallway—and hear what others suggest. Heading into a class with some skepticism about whether the students have done the reading? Not to worry. We've got you covered.

This book is structured to mirror the experience of teaching: designing the shape of the course all the way through assessments and then beyond that to figuring out how to make teaching count both personally and institutionally. As such, the book has four sections: The Philosophy Course, The Philosophy Classroom, Exercises and Assessments, and What Comes Next. What do you want your course to accomplish? How should you run your class to accomplish those goals? What do you want your students to be able to do, and how should you evaluate them when they do it? How can you reflect and report on what you've done?

Importantly, the contributors are not telling you what you should do or how your class should go. They are instead discussing how *they* think of these questions, giving readers time and space to reflect on whether and how that might work for their own classes. These chapters offer ideas, but they also offer inspiration. What a particular teacher does in their class may not work for you, but the creative spark each contributor lights certainly will. The length of the chapters here reflects our limitations as people with whole lives; the creativity of these chapters reflects our limitlessness as teachers.

The Philosophy Course

Teaching a course begins with the course design. Before entering the classroom or even crafting the syllabus, we have to consider what we hope to accomplish. Given the power dynamic between professors and students, instructors reasonably have a justificatory burden in designing their class, in terms of setting goals, selecting readings, setting deadlines, designing how the day-to-day class will run, and so on. They ought to have good reasons for designing the course the way they do.

The chapters in this unit explore questions ranging from the broad to the specific. For example, you might be thinking in terms of big-picture values, like what you ultimately hope students take away from your class. Karen Adkins shares how she encourages students to engage directly with one another about deep questions about what philosophy is and ways she designs her syllabus to reflect those deep questions. Corey Reed makes a case for thinking of our classes as teaching students to pursue capital-T Truth, in service to the pursuit of freedom, and this "freedom anchoring" should shape how we approach content selection and course design.

If you're thinking about the structure of your class, Rima Basu explains how we might conceive of syllabus design as world-making in roleplaying games, with quests and opportunities for students to level up. Christopher Blake-Turner shares their take on how to think about deadlines, both in terms of what's most beneficial for students and what's most manageable for the faculty juggling feedback schedules.

Perhaps you're focused on content selection and ways to engage students in the project of doing philosophy. Meg Wallace explains how she uses spectacle—specifically the circus—to encourage students to practice thinking in ways that are new and surprising to them, offering ways to think about including first-person performance, art, and play into the class. With so many of us teaching classes that satisfy core curriculum requirements, K. Lindsey Chambers offers a way of constructing such a class that can effectively demonstrate to non-majors why philosophy matters to them in their daily lives.

Heather Anne Phillips helps readers think about how *much* content is useful to schedule if teachers want to leave room for practicing the skills of philosophy, while John Torrey tackles the question haunting many in the discipline right now: what *can* I teach? In the face of constantly shifting political winds and mandates, how should teachers think about content selection?

Zyaire Hadrian Agee concludes this section by offering his perspective as a student. His discussion focuses on what it's like to be a student and encounter all of these decisions that have been made for you before you even walk into the classroom, including what it means to do philosophy, what sorts of questions matter enough to explore during the semester, and what it means to have answered those questions well. Importantly, he reflects on what it's like to disagree with those decisions.

The Philosophy Classroom

Of course, the classroom is distinct from the course design. We craft the course in our minds, but then we still face the day-to-day task of running the class. How do we balance lecture with discussion? When we lecture, *how* do we go about doing that? What are our goals? When we're leading a discussion and a student says false things, what should we do? What should we do if we notice that men are dominating the discussion? In a discipline in which we routinely push students to challenge their most deeply held values, how can we cultivate trust in the classroom space? What do we do when students aren't completing the course readings? These are challenging questions that often emerge in the moment we're teaching, and each class is different. Giving these teaching puzzles some thought ahead of time can help us better respond to the actual classroom environment as it evolves.

The actual teaching of a class can be daunting for many reasons, not least of which is that how well the class goes depends on the students in the room and how much we can—or should—trust them. We lose a bit of control from the course design phase to the classroom instruction phase. Our classroom can mimic dynamics that emerge in broader society, or it can teach students new ways of engaging with one another. Or it can do both! The contributors in this section offer their thoughts on what works (or doesn't) for them in the classroom itself.

Jimmy Goodrich explains how he conceives of the role of lecture in class to help students engage more meaningfully with both the professor and the material. W. John Koolage offers his reasons for thinking that extending more trust to students benefits everyone in the room, including the teacher. Similarly, Barrett Emerick also focuses on how to build different types of trust in the classroom in order to create the type of learning environment described by Paulo Freire. Of course, one natural worry is whether students will do the work we trust them to do. Alida Liberman offers thoughts on what to do when students don't do the reading assignments, while Russell Marcus and Alessandro Moscarítolo Palacio offer their diverging views on how to respond when students say false things during class discussion. Harry Brighouse helps readers think about how to respond if in-class discussion mirrors broader social gender dynamics, and how to help anyone who's speaking make more productive contributions to the discussion.

Philosophy is hard, and it is often new to our students. Rebecca Scott reminds us of why and how to cultivate playfulness into our classroom environment, and Greta LaFore suggests a way of framing philosophical discussion as a role-playing game to encourage student engagement and active learning. Karen S. Emmerman explains how the tools of Philosophy for Children (P4C) can help teachers facilitate community building and joy in college classrooms, as well.

Many philosophy teachers—myself included—focus on developing certain dispositions, and those must be modeled and practiced in class just as any other skill. Stephen Bloch-Schulman explains how he incorporates gratitude practice as part of students' participation, and I present my own approach to modeling and cultivating humility.

Anna Ulrey concludes this section with her student perspective on the classroom experience, including how she as a student experiences trust, active learning, and engagement. Importantly, she considers how what she learned in the philosophy classroom shaped how she learns outside of it, as well.

Exercises and Assignments

Whereas the first part focuses on shaping the course goals and content and the second part focuses on cultivating and managing in-class dynamics and dispositions, this unit focuses on what we ask of students and how we respond to what they give us. How might we think of constructing final exams, or even final products more broadly? How can we help students improve in discussion, and how can we assess their discussion engagement in ways that are both fair and manageable? How might we rethink what students should demonstrate in their work, and how can we craft assignments that help them take what they are learning beyond the classroom walls? Here, contributors offer some of their favorite in-class exercises, assignments, and feedback strategies.

David W. Concepción defends both the value of assessing dispositional growth and the practicality of such assessments. Kristopher G. Phillips explains how teachers can think about assignment design and assessment that can address both skills and virtues development, and how we can communicate our assessments to students in ways that model those virtues. Monica Janzen and Ramona Ilea give specific examples of ways they have encouraged student transformation using civic engagement projects in their own classes. Christopher Blake-Turner offers their strategy for encouraging students to engage more productively in discussion and to be more thoughtful about the ways they interact with others, as well as suggestions for how to assess those discussions.

Several contributors in this part offer methods that can help students approach and engage with a wide variety of content. Maralee Harrell explains how and why she uses argument diagramming to help students develop and strengthen their reading, writing, and analytical skills throughout the course, and Russell Marcus gives an overview of how teachers can use jigsaw lesson approaches to help students develop mastery of complex subjects while collaborating with one another. David O'Brien offers suggestions for using puzzles to help students engage without feeling overly protective of their own views but rather invested in the project of finding the truth, a project in which the teacher is a collaborator rather than an adversary or judge.

It is not uncommon for philosophy teachers to have a particular exercise they use to land a specific point while instilling in students a deeper appreciation for the *importance* of that point. Stephen Bloch-Schulman presents a specific exercise he uses to help students independently come to question their own intellectual (if not altogether sincerely held) commitment to naïve relativism that also invites them to reflect on the difference between verbally endorsing a view and being committed to that view in a deeper sense. Joshua DiPaolo shares an activity he uses in class that helps students both practice reasoning by engaging in either the Prisoner's Dilemma or Prisoner's Delight exercise and recognize that people who endorse different views than they themselves endorse may simply face different circumstances or have different information rather than being entirely different *sorts* of people. Harry Brighouse gives an in-class exercise he uses to help students both see that the gendered division of labor is at work in their own lives (and likely will continue to be) and resist the temptation to think that particular social problems merely reflect the moral failings of previous generations. Susan Kennedy shares her spin on a Rawlsian Original Position Exercise that helps students both understand feminist critiques of Rawls' work and better understand the power of priming and defaults in shaping their own worldviews.

Of course, a significant part of teaching is grading. How might we design assignments that both demonstrate what the students have learned and are manageable and—dare we dream—even *enjoyable* to assess? Dustin Locke shares his "Clear and Concise AF" assignment, which both helps students learn to write better generally (as opposed to learning to make this specific paper better) and helps make the instructor's grading more efficient. If you're considering trying alternatives to essays as assessments, Claire Katz discusses her own experiments using social media assignments to help students demonstrate content mastery and their own clever creativity. C. Thi Nguyen gives ideas for crafting exam questions that give students a chance to show off their engagement with the material while making their final interaction with the class a fun one, and Stephen Bloch-Schulman encourages readers to think about extending the final project beyond the classroom in ways that are genuinely meaningful to the students themselves.

When we design assessments, we are often asking ourselves what we want students to learn and how we want them to demonstrate having learned it. Micah Williams concludes this part with a student's perspective about how what he learned in philosophy classes has shaped who he is as a person and what he sees as his life's work going forward.

What Comes Next

Finally, the class ends. Despite submitting the grade, the work of teaching continues. Philosophy teachers mentor students both during and well beyond their time in class, and ideally, we also continue to develop as teachers and philosophers. In this final section, Emma Prendergast argues that given the nature of what we teach and discuss, philosophy teachers are especially well poised to serve as mentors and offers practical advice for how to do this mentoring work well. Britta Clark and Gina Schouten consider the apparent undervaluing of teaching in higher education and offer a discussion of practices that can help making teaching count, both for an individual philosophy teacher and—in the long run—in the profession as a whole.

Concluding Thoughts

Hallway chats about teaching have shaped who I am as a teacher since I started graduate school nearly twenty years ago. For many of us, friends and colleagues serve as the most significant resource in our teaching toolbox. Some teachers in the field may have benefited from sustained, effective professional development focused on teaching, and some no doubt enjoy institutional support and incentives for developing their skills as a teacher. Even with those support systems in place, however, many of us rely on hallway chats with our friends and colleagues.

Between the demands of life and the profession, there are far too few opportunities to sit and reflect on who we want to be as teachers and what we hope to accomplish in our teaching. The discipline is *loaded* with outstanding teachers who think carefully about what they do and why they do it. Whether that means asking for a few pointers or rethinking your role in the classroom and your class's role in the education of others, friends and colleagues are an invaluable resource. I am deeply grateful the contributors to this volume agreed to offer their thoughts and talents to those of us lucky enough to learn from them.

Teaching is a moral enterprise through which we reflect our most deeply held values and which reflects tremendous social trust in us. It matters that we do it well. See you in the hallway.

Part I

The Philosophy Course

1
De-centering the Professor (Not by Design)

Karen Adkins

I have been teaching college philosophy since 1991, and as such thought I had a pretty settled pedagogy that I mostly tinkered with around the edges (indeed, I wrote this almost verbatim in my last post-tenure review, submitted mere months ago). And yet, two of my recent experiments with my intro course, which were adopted for different reasons, ended up not just succeeding in their intentions but each contributing to another significant benefit. They de-centered the classroom, by which I mean discussion became nontrivially more student-driven, and crucially, student-to-student. In doing this, they've caused me to think about my assumptions about why a de-centered philosophy classroom matters, and how to go about getting there.

The idealized version of philosophy as practiced by seminar—vigorous give-and-take in discussion, positions that get modified, complicated, questioned, or rejected as discussion morphs and extends—is extremely difficult to enact in the introductory classroom. Far more common, no matter how gifted the pedagogue, is the more dyadic call-and-response form of discussion, where students participate mostly in response to a professor's questions or comments.[1] In my view, this ends up still putting too much pressure, and presence, on professors' organizing ideas and themes in a class, and makes it harder for students to experience their own sense of discovery in philosophy. While academics have advocated for strategies for de-centering the classroom since Paolo Freire's work in the 1970s, philosophy has seemed slower to de-center than other disciplines.[2] Recently, scholars have offered practical ideas for how to de-center the classroom (see Capps 2018; Englert

2020; Rempala, Sifferd, and Vukov 2021). These are exciting ideas, but some seem less well-suited to the introductory classroom, which is often filled with students there by requirement, not choice, who may have no intrinsic excitement for the material or the work. I want to talk about two different strategies I've experimented with recently that have had the benefits of de-centering the classroom. The first is diversifying the curriculum, and the second is Team-Based Textual Discussion and Analysis. Crucially, I adopted both strategies not for purposes of de-centering the classroom; this was an additional and unanticipated benefit in both cases.

My first experiment was Covid-induced; I chose to start diversifying the curriculum while preparing for my Fall 2020 course. Of the basic approaches to intro curricula (historical survey, major questions survey, deep dive into a few original sources), I have used a version of the deep dive approach virtually my entire career. I think there is value in students appreciating how hard it is to put together a series of philosophical positions that form a coherent worldview; students can appreciate how different philosophers have different starting assumptions or oversights when they look at their work in depth; choosing original sources carefully can create themes and debates that can emerge over the semester. But one trade-off to this approach is the relative loss of breadth and diversity[3] of reading material; with so many fewer sources used in the course, there are just fewer opportunities to have a wide range of authors and traditions represented.

When I was planning my first Covid class for Fall 2020, I realized that reading a few original sources in their entirety was not realistic in a semester where students would likely be jumping in and out of class regularly because they were in quarantine or sick. So I switched to a survey approach based on three major questions in philosophy, and took advantage of resources like the "Diversity Reading List" and the APA's "Diversity and Inclusiveness Syllabus Collection" to develop a significantly more diverse reading list for students.[4] One of the results I saw immediately in that semester, and continue to see in successive semesters where I use this syllabus, is a more participatory class, and in particular, one where students participate from a position of authority.

Let me speculate a bit about why too many of us are too slow about diversifying our syllabi. As many people note, most graduate programs in the United States focus on the Western philosophical tradition. Further, whichever of the methods of intro organization people choose, I think it is inevitable that we choose from a position of deep familiarity. We choose the texts, questions, or authors with whom we are most comfortable, or who interest us the most. But this puts us in a conventional position of expertise. The corollary here is that it can seem intimidating to take on many texts with which we haven't had meaningful exposure or expert guidance, and faculty can be worried about doing the work badly (not doing justice to the argument or position, not understanding enough background context). While resources exist to give faculty the background tools to address these gaps—the APA maintains an extensive list of organizations, articles, and other resources—I suspect that this can seem like a big lift for too many faculty.[5] And while I did background reading to give myself familiarity with authors before the semester started, I definitely felt the gap between my "back pocket" authors whose work was deeply familiar to me, and those where I had less confidence in what I was doing.

What I hadn't anticipated, and what I greatly welcomed, was the collaborative way in which students responded to this. I announced on the first day of the first class I taught with this syllabus (and have done so every time since) that this was an experiment for me, and that I was teaching authors and works with which I had varying levels of comfort and familiarity. In each semester, students have responded by talking about what they've learned about authors or traditions in their own reading or in other classes. For instance, when teaching Amy Olberding's article about how Confucianist ethics helps illuminate an ethical orientation in everyday life that Western ethics misses (2016), one of my students who was a history major put the Confucian approach into historical context, describing the ways in which Confucianism changed throughout the dynasties. It was valuable for students to see the ways in which ideas and beliefs form and change throughout political moments. Students brought other kinds of expertise to the class as well, and were free about offering it; a neuroscience major pushed hard on discussions about free will, a student whose spouse was from a different ethnic group resonated deeply with discussions of epistemic injustice, having witnessed small testimonial injustices when their family was in public spaces. Students seemed to find more entry places, whether from their academic experiences or their personal lives, to engage with the ideas we were discussing, and the class felt freer as a result.

My second experiment was also a result of Covid, specifically, our return to what we hoped would be "normal" in-person courses after the worst of the pandemic. Team Discussion and Analysis Assignments (TDAAs) were first created by one of my colleagues, Dr. Rebecca Vartabedian in 2018, and she has used them quite successfully in every intro course she has taught ever since. (We teach at a small Jesuit university where philosophy is a required core course, and thus each of us teaches at least one section of intro virtually every semester.) Most basically, this technique puts students into small discussion groups (membership stays the same for the whole semester), and the groups meet on their own as a replacement for a normal class session periodically throughout the semester (anywhere from four to eight times) to complete a focused group discussion prompt. Prompts can vary between deeper dives into texts students are reading for the class, or discussion of an applied or current issue that is related to the material for the course. Students are encouraged to meet in places where they can speak freely and sociably (i.e., meeting for lunch or coffee, or under a tree if the weather is nice). In other words, TDAAs are an attempt to simulate the parts of Socratic dialogues that get the most positive attention (minus, one hopes, the occasional drunkenness and overly aggressive questioning of interlocutors), and aim to give students a taste of the pleasures and benefits of free(r) intellectual inquiry. Students write up their notes from discussion and submit them for grades, to build some accountability into the practice. I incorporated this technique into my intro syllabus for the Fall 2021 semester, largely because this was my first in-person semester since the onset of Covid, and because I'd learned from a student affairs officer that our incoming first-year students were craving the sociality of college, and had missed many of these opportunities in the last eighteen months of online school. (No surprise there, as many faculty felt similarly.) In other words, I added this assignment to the class for largely social and developmental reasons, thinking it would benefit students to have more and more sustained opportunities for engaging with one another, and did not anticipate spillover benefits for "normal" classes where we were all together discussing the reading. Dr. Vartabedian and I have written elsewhere about some of the pedagogical and philosophical benefits of TDAAs, with more detail about how they work and how they can be adapted (Vartabedian and Adkins 2023), but here I want to talk about what was a very unexpected but welcome benefit for me of this addition to the classroom—the way in which TDAAs de-centered our full-class discussions.

While I have emphasized discussion in my introductory courses from the start of my career, and have adopted practices to make its value explicit (such as counting participation in discussion for a nontrivial part of the semester grade, using criteria to guide credit for participation, sending out periodic updates on how students are doing with respect to participation, designing both small-group and full-class discussion exercises that lead to writing exercises, etc.), it was still by far the exception rather than the rule for students to speak and debate with one another in our courses, as opposed to them speaking with me. But during the TDAA semester, students started responding to each other's observations with questions and alternatives almost immediately after the first TDAA, and it continued most days of the class. I think that the TDAAs helped in terms of opening up perspectives in the room.

What do I mean by this? When students develop significant familiarity with one another, they start to see each other as sources of knowledge or perspective. Because students met with the same group five times in a semester for an hour to ninety minutes each time, they were able to get more of a sense of how their partners thought about problems. Typical ways of organizing in-class discussion—random sorting into groups by techniques like counting off, or letting students organize themselves—do not guarantee any kind of continuity in discussion, or growing familiarity with discussion partners. In addition, because we did full-class debriefs of TDAAs in the session after students held them, we got to discuss this variety of responses and reactions people had to the prompts (both singly and in groups). Students could see that the variety of perspectives went beyond simply what the members of their own group thought and could recognize the ways in which different groups responded to prompts. And crucially, because students got additional depth and exposure to one another's ideas and beliefs in those TDAAs (particularly cumulatively), the idea that there were multiple ways to look at an issue or consider a question became more expected for students. To be sure, I think the unsupervised and un-surveilled nature of the TDAAs helps students take ownership of the prompts and encourages them to develop their own perspectives. But one of the side benefits of this ownership is a de-emphasizing of the importance of professor as philosophical tour guide, as students become more habituated to thinking of each other as sources of perspective and analysis. Indeed, in course evaluations, students universally encouraged me to keep doing the TDAAs, and one of the reasons that was cited multiple times in comments was the way in which doing the TDAAs opened up perspectives on the reading and issues we were covering. Through sustained conversation with the same discussion partners throughout the semester, students were appreciating reasonable ways people could develop different approaches or interpretations of philosophical texts or questions. It opened up the classroom.

Now, I want to be clear; these are both newer techniques for me, and it could be that I've simply been fortunate enough to have particularly chatty classes since Fall 2020, who would have been well primed for discussion with one another regardless of my assignments. But my observations here are less about just the quantity of student participation, but also about the quality. With both of these techniques, I've observed that the quality of student discussion with one another was comparable to if not better than other introductory courses I have taught, including Honors courses where I had students take turns as discussion leaders (which you would think would facilitate exactly that sort of regular, respectful peer-to-peer exchange).

De-centering is just one of many pedagogical objectives professors can have, so let me close by making a pitch as to why it matters. One of the texts I use in most of my introductory courses has been Jacques Rancière's *The Ignorant Schoolmaster* (1991). This brief book tells the true story of an aged French bureaucrat and school leader, Joseph Jacotot, who in the early nineteenth century is sent to Flanders to teach ambitious would-be civil servants French. Because the old pedagogue speaks no Flemish, he resorts to finding a facing-pages translation of a book and hoping the students can teach themselves, and he is astonished when the students not only are able to teach themselves French, but produce interesting and varied work as a result. There's a lot in this book (it's as much about equality and the state as it is about education), but I fundamentally love and teach this book because it is a defense of meeting one another directly, and it is this spirit I try to inculcate in my classroom. Both of these techniques—diversifying the curriculum and TDAAs—are different ways of explicitly de-emphasizing the importance of the professor in the learning process. I'm an old enough colleague that my graduate school training in teaching was relatively simple (the hot idea back then to stimulate discussion was to put the chairs in a circle). Both of these strategies are ways of producing what to me is most radical about Rancière's book: structuring the class so that students own their education, and experience the class as a collective enterprise of learning. Jacotot also didn't intend this outcome (he de-centered not by design), and the impact was transformative for him and for his students.

To be clear, these are both still experiments in the sense that they are both works in progress. There are steps I want to take to improve both of these strategies. And it's important for me to acknowledge that one commonality between these two strategies is me giving up control and direction of the course in some way, and that that is an easier thing to do for someone like me—a full professor, in her fifties, white, and at an institution that gives faculty lots of freedom to devise and revise their own syllabi—than for folks who are more precariously situated at their institutions or in the profession writ large. The main reason so many of us teach those "hip pocket" texts for intro is because of the comfort of expertise; we can anticipate and will be ready for the kinds of questions students are most likely to ask about the arguments or authors. I would not pretend that it's easy to give up this kind of security, or that faculty at all institutions would have the freedom to experiment with their syllabi or assignments.

But at least one workaround to this problem is captured in Luvell Anderson's and Arlen Erlenbusch's exploration of the ways one can diversify an introductory syllabus (2017), and that is simply the philosophical value in making our pedagogy explicit and invitational to students. They note that our decisions about what to include and exclude from our intro syllabi "inevitably also craft a story about what philosophy is. Rarely, however, do we make explicit and subject to scrutiny our commitments and presuppositions concerning the nature of philosophy" (Anderson and Erlenbusch 2017: 17). Doing this work openly with the students—telling them what we think philosophy is, and the way in which the work of philosophy has been contested and revised over the centuries—invites them into a conversation. I have practiced a small version of this invitation and transparency for years (predating both of these particular experiments). I've made it a point to highlight when I'm doing something different in a course, to explain why I'm doing it and what I hope to achieve, and to solicit student feedback (both generally when I first announce this, then explicitly later in the course, usually through a mid-term evaluation done anonymously through an electronic polling platform). Even when an experiment doesn't quite succeed or needs modification (and they sometimes do), this work functions to make the course open and give students co-ownership of the learning. I am telling them what I think is important in the course and for their learning, and how we might achieve it, and I make clear that I see their participation and contribution as essential to this work. And most crucially, I'm indicating that my perspective is provisional and revisable, which doesn't just allow but insists upon students thinking about what ideas are important to them. These experiments produced benefits I didn't anticipate but really welcome. Building space for us to be surprised by our work in the classroom invigorates education for everyone.

Notes

1. I say this as someone who has taught philosophy at the college level for over thirty years, and who has observed dozens of classes of colleagues. Even in the cases where small groups discuss material and report back to a larger group, reports are generally made to the professor; between-group dialogue and discussion is the exception, not the norm.
2. Casual discussions of why philosophy de-centers slowly often cite the abstract nature of the concepts or the difficulty of the readings as good reasons for the continued centrality of the lecture. While these are good reasons, it is striking that natural sciences like physics (which nobody would accuse of lacking abstract material or dense readings) have been able to incorporate de-centered or flipped classroom strategies.
3. I'm using "diversity" here to indicate both a greater representation of identities of the authors students read, and ideas and perspectives from non-Western traditions.
4. See "Diversity Reading List" and American Philosophical Association, "Diversity and Inclusiveness Syllabus Collection."
5. See American Philosophical Association, "Resources on Diversity and Inclusiveness."

References

American Philosophical Association. "Diversity and Inclusiveness Syllabus Collection." https://www.apaonline.org/members/group_content_view.asp?group=110430&id=380970. Accessed February 1, 2023.

American Philosophical Association. "Resources on Diversity and Inclusiveness." https://www.apaonline.org/page/diversity_resources#:~:text=APA%20Diversity%20and%20Inclusiveness%20Syllabus%20Collection%20The%20Committee,philosophy%20to%20create%20more%20diverse%20and%20inclusive%20courses. Accessed February 1, 2023.

Anderson, Luvell, and Verena Erlenbusch (2017). "Modeling Inclusive Pedagogy: Five Approaches." *Journal of Social Philosophy* 48(1): 6–19.

Capps, John (2018). "The Case for Discussion-Intensive Pedagogy." *APA Newsletter on Teaching Philosophy* 17(2): 167–73.

"Diversity Reading List in Philosophy." https://diversityreadinglist.org/. Accessed February 1, 2023.

Englert, Alexander (2020). "Philosophical Think Tanks." *Teaching Philosophy* 43(4): 357–81.

Olberding, Amy (2016). "Etiquette: A Confucian Contribution to Moral Philosophy." *Ethics* 126(2): 422–46.

Rancière, Jacques (1991). *The Ignorant Schoolmaster: Five Lessons in Intellectual Emancipation*. Trans. Kristin Ross. Redwood City, CA: Stanford University Press.

Rempala, Kit, Katrina Sifferd, and Joseph Vukov (2021). "Philosophy Labs: Bringing Pedagogy and Research Together." *Teaching Philosophy* 44(2): 187–206.

Vartabedian, Becky, and Karen Adkins (2023). "Building Autonomy and Trust in the Introductory Classroom: Team Discussion and Analysis Assignments." *APA Studies in Teaching Philosophy* 22(2): 2–8.

2

Freedom Anchoring: Teaching Philosophy as a Dialogic Endeavor

Corey Reed

How can we improve our instruction and facilitation of topics concerning lived experiences like race, sex, class, sexuality, ability, etc., in philosophy classrooms, specifically in introductory courses and courses that do not address these issues in their title or course objectives? My proposition is that we should first examine how we, the instructors, are construing the purpose of academic (undergraduate) philosophy and what overarching thematic outcomes guide our courses. I take this as a starting point to address what I call the *sprinkling* problem, where issues regarding oppressed agents, marginalized philosophers, and questions about applied theories of resistance and revolution are at best *sprinkled* into a course to diversify it. If the topics are addressed at all, they are periphery to the main objectives of the course, and how philosophy is being construed. In order to decolonize[1] this, I argue that we must change our approach to philosophy as a Higher Education major, a field of the Academy, and whatever its raw definition is (we often gesture to its Greek meaning *philosophia* or *the love of wisdom*). To accomplish this decolonial work, and open space for marginalized conversations to become central, and not secondary, I argue that a good starting place is thinking of philosophy as a dialogic endeavor: an academic pursuit of truth shaped as a journey toward greater freedom through dialogue.

Philosophy has always prioritized the pursuit of truth since its ancient origins, not just in the Western tradition of the ancient Greeks, but also in ancient Egyptian texts like "The Declarations of Innocence" in *the Book of the Dead* (1500 BCE) which says, "Hail, Lord of Right and Truth, who comest forth from the city of Right and Truth, I have not been an eavesdropper … I have not stopped my ears against the words of Right and Truth" (Budge 1895: 347–9). Coupled with *Truth* (capitalized here on purpose, which suggests the meta-normative version of the epistemic term), *Right* is understood in its meta-normative, moral connotation. If we examine these terms together, the pursuit of *rights* and *truths* likely leads to a confrontation of knowledge that is unknown or restricted, suggesting that epistemology and morality lead to issues of domination and isolation regarding *rights* and *truths*. Philosophy, from this perspective, can be understood as a pursuit of liberation: moral, epistemic, or otherwise. We are trying to free ourselves from ignorance by expanding our knowledge.

To use a more contemporary example, we can think about freedom's relationship with philosophy in the Beauvoirian sense, where the "supreme end at which man must aim is his freedom, which alone is capable of establishing the value of every end" (Beauvoir 1948: 121). Beauvoir thinks of freedom as that "end of all ends" because of the imposed restrictions the world, and those within it, constantly ascribe to agents (a form of *immanence*), and our journey is to *transcend*, or to constantly go beyond those restrictions that are proposed as givens in our reality. Whether that restriction is a direct oppression, signified by suffixes like – ism and – phobia, or something indirect, like the difficulty reaching for certain truths, philosophy is largely a project of freedom.

I take my position regarding philosophy's dialogic nature from Paulo Freire, whose definition of dialogic education I utilize, and bell hooks's conceptualization of theory as a liberatory practice. First, Freire gives the following statement:

> I consider the fundamental theme of our epoch to be that of *domination*—which implies its opposite, the theme of liberation, as an objective to be achieved … In order to achieve humanization, which presupposes the elimination of dehumanizing oppression, it is absolutely necessary to surmount the limit-situations in which people are reduced to things.
>
> (Freire 2000: 103)

Freire's dialogic framework comes from the idea of *dialogue,* or to foster conversation where the oppressed, to some extent, get to be "masters of their thinking" (Freire 2000: 124). We know that the "history of [Western] philosophy" has often been construed as an ongoing (isolated) set of dialogues, where medieval philosophers like St. Thomas Aquinas and St. Augustine respond to the ancients, and Descartes responds to them, and Kant responds to Descartes, and so on. However, there are clear voices missing, ignored, or silenced in these dialogues. We get the opportunity to reclaim some of this by centering freedom as a point of departure for the endeavor of Philosophy. Without dismantling these isolated conversations, our curriculum's diversity measures become *addendums* to core problems instead of *eliminating* core problems. I take a decolonial approach, instead of a diversity one, because diversity still perpetuates the centering of a singular conversation, or way of knowing. In diversifying, those voices would be integrated, but not centralized, or regarded as representative of philosophy generally.[2] Part of the issue is that the discipline of philosophy (lowercase *p*) is often regarded as synonymous with the Western canon, and Philosophy (the meta ideal captured as capital *P*), whether that represents a set of methods for inquiry and analysis or simply an unconfined *love of wisdom*, needs to be recentered.

Following Freire, hooks asserts that "[t]he classroom remains the most radical space of possibility in the academy" (hooks 1994: 12). This is key to understand in conjunction with her later assertion in *Teaching to Transgress*:

> If we examine critically the traditional role of the university in the pursuit of truth and the sharing of knowledge and information, it is painfully clear that biases that uphold and maintain white supremacy, imperialism, sexism, and racism have distorted education so that it is no longer about the practice of freedom.
>
> (hooks 1994: 29)

Philosophy, as a discipline within the university, is not exempt from this. In fact, with it being the discipline from which the others derive, there is something essential about hooks's assertion as it pertains to philosophy. In its generalized pursuit of a certain *kind* of truth, it has participated in the imperialization of other ways of pursuing *Truth* and *Right*.

A dualistic purpose comes from this problem: (1) that centering freedom addresses the imperial history of Western philosophy, making racist, sexist, classist philosophies and philosophers face themselves in our approach to the content, and (2) that centering freedom addresses our issues in contemporary university approaches to knowledge, by embracing philosophical ideas that may not follow certain historical conversations, but push us toward freedom in that subject, nonetheless. The latter is what Kristie Dotson is thinking through in both "Concrete Flowers: Contemplating the Profession of Philosophy" and "How is this Paper Philosophy?" She asserts that "[p]hilosophy simply cannot survive as a discipline without the continuous creation of new ideas" (Dotson 2011: 408) and so she also suggests that philosophy needs a *culture of praxis* that has

> (1) Value placed on seeking issues and circumstances pertinent to our living, where one maintains a healthy appreciation for the differing issues that will emerge as pertinent among different populations and
>
> (2) Recognition and encouragement of multiple canons and multiple ways of understanding disciplinary validation.
>
> (Dotson 2012: 17)

Both of these points from a *culture of praxis* are products of centering a concept of freedom. Theorizing freedom helps us to see and address issues "pertinent to our living," and recognizes that philosophy itself needs to be freed from the West into its larger ideal, which embraces multiple ways of knowing and being without a geographic center.

This is why diversifying the actors in a syllabus is only step one and not decolonization in itself. As Lewis Gordon states:

> reducing philosophy to epistemology and logical analysis is a distortion of philosophy. Rejecting those reductions also leads to the question of what other dimensions of philosophy to reject as practitioners of the discipline reach out beyond questions of what they can know and support with formal argumentation.
>
> (Gordon 2021: 57)

Truth, in its definition and our pursuit of it, is often construed in a limited set of ways, and we teach with those approaches largely because those are the tools we were given in our training, and we want to prepare our students to engage the same metrics of knowledge we faced (graduate school). However, that is not the totality of philosophy. We choose our methodologies and the philosophers to cover with the same problem Sylvia Wynter highlights in her concept of *poetics*, where "*Poetics* [is] (Western/real/true poetics) [and]—Ethnopoetics—The Other Poetics" (Wynter 2022: 437). Philosophy is a *Poetics*, a discourse of naming and signifying the world, and thus, our approach to philosophy must recognize this distinction and be honest in seeing the restriction we help to facilitate. Philosophy is not decolonized until "Ethnophilosophies," or the philosophies that are *othered*, are usurped by what Wynter calls "the concretely human global, the concretely WE" (Wynter 2022) as opposed to the tribal "We." That is a freedom project. In order for our students to experience philosophy in our classes without continuing traditions of restriction, silencing, and devaluing various ways of knowing, and for us to decolonize our university's/discipline's colonial remnants, we should center freedom.

By *centering (anchoring) freedom*, I am suggesting that we make philosophy an introspective endeavor, where we (academic philosophers), and our students, turn the canons of philosophy against whatever we take its meta-objective to be, hoping to expand (and free) philosophy from the restraints that have been historically put on it. To illustrate what I think centering freedom does to Philosophy courses, I provide the following eight subclaims:

1   Freedom anchoring can create space for any domain or approach to philosophy to discuss sociopolitical issues.

In teaching Africana Philosophy as my department's capstone course, I taught two of Anton Wilhelm Amo's texts regarding what we call "Philosophy of Mind." He has a small section on "Liberty" in *Philosophical Disputation Containing a Distinct Idea of Those Things That Pertain Either to the Mind or to Our Living and Organic Body* (1734) where he says, " … with respect to the whole man[,] liberty is the absence of an impediment in the mind's operation by means of the body" (Amo 2020). I want to draw a few things from this quote and Amo generally: (1) Amo is in direct dialogue with Descartes, and yet he is rarely taught. The argument could be that his thought does not yield the same benefits as others, but as an eighteenth-century African figure that *is* in the dialogue already, it is interesting that he is avoided or unknown; (2) the sociopolitical value of this quote regarding slavery and colonial restrictions of the mind/body is evident, and ignoring that value could be an opportunity lost and a missed component to Amo's contribution to the field of "philosophy of mind;" and (3) although he uses his legal training and his familiarity with Descartes to formulate his argument, his preservation of the spiritual in his philosophy of mind is an important interjection into this domain of philosophy. Anchoring *freedom* thematically allows Amo and others to be utilized, not because of their contribution to the Western canon (although that is relevant for Amo), but because their philosophies push humanity toward greater freedom, and the utility of that coincides with the theme of the course, making the figure and the philosophical contribution central to the project of the course.

2 Freedom anchoring can conceptualize inquiry and critique as a liberatory praxis because philosophy's pursuit of [T]ruth is anchored in making humanity freer.

bell hooks thinks theory should be a liberatory practice, although it is " … not inherently healing, liberatory, or revolutionary. It fulfills this function only when we ask that it do so and direct our theorizing towards this end" (hooks 1994: 61). Patricia Hill Collins, in her text *Intersectionality as Critical Social Theory*, states, "Existential freedom is meaningless without critical praxis, yet critical praxis needs theoretical ideas such as existential freedom" (2019: 220). The theoretical is bound up in the applied, and vice versa. Anchoring freedom as the purpose behind our philosophical endeavor allows for this symbiotic relationship between the most complicated theories to sociopolitical situations of oppressed people. She also states:

> Dialogues are essential because no one individual or interpretive community can wrap its arms about the magnitude of intersectionality itself, nor can the arguments of a small number of intellectuals or the practices of one resistant knowledge project become the template for intersectional theorizing.
> (Collins 2019: 221)

A dialogic approach is relevant here. When I teach Feminist Theory, I make it clear that even within women's liberation frameworks, there are multiple canons we must address because of the complicated and intersectional issues of sexism, racism, classism, etc. We need Black Feminism, Womanism, Third World Feminism, Transfeminism, etc., to conceptualize and address not just women's issues, but philosophical conceptions of defining the *human*. It cannot be singularly construed, meaning that it cannot be only one thing and it cannot be signified and analyzed by only one group. Freedom anchoring demands a collective praxis in pursuing freedom via knowledge. That collective project embraces cross-disciplinary philosophies, analyses beyond geographical borders, and an open epistemology, where everyone can contribute to what knowledge is.

3 Freedom anchoring can make the applicability of philosophy more visibly evident to our students.

We are facing a "why is philosophy relevant?" conundrum as it pertains to students majoring in the subject and taking our classes. I share the worry of Martin Luther King, Jr. where he says:

> Every man lives in two realms, the internal and the external. The internal is that realm of spiritual ends expressed in art, literature, morals, and religion. The external is that complex of devices, techniques, mechanisms and instrumentalities ... Our problem today is that we have allowed the internal to become lost in the external.
>
> (King 1968:181)

We address this university-wide focus on the *external* by coming into a contemporary understanding of the *internal*. This means that philosophy, understood *through* a social justice lens, should focus on issues of race, sex, class, etc., not because they are trendy in Higher Education currently, but because they speak to this lived moment and experiences of our undergraduates and they are central to our discipline. We must focus on philosophy that speaks to them, and all of it can if we anchor it and direct it in certain ways. Philosophy, as a major, may not appeal to students captivated by the capitalistic project (even though many departments have shifted their advertisement because of this to law school training, etc.). However, for the students who came to college to study, or discovered during their studies, issues and causes that they care deeply about, philosophy is a great discipline to examine those issues and causes through. It requires us, however, to be honest about our discipline's history regarding certain oppressions. For example, I teach the historical parts of "Philosophy of Race and Racism" twofold: (1) the general, historical development(s) of the term "race" by Johann Friedrich Blumenbach, Charles Darwin, and others, and (2) the explicitly philosophical contributions to race and racism in Kant, Hegel, and others. I do a similar analysis of philosophy in Biomedical Ethics, where I center Black and Brown women's experiences in the course and confront philosophy's contribution to the epistemic injustices these agents face. Decolonizing philosophy means we must address its role in perpetuating oppressions. It is up to us to show the connection between the method/tradition we are teaching and the causes they care about. I think that is done best when we center philosophy as a dialogue about freedom.

4 *Freedom anchoring can help facilitate the incorporation of ignored, silenced, and denigrated voices.*

My students had not heard of Bayard Rustin prior to my class, and his historical silencing is likely due to him being a queer, Black political philosopher. That is an intersectional problem in itself, but I highlight him as an interesting case for political philosophy. It would be easy to say that because he does not fit into social contract theory, Marxism, or similar political philosophy paradigms well, he should not be considered a social/political philosopher. However, when we get to meta-ideals of political philosophy—the Aristotelian *polis* and the structuring of a city-state, organizing laws, natural and socially constructed rights, varying types of justice, and the like—Rustin is a critical theorist to engage as he simultaneously thinks about race, class, sexuality, and politics in his theories and applies them to the varying methodologies of protest. His 1977 speech entitled "A U.S. Coalition on Human Rights" discusses the moral imperative to combat injustice across nation boarders to prevent infringements on "Freedom of Speech … assembly and association, including the right to form trade unions … An independent judiciary … Freedom of artistic and intellectual expression … [and] Religious liberty and freedom of movement" (Rustin 2003: 328). He gives vital insights into democracy, justice, and nonviolent protest.

However, like Alain Locke and others, despite his comments on political philosophy, he is rarely utilized. The counterargument could be that he is not historical, meaning that his work does not inform future political ideas in the same way as John Stuart Mill's *On Liberty* does, for example (which I often pair them together). My first response would be that construing philosophical relevance via historical influence is a flawed approach for the reasons I mentioned earlier about ignored and silenced voices. My second response would be that coupling historical texts (and by this I simply mean texts that inform later texts, but may or may not fit into the Western History of Philosophy proper) with contemporary texts on political themes is a decolonial approach worth investigating if and only if they can be evaluated as texts of equal relevance. For example, W.E.B. Du Bois's "Of the Ruling of Men" from *Darkwater* coincides well with Aristotle's questions of the responsibility of the citizen, or full member of the *Polis*, in his *Politics*. Pairing these two texts raises important questions about voting rights and education in political philosophy. This pairing is done best when the themes are coinciding toward some metanarrative or overarching goal, and I suggest freedom to be the target that makes these texts from varying historical points come into philosophical harmony for our students. Each text would be read as an evaluation of openings and closings of freedoms for humanity, our society, or individual agents. Anchoring freedom allows silenced voices to emerge and that content to be recognized as *equal* philosophy to Western traditional texts.

5 Freedom anchoring can encourage philosophy to be practiced as a revolutionary act in our students' future occupations.

I tell my students that because philosophy is a critical discipline, whose purpose is primarily to question structures, systems, beliefs, ideologies, etc., this enterprise is a risky one. I view myself as a philosophical "optometrist" of sorts, and my job is not to tell you what to think, but to give you a variety of glasses by which to see the world. There are some glasses that will fit the worlds they will enter into well, and there are some that will help them see *through* those worlds and wrestle with the problems underneath that many try to avoid or exist ignorant of. I let my students decide, like the *Matrix* (1999) red pill/blue pill choice, but the one thing I ask my students to do throughout the course is "throw everything into the fire and see what comes out." My hope is that even those who choose to stick with their dispositions that are oppressive have taken more time to critically assess *why* they believe what they believe.

We joke about Socrates's accusation of "corrupting the youth," but in this dog-whistling war against Critical Race Theory and the like, corrupting the youth is exactly what we must do. Not corrupt them into thinking monolithically or dogmatically but corrupt them as in facilitating the questioning of socially constructed ideas that they take for granted. As Fanon ends his text *Black Skin, White Masks* with the declaration, "O my body, make of me always a man who questions!" (1986: 232), so, too, does Socrates take questioning to be essential as he famously states, "the unexamined life to not be worth living" (Plato 1984: 92). Philosophy pushes critical questioning, and anchoring our courses with the concept of freedom allows our students to critically engage their future occupations and determine how they want to exist in them. This is a clear task when teaching Biomedical Ethics, Business Ethics, Tech Ethics, etc., to students majoring in those fields. However, this is also a key concept for courses that do not, by title or objective, speak to their future occupations directly. We can inspire change by pushing our students to prioritize freedom as the anchoring question from which we explore. However, when we address oppressions directly in these courses, the realities that are uncovered are serious, and the potential recoil for junior faculty is dangerous. Revolution always is, which is why I think many shy away from thinking of philosophy in such a way. However, if wisdom is bound up in the task of freedom, then it is likely true that philosophy, understood through wisdom and freedom, should address that which is revolutionary, disruptive, countercurrent, and occasionally violent.

6 Freedom anchoring can unify philosophy in a way that allows for social justice to be the focus across courses and activism to be part of the philosophical project of the classroom.

This is not the approach of all philosophers; there are many that may not think of philosophy as a social justice enterprise across its subdomains. However, there is something to the connection between social justice, activism, and philosophy. I want to evoke the legacy of Kwame Ture, Huey P. Newton, and Angela Davis. All three of these scholars and social justice theorists are formally trained in the discipline of philosophy. Angela Davis, in her "Lectures on Liberation," begins with the following statement:

> The idea of freedom has justifiably been a dominating theme in the history of Western ideas. Man has been repeatedly defined in terms of his inalienable freedom. One of the most acute paradoxes present in the history of Western society is that while on a philosophical plane freedom has been delineated in the most lofty and sublime fashion, concrete reality has always been permeated with the most brutal forms of unfreedom, of enslavement.
>
> (Davis 2018: 110)

This passage from Davis is in direct conversation with the Hegelian Master-Slave (Lord-Bondsman) dialectic. Angela Davis also gives this important account regarding her time as a philosophy professor:

> I was hired by UCLA's Department of Philosophy to teach courses in Continental Philosophy, I welcomed the opportunity to teach courses in the tradition forged by Kant, Hegel, and Marx. Such courses would allow me to put to good use my training as a student of Herbert Marcuse and Theodor Adorno. But I was also deeply interested in the emergence of Black Studies … Consequently I decided to design a course that I called "Recurring Philosophical Themes in Black Literature" … The overarching question I considered in the course was that of liberation. I intended to think about liberation both in broad philosophical terms and in the way the theme of liberation is embedded in the literary history of black people in North America.
>
> (Davis 2012: 194–5)

Liberation was not only her approach to philosophy and literature but to her career as an academic instructor. For Davis, it is critical that the theoretical ideals of philosophy explicitly engage the issues of people's lives. Her training in, and approach to, philosophy has clear influences on her abolitionist, socialist, feminist, and Black radical political ideologies.

A similar statement can be said of Kwame Ture (formerly known as Stokely Carmichael). Ture's 1966 "Black Power" speech cites Albert Camus, Jean-Paul Sartre, and Frantz Fanon to question if one can condemn themselves, and he sides with Fanon saying that condemnation is not internal, but externally imposed. He suggests that "[i]n order to escape that oppression we must wield the group power we have, not the individual power that this country sets as the criterion under which a man may come into it" (Ture 1966). Freedom from oppression comes from the unraveling of individuality and focusing on group coalition. In *To Die for the People*, a collection of Huey P. Newton's writings, Newton evokes three political philosophies that do a sort of freedom anchoring: intercommunalism, revolutionary love, and revolutionary suicide. Newton, in conversation with Marx and Lenin, believes in an intercommunal redistribution of material resources to all communities, especially the disenfranchised. Revolutionary love[3] is what makes "common cause with these oppressed communities" (Newton 1972: 22) and revolutionary suicide, predicated on a revolutionary enthusiasm, or an optimism predicated on dignity and courage, is when one makes the ultimate self-sacrifice for the people and the movement (Newton 1972: 40). Newton and the Black Panther Party utilized a "dialectical materialism as [their] analytical method" (Newton 1972: 44), which showcases the philosophy behind their resistance methodology, but what anchors Newton's pursuit of *truth* and *right* is the concept of freedom.

I want to resist, however, the urge to include people like Davis, Newton, and Ture in the canon of philosophy simply because they can cite, and be in conversation with, Western philosophers. I also do not take their formal training in the discipline as a necessary condition for them to be canon philosophers. Instead, I highlight them because they have a deep understanding between philosophical methodologies like dialectics and misrecognition (Davis), existential restraints on freedom (Ture) and intercommunalism (Newton). I give these three examples to demonstrate how their philosophical training intertwines with their activism. Their activism is not philosophical because it focuses on Hegel, Sartre, Marx, or Camus; it is philosophical because it utilizes methodologies of philosophy to create communal change. They demonstrate what can come about when the approach to philosophy is one of freedom.

7 Freedom anchoring can help marginalized students see themselves in philosophy through their lived experience.

In the few times I have persuaded underrepresented students to shift their major or minor to philosophy, they attribute the change to being able to *see themselves* in my course and the materials thereof. A quick move is to think that this was accomplished solely by the wide array of voices I include regarding race, sex, sexuality, etc., or my presence as a Black professor. Although important, those are often not their first insights. They usually speak to the media (television, film, music, and news) that I bring into class to couple with the readings. They see the issues they care about, and they engage them philosophically using theorists and philosophies they relate to. Both components are necessary. The beauty of philosophy is that it gives a name to things we already know phenomenologically. "Testimonial injustice" and "hermeneutical injustice" are terms that most of my students snap their fingers and exclaim, "so that's what that is?" after we define it. They are already *living* philosophy, we simply give them tools to think through life with. When I teach these terms, I show the trial examination of Trayvon Martin's girlfriend, Rachel Jeantel, and questions arise about education, respectability politics, disbelieving women, and various forms of credibility deficits from the students. They are evoking Sojourner Truth's social epistemology when she asks rhetorically, "Ain't I a Woman?" This is philosophy that allows the student to participate with a present moment, and experiences they know too well, which makes them part of the dialogic endeavor. As José Medina describes the "Imperative of Epistemic Interaction,"

> The aim of epistemic interaction in which resources are pooled and experiences and imaginations are shared, compared, and contrasted is both practical and epistemic … Democratic sensibilities require free and equal epistemic interaction among the heterogeneous groups that are part of society.
>
> (Medina 2013: 7)

In other words, for knowledge to grow and theories of freedom to be refined, there needs to be an equal exchange of ideas in which he calls productive "epistemic friction" (Medina 2013: 56). Philosophy classrooms should facilitate a space for these kinds of exchanges: student-to-student, student-to-professor, and student-to-text. When students see themselves as true producers of knowledge and philosophers in their own right, they can work toward pushing these theories forward; however, it is often our marginalized students that do not feel like they can produce, or even critique, knowledge because of both their position in the room as a marginalized agent and because the philosophies and philosophers do not look, exist, and operate like them.

8 *Freedom anchoring helps free philosophy from itself.*

I think that it is fruitful to think about embracing marginalized-identity-questions like Stefano Harvey and Fred Moten do in the book *The Undercommons: Fugitive Planning and Black Study*. According to them, to question and critique beyond the bounds of professionalization is a fugitive act, a criminal one, and it is an approach that makes the university, as an institution, and the discipline of philosophy, uncomfortable. Their comments on abolition seem especially important for philosophy, as they claim:

> What is ... the object of abolition? Not so much the abolition of prisons but the abolition of a society that could have prisons ... slavery ... the wage, and therefore not abolition as the elimination of anything but abolition as the founding of a new society.
>
> (Harney and Moten 2013: 42)

Let me rephrase it. What is the object of decolonizing academic philosophy? Not so much about eliminating authors or disassembling traditions but addressing how philosophy came to be a discipline that silenced, ignored, and deemed savage other ways of doing critical inquiry. Therefore, this is not a praxis of elimination, but one of imagination, the founding of a new discipline. When I say that philosophy must free itself from itself, I speak to freeing philosophy from centering any tradition, and in our current moment, that is the West's tradition(s). It is my hope that we take Mariana Ortega's sentiment seriously, where she says:

> let's reconstruct the way we do philosophy; let's drop false idols and break the imposing statues that are gatekeepers of the profession; and let's ignore the empty promises of justice and neutrality and not allow those who have no disposition for understanding each other's way of life define what really should be a love of wisdom, not of exclusion.
>
> (Ortega 2016: 220)

Knowledge, and the love of wisdom, should not be colonial, meaning that it should not be imperialized, owned, gatekept by power, defined and valued by a limited group, or made in a group's image. It must be rhizomic (not hierarchical), multiplicitous, embracing of tension and contradiction, speaking truth to power, and it must constantly reevaluate itself. Philosophy frees itself by anchoring its project in freedom: an evolving, transcending, never-ending project of pursuing horizons and new beginnings.

Conclusion

In Bryan Van Borden's text *Taking Back Philosophy: A Multicultural Manifesto*, Van Borden gives the following assessment of philosophy *now*: "We are doing philosophy when we engage in dialogue about problems that are important to our culture but we don't agree about the method for solving them" (2017: 142). Van Borden makes the important distinction that there are no evident necessary or sufficient conditions for defining philosophy even when centered in the West (2017). However, he later addresses what he calls "Less Commonly Taught Philosophies" or LCTPs. These include, but are not limited to, "African American, Christian, feminist, Islamic, Jewish, Latin American, and LGBTQ philosophy" (2017: 149). If philosophy is a dialogic endeavor, where dialogue emphasizes the pursuit of freedom, then we can start to eliminate the LCTP problem, or what I call the *sprinkling* problem. Our discussion on these difficult but relevant questions is often limited because the course itself is not shaped in such a way to relate these questions to all of the readings. This is why I suggest freedom anchoring in course objectives, student learning outcomes, assignments, lesson plans, and as a common narrative thread that not only guides the curation process for our courses, but guides what we want students to take away from the class. One of the best moments in my classes involves the students evaluating how much freedom they think is the correct balance between individual autonomy/agency and the necessary sacrifices and forfeited freedoms for a social, governmental structure that they would feel safe in. It becomes evident to them that freedom is a question that permeates through the different methodologies and traditions we engage, whether that is metaphysical and logical philosophies, American Indigenous and African American philosophies, analytic and continental philosophies, inductive and deductive reasonings, etc.

There are other concepts that may accomplish the goals stated in this chapter, like *justice* or *peace*. However, they, too, are interwoven with freedom. As Kwame Gyekye states, philosophy "is a conceptual response to the problems posed in any given epoch for a given society or culture" (1997: 27). This definition not only opens philosophy for the African experience, but for all experiences. He ends *Tradition and Modernity* claiming that this intellectual and cultural project called philosophy ultimately returns to the issue of choice, namely, the values we hold and the "rational and moral choice that human beings are free to make" (2017: 297). We, the philosophy professors, are curators of an experience of reflection. Our students should reflect on the world, on themselves, and everything in-between and beyond, understanding that choice is at the center of being human. By extension, that very freedom is key in the project of philosophy, and it is what links all of the branches of philosophy, all of the geographical divides of philosophical thought, all of the sub-disciplines, and this so-called analytic-continental divide. The objective is to examine choice, and philosophy classes are excellent spaces to explore *choice*, because philosophy is intellectually and culturally bound up in meta and applied questions of freedom.

Notes

1. Let me make a distinction between diversifying and decolonizing as it pertains to philosophy and Higher Education. As the study by Arshad et. al. suggests, diversifying is a form of inclusion, an adding on to a paradigm. However, decolonizing requires a dismantling of the *othering* that the paradigm creates and fosters. Decolonizing addresses the paradigm, institution, or discipline itself, requiring that the vehicles for exclusion be eliminated. This is more than an inclusion of marginalized perspectives. As it pertains to philosophy, the examples are numerous: *Decolonizing American Philosophy*, edited by Corey McCall and Phillip McReynolds (2021), *Black Existentialism and Decolonizing Knowledge: Writings of Lewis R. Gordon*, edited by Rozena Maart and Sayan Dey (2023), *Fanon and the Decolonization of Philosophy*, edited by Elizabeth Hoppe and Tracey Nichols (2010) are anthologies full of examples of why philosophy needs decolonization instead of diversity. However, I will summate those responses with Gordon's following statement:

    The struggle with reason, then, becomes a form of reason beyond reason as presently conceived, and, in turn, it leads to metaphilosophical reflection of Africana and other anticolonial philosophy as the paradox of philosophy being willing to transcend itself. This effort is, in effect, a call for the decolonization of philosophy, which means, then, that a critical consequence is one against philosophical parochialism (false claims of universality) and a demand for ongoing, universalizing philosophical practices in which ideas connect across disciplines, fields, and peoples without collapsing into delusions of completeness.... Philosophy understood in this way, despite protest throughout the ages, is also an expression of humanity's search, at the level of ideas about our relationship with reality, for a home to which one does not return; it is what one builds along the way through and alongside decolonization.

    (Gordon 2019: 25–6)

2. My thought here is that diversity rests its hope for change in a *critical mass of inclusion*, and the hope is that what is included overshadows the problems within the paradigms themselves. I find this to be largely unsuccessful. Even a course with a significant number of marginalized

philosophers in their syllabus can still be unsuccessful at decolonizing their syllabi if those voices are considered *marginal* (marginal in the sense of relevance, not just identity) to the overarching project of the course of philosophy broadly.
3. "Revolutionary Love" can also be understood in the academic sense via Clelia Rodríguez's concept of "decolonial love," where Rodríguez says, "In this course, we will experience decolonial love through transformative lessons to teach us how to liberate ourselves from colonial notions of what violence is and who is violent" (Rodríguez 2018: 31).

References

Amo, Wilhelm Amo (2020). "Philosophical Disputation Containing a Distinct Idea of Those Things That Pertain Either to the Mind or to Our Living and Organic Body (1734)" in Stephen Menn and Justin E.H. Smith (eds), *Anton Wilhelm Amo's Philosophical Dissertations on Mind and Body*, 199–226. New York: Oxford University Press.

Arshad, Muminah, Rachel Dada, Cathy Elliott, et al. (2021). "Diversity or Decolonization? Searching for the Tools to Dismantle the 'Master's House.'" *London Review of Education* 19(1): 1–18.

Beauvoir, Simone de (1948). *Ethics of Ambiguity*. Trans. Bernard Frechtman. New York: Open Road Publishing.

Budge, (Sir) Earnest Alfred Thompson Wallis (Trans.) (1895). *The Book of the Dead: The Papyrus of Ani in the British Museum*, 347–9. London: Trustees of the British Museum.

Collins, Patricia Hill (2019). *Intersectionality as Critical Social Theory*. Durham: Duke University Press.

Davis, Angela (2012). *The Meaning of Freedom: And Other Difficult Dialogues*. San Fransisco: City Lights Books.

Davis, Angela (2018). "Lectures on Liberation" in Neil Roberts (ed.), *A Political Companion to Frederick Douglass*, 107–34. Lexington: University Press of Kentucky.

Dotson, Kristie (2011). "Concrete Flowers: Contemplating the Profession of Philosophy." *Hypatia* 26(2): 403–9.

Dotson, Kristie (2012). "How Is This Paper Philosophy." *Comparative Philosophy* 3(1): 3–29.

Fanon, Frantz (1986). *Black Skin, White Masks*. Trans. Charles Lam Markmann. London: Pluto Press.

Freire, Paulo (2000). *Pedagogy of the Oppressed*. New York: Bloomsbury Academic.

Gordon, Lewis (2019). "Decolonizing Philosophy." *Southern Journal of Philosophy* 57(1): 16–36.

Gordon, Lewis (2021). *Freedom, Justice, and Decolonization*. New York: Routledge.

Gordon, Lewis (2023). *Black Existentialism and Decolonizing Knowledge: Writings of Lewis R. Gordon*. Eds Rozena Maart and Sayan Dey. London: Bloomsbury Academic.

Gyekye, Kwame (1997). *Tradition and Modernity: Philosophical Reflections on the African Experience*. Oxford: Oxford University Press.

Harney, Stefano, and Fred Moten (2013). *The Undercommons: Fugitive Planning and Black Study*. Brooklyn: Minor Compositions.

hooks, bell (1994). *Teaching to Transgress: Education as the Practice of Freedom*. New York: Routledge.

Hoppe, Elizabeth Anne, and Tracey Nicholls (eds) (2010). *Fanon and the Decolonization of Philosophy*. Lanham: Rowman and Littlefield.

King Jr., Martin Luther (1961). "Seminar in Social Philosophy, Morehouse College, 1961–1962" in *The Inventory of the Martin Luther King, Jr. Collection* #127 Howard Gotlieb Archival Research Center: Box 10, Boston University.

King Jr., Martin Luther (1968). *Where Do We Go From Here: Chaos or Community?* Boston: Beacon Press.

Medina, José (2013). *The Epistemology of Resistance: Gender and Radical Oppression, Epistemic Injustice, and Resistant Imaginations*. Oxford: Oxford University Press.

Newton, Huey P. (1972). *To Die for the People: The Writings of Huey P. Newton*. New York: Vintage Books.

Ortega, Mariana (2016). *In-Between: Latina Feminist Phenomenology, Multiplicity, and the Self*. Albany: State University of New York.

Plato and Aristophanes (1984). *Four Texts on Socrates*. Trans. T. West & G. West. Ithaca: Cornell University Press.

Rodríguez, Clelia O. (2018). *Decolonizing Academia: Poverty, Oppression, and Pain*. Black Point: Fernwood Publishing.

Rustin, Bayard (2003). *Time on Two Crosses: The Collected Writings of Bayard Rustin*. Eds D. Carbado and D. Weise. New York: Cleis Press.

Ture, Kwame (Stokley Carmichael) (1966). "Black Power." Speech in Berkeley, CA. http://www.sojust.net/speeches/stokely_carmichael_blackpower.html.

Van Borden, Bayard (2017). *Taking Back Philosophy: A Multicultural Manifesto*. New York: Columbia University Press.

Wynter, Sylvia (2022). "Ethno or Socio-Poetics" in Demetrius L. Eudell (ed.), *We Must Learn to Sit down Together and Talk about a Little Culture: Decolonising Essays, 1967–1984*, 421–44. Leeds: Peepal Tree Publishing.

3

Syllabus Design and World-Making

Rima Basu

The first time I drafted a teaching statement, one of my cohort commented that the way I talked about students sounded like the field notes of an alien observing a new species. Perhaps knowing that story will make what comes next less surprising.

When designing a course it's not much of a stretch to say that you're designing a world, a world that's governed by conventions that need to be made explicit. It's similarly not much of a stretch to say that the world of a college classroom can be an alien environment for many students. The rules and conventions can be hard to grasp. It has been well-documented that the unstated norms disadvantage students unfamiliar with the space. For example, in high school going to the teacher's office means you're in trouble, you need help. It's something bad, something to be avoided as much as possible. In college, on the other hand, going to office hours is good, it's encouraged. The document that's supposed to make the conventions and expectations of the world explicit is our syllabi. However, syllabi have come to resemble long legal contracts, and so it should be no surprise that students frequently don't read them. When was the last time you read the terms and conditions?

In thinking about how to design my syllabus, I was struck by the following realization: there are many commonalities between the framework of tabletop roleplaying games (TTRPGs) such as Dungeons & Dragons (D&D) and what we do when we're designing a course. The professor (the dungeon master) selects a number of readings with some end goal in mind (the campaign). Along the way the students are expected to be active participants (roleplay) and the professor designs progressively harder assignments (quests) in order to test the students' abilities and to promote learning and growth (leveling up). This structural analogy prompted me to investigate how such a framework could be implemented more explicitly in a class. That is, if I took a step back and started from scratch, if I threw out what I previously thought a syllabus should look like, how would I explain all the elements of the course—e.g., the course goals, the set-up of the readings and assignments, the unstated norms of etiquette that govern classroom discussion—to someone new to the space?

There are some superficial ways in which designing a class is like designing a TTRPG or the start of a good fantasy book. For example, you have to think about the narrative arc of the course. That is, when designing syllabi we think about how to structure readings and assignments so that assignments get progressively harder and build upon skills from previous assignments. Similarly, we think about what students will need to read at the start of the semester to be in the best position to tackle the readings at the end of the semester. A good dungeon master has their players fight low-level bosses before they get to the big boss. A good professor, like a good DM, thinks about how to encourage that path of growth and improvement over the course of the semester and how all the pieces of the course will fit together in a satisfying way. Each quest, each reading, each assignment, although not always obvious to either players or students, plays a role in a larger campaign, in a larger story.

Another lesson from TTRPGs is that you're not in this alone. Our individual success depends on the success of others. A successful learning environment also requires students to recognize that they're not in this alone. To do well they must work together, respect one another, recognize each other's strengths and weaknesses, and cooperate successfully to not only defeat whatever assignments that we put in their way, but also grow as characters and develop the skills they need to tackle harder classes. With the general motivation now laid out, let me get into the specific elements of the class that resemble a traditional TTRPG, including the game we play as part of the class.

Character Sheet

When you start a D&D campaign you create a character by filling out a character sheet. You choose a name, a race, a set of skills and abilities, and create a history for this character. Translating this exercise to the classroom environment, I have my students fill out a modified character sheet that I've created in a shared folder that they all have access to. This way they can just make a copy of the template, fill it out, and it'll automatically save in that shared folder so everyone can see each other's character sheets. This way I get to know them a bit better, and they also get to know each other a bit better.

On the character sheet I ask them for basic info like their name, alias (if they go by another name or if people commonly mispronounce their name they can put the pronunciation), and their preferred pronouns. In addition, I ask them to attach a picture and answer the following five questions:

1. Background: Who are you?
2. Ideals: What drives you? What are the fundamental moral and ethical principles that compel you (if any)?
3. Bonds: Why did you choose CMC? Why did you choose this class? What do you hope to gain?
4. Personality Traits: What makes you *you*?
5. Weaknesses: What do you want to work on?

Our first class session then becomes a discussion of their answers to these questions and we all leave with a better understanding of one another.

Character Classes

When playing D&D you also choose a class for your character, e.g., whether to be a ranger, a druid, a wizard, a barbarian, etc. I thought this element of D&D was best translated into a way to rethink the grading system for the class. That is, I provide a description of the various character classes, and students can choose for themselves what they want to aim for. Within each class there's a certain number of a mix of high- and low-stakes assignments students must complete to either level up within their character class, or to level up to the next character class. The character classes I chose and their descriptions are as follows.

The Ranger (C– to C+)

To achieve this grade students must complete at least half the assignments with at least a passing grade. I describe this path to students as follows: for the ranger there are a range of low-stakes assignments. Upon completion of the course I trust that you'll know right from wrong, be able to think about complicated moral and political issues in a more nuanced way than before, have the tools to recognize how it is that humans commit evil actions, and have a deeper understanding of your own nature and motivations. Only you can answer for yourself what you'll do with your life and the skills you've gained from this course.

The Paladin (B– to B+)

There are three levels to the Paladin. One begins as squire (B–), and then can progress to a knight (B) and then a lord (B+). Each level requires more assignments and more demonstrated mastery of the material. The description for the Paladin is as follows: Paladins are skilled warriors with a commitment to what is right. What is right is rarely easy, and thus Paladins are always ready to make great sacrifices. Upon completion of the course I have faith that you'll not only know right from wrong, but also always do the right thing. You have the skills to persuasively argue for the view you believe to be correct, and you've engaged in deep reflection about yourself and humanity and have a better understanding of both yourself and what it is that drives others to commit evil actions.

The Wizard (A– and A)

One does not become a wizard right away. First one must demonstrate the skill and mastery of a scholar (A–), and then after completing almost every assignment and receiving an A on most assignments, students can rise to the rank of Master (A). Here's how I describe this level of mastery to my students: Wizards dedicate their lives to the acquisition of knowledge (sometimes to the end of good, sometimes to evil). Upon completion of the course *I am most concerned about you.* You will know right from wrong, but I'll have equipped you with the tools to persuasively argue for any position. Only you know your true motivations, and although you may say you know right from wrong, it could be a clever illusion. You have the ability to shape the world to better reflect how you think it should look, but will you shape it for good or for evil? I hope you'll fight for what's right, but will you?

Skills and Course Objectives

When designing a character for D&D you also need to settle on some skills that your character will have. I incorporate this into my courses by first converting each course goal and objective into an explicit skill. Then when designing assignments I explicitly note what skill/s (i.e., course objective/s) that assignment is designed to develop. For example, here are the course goals and objectives for one of my classes:

- You will be able to identify the main arguments and discriminate objections of varying strengths. Skill: Wisdom
- You will be able to identify the structure of arguments found in the readings and in turn persuasively argue for a point. Skill: Dexterity
- You will be able to draw connections between the various materials discussed in class. Skill: Insight
- You will be an active participant in the classroom applying what you've learned in the readings and demonstrating effective engagement with critical ideas. Skill: Charisma
- You will be able to recall, reproduce, and demonstrate an understanding of foundational and contemporary work relating to the challenge evil poses to our development as moral agents. Skill: Comprehension

Assignments and Building a Community

First, assignments in this class aren't worth percentage grades that add up to 100 percent. Instead, I break up each final grade into a set of assignments that must be completed to a certain level of mastery to attain that final grade. As I explain to my students, this allows me to assess different skills in both low- and high-stakes scenarios and to make adjustments as needed. Second, students have some freedom to choose which assignments to complete. This puts them in charge and lets them choose how to engage with the material. However, the freedom to choose is not complete freedom, the freedom is limited. Too much freedom in choosing assignments can itself be a source of debilitating stress. Roleplaying games are highly structured, but there is also freedom in that structure.

The range of assignments fall into the following three categories: (1) Adventurer's logs, (2) Individual Quests, and (3) Group Campaigns. Adventurer logs are short pieces of writing that are more personal in nature. In this category are character sheets (explained in more detail above), reading reports (short responses to the readings due before the start of class), and journal entries (end-of-the-week reflections on the class and class material). Individual quests are familiar paper assignments, each one longer and more difficult than the one before. And finally the group campaign is the assignment I use to explicitly play a roleplaying game in class to build community. As I explain in the syllabus: campaigns serve the function of building community and maybe even making some new friends or solidifying old friendships. They'll also require you to put into practice and test out philosophical concepts we've discussed in class.

To say more about the group campaign, halfway through the semester I ask the class for their preferences regarding people they'd like to work with, who they would not like to work with, and I ask them to fill out a WhenIsGood for their availability outside of class time. Using that information I break them up into parties of 3–5 who together share at least a two-hour period of unscheduled time outside of class to play Microscope RPG. I also set aside three in-class sessions for playing Microscope and we play one large game together as a class so they can learn the rules and the basic moves.

Microscope RPG is a roleplaying game where you design your own world, and most importantly, it is collaborative and requires no dungeon master. This means all the players have equal power to affect the story and the gameplay. Together students determine how their timeline begins, how it ends, and everything that happens in between. Together they decide the rules that govern how to navigate the world they create, e.g., what it's like, how it works, the big events that shape it, what kinds of people get ahead, and which get left behind. Over the course of fleshing out the details they are also prompted by me to develop and test ethical systems in those worlds. For example, does their world contain a universal objective morality? Is there a God or Gods? Are there any upheavals that change the prevailing ethical system/s? Ultimately: how does one be a good person in their worlds? To get them to engage in this kind of reflective thinking, I ask them to submit campaign reports. These reports not only provide an overview of the key events of the worlds they create, but I also explicitly ask them about what kind of people flourish in their worlds, what it means to be good in the world they've created, and how their answers connect to the readings we've covered in class. In addition, I ask them what they've learned about each other. Usually they discover that they're more creative than they thought.

Finally, in addition to reading the rulebook for Microscope RPG, the students also read *Consent in Gaming* by Reynolds and Germain. The first tells them about the game, the latter about how to handle interpersonal conflicts that might arise as some of the gameplay will occur outside of class time under their own supervision.

Games and Distance

Finally, there are some *human* reasons in addition to the pedagogical reasons for structuring the course in this way. I use this structure primarily in my class that is on the topic of evil. The class comes with a trigger warning because it is a class about the worst things humans have done to one another and it explores the question of how we're capable of committing such atrocities. To be fully engaged, to fully take on the depth of human evil is a lot. By "gamifying" the course structure in the ways outlined above, part of my goal is to provide a way to maintain some critical distance from the material. That is, a way for students (and myself) to step back from the material and apply a familiar gaming framework of skills, XP (experience points), and leveling up. This is done not with the aim of trivializing the material, but with the aim of giving them the resources to escape when they need to escape. We can put down books when they become too much, we can pause movies when we need to breathe. It's harder to do so if one feels one has to keep going because one's grade depends on it. That said, I've briefly stopped teaching the class because I too needed a break from the material.

Final Words

I want to end by noting that in many ways I've been lucky and that the implementation of TTRPG strategies into either syllabus design or in-class assignments may not work for everyone. First, I am a giant nerd and I bring that energy into the classroom. Second, I've been blessed with small classes that are heavily discussion based. Third, the class in which I incorporate the most of these elements is my first-year humanities seminar, which has a lower cap than other courses and is composed entirely of first-years. As a result, students are more open to experimentation with classroom design because the course itself is a little bit odd in that (1) it's not discipline specific, i.e., we read from philosophy, sociology, religious studies, psychology, and more, and (2) the class is only for first-years. That structure I think gives me liberty and license that I usually don't have in upper-level classes (where there is more expectation of what a college class in the major is supposed to look like) and more liberty and license than if I were teaching a large lecture class to a room of a hundred or more (where this level of personal attention is simply not achievable).

In closing, although I can only speak to my experience in my classrooms my hope is that those in different sorts of classrooms can still find something valuable in this report.

4

Deadlines, Learner-Centeredness, and Nonideal Pedagogy

Christopher Blake-Turner

1 Introduction

This chapter has two goals.[1] First, I want to think aloud (apage?) about deadlines and how to approach them in a more deliberate way. Deadlines can be something of an afterthought, both in my own experience and in that of instructors I respect. We spend meticulous time backward designing course and lesson content, assignments, in-class work, and thinking about grades. But deadlines sometimes get short shrift. What might it look like to approach deadlines with some of the same care we approach other elements of course design?

Second, deadlines provide a good opportunity to think about what I'll call *nonideal pedagogy*. When we think about learner-centered pedagogy, we rightly center learners. But in the nonideal teaching contexts many (most—all) of us find ourselves in, it's just not possible to put some pedagogies into practice. It's not that we should abandon learner-centered pedagogy. But I do want to encourage, or at least provoke, a conversation about the limits of learner-centeredness in nonideal contexts, and a shift to a pedagogy that is both learner-centered and instructor-sensitive.

2 Deadlines from a Learner-Centered Perspective

What's the point of deadlines from the point of view of learning? Here's a suggestion:

> Deadlines provide structure for learners so that they can complete learning tasks on a schedule constrained both by: (i) learning outcomes; and (ii) external factors.

Even from the most learner-centered perspective possible, there are external constraints imposed on any course. For instance, in the vast majority of courses, final grades have to be assigned by some specific time. And instructors will often need some time to grade. So, even aside from any considerations of learning, structure needs to be imposed on the course in order to ensure that learners do whatever they need to do for assessment.

But learning outcomes themselves impose scheduling constraints. For instance, consider the outcome *learners will be able to integrate feedback into written work*. Such an outcome requires that learners receive some feedback to integrate. That means they'll need to submit something to get feedback on. Both the giving of the feedback and the integrating will take time. That imposes constraints on scheduling.

So, deadlines help structure a course in order for learners to complete the tasks they need to, as required by the constraints generated both by the course's own learning outcomes and external factors. I stress this because it's easy to think of deadlines as a necessary evil, as something that it would be better to do without if possible, but that sometimes have to get imposed for reasons beyond an instructor's control. I'm sympathetic to being flexible with deadlines (more on this below), but it's worth realizing that deadlines can sometimes help rather than hinder learner success. Here are two, related ways this can happen. First, regular deadlines keep a course in the minds of learners. They help learners check in regularly with the course rather than putting it on the back burner and prioritizing other things.[2] Second, the more sparse deadlines are, the more assignments evaluate learners' executive function, rather than whatever the assignments are supposed to be evaluating (D'Agostino 2023). If executive function skills are what we want to assess, we should be deliberate and transparent about that. If they're not what we want to assess, we should not design our assignments in ways that heavily depend on them. This is borne out by a growing body of evidence suggesting that learners in college settings do better with more deadlines, rather than fewer (Miyake and Kane 2022; Svartdal et al. 2020). Here's a theoretical argument to support the empirical evidence. Deadlines are a kind of scaffolding. Rather than scaffolding a skill that's usually targeted explicitly for improvement in the course—critical reading, say—deadlines scaffold executive function, and in particular time management. Time management is a complicated skill that takes practice to master, so it makes sense that scaffolding it helps learners who haven't yet developed the skill to a high degree. Fewer deadlines thus allow for more procrastination, which can be harmful to learning.

This rationale for more deadlines does not straightforwardly support making deadlines more rigid. We should separate deadline *rigidity* from deadline *frequency*. Call the complete schedule of deadlines over a course the *deadline pattern*. On the one hand, the rigidity of the deadline pattern concerns how forgiving or not the deadlines are.[3] Think of it as a spectrum. At the hard extreme of the spectrum, an assignment is awarded zero (and perhaps not even given any formative feedback) if it is submitted even a second late, and there is no possibility of extension. At the soft extreme, there is no penalty at all for missing the deadline. The rigidity of most deadlines falls somewhere between these extremes. The frequency of the deadline pattern, on the other hand, concerns how many deadlines there are, and how they are spaced out. The evidence of the previous paragraph suggests that even fairly soft deadlines help learners with procrastination. And softer deadlines are more forgiving to those learners whose lives impose on their ability to complete course content in various ways: family emergencies; job demands; and so on.

Two arguments are often given in favor of greater deadline rigidity. First, deadlines are hard in the "real world" and, given that we should be preparing learners for the "real world," deadlines should also be hard in our courses. I reject both claims that this argument depends on. Deadlines aren't usually very hard in the "real world" (Warner 2019). Much more important in that context is to be able to communicate effectively and ask for extensions if needed. Yes, there are times when a project simply must be due—just as final grades have to be submitted by a certain point. But very often, work quality is more important than a set time of completion. I also reject the claim that we should be preparing learners for the "real world," where that is interpreted solely in terms of employment. Philosophy absolutely should have a bearing on learners' current and future lives. But it should have a bearing on their whole lives—their flourishing as entire human persons—and not just the narrow part of their lives bound up with work. If softer deadlines help learners do work that makes them more creative and full thinkers, questioners, and humans, then I'd much rather encourage that.

The second argument for rigidity is based on fairness. The thought is that giving flexibility to some learners is unfair to those who don't take advantage of the flexibility. Learners who don't take advantage of flexibility have to turn in assignments that they've had less time to work on. I'm sympathetic to this concern, but some of it can be mitigated by communicating effectively to learners about how your deadline flexibility works.[4] If everyone knows to what extent the deadlines are flexible, then this curbs the unfairness that arises from ad hoc extensions and the like. Two worries remain, however. First, even with the flexibility made clear, learners with more confidence and cultural capital are going to take greater advantage of certain policies than other learners. For instance, suppose you have a policy to the effect of: *I'll work with you however I can to meet your time constraints, as long as you contact me before the official assignment deadline.* The learners that need the flexibility most because of their life circumstances are likely to be the learners least able to take advantage of it. That's partly because whatever is going on that makes it harder for them to complete the assignment will also make it harder for them to reach out, and partly because learners with less cultural capital are more likely to be affected by circumstances for which deadline flexibility will be especially helpful. I think the best we can do here is to try and build the flexibility into the deadline pattern as much as possible in ways that don't require learners to *do* something to take advantage of it. For instance, many of my assignments have a no-questions-asked grace period, during which work can be submitted late without penalty.[5] And after that, a gently tapered late penalty can help learners who are really struggling to still gain some credit.[6] The second lingering worry is that sometimes shit really does happen. A learner has a mental health crisis, or is bereaved—some crisis renders them unable to meet even a very flexible deadline policy. In such circumstances, softening the deadline further would have to be ad hoc, and this risks unfairness to other learners. My sense here is to prioritize the learners in crisis over their peers. Learners in crisis should be met foremost with compassion and care. Whatever putative unfair advantage they have from extra deadline flexibility is probably offset by the disadvantage of being in crisis. Even if it's not, I'd rather prioritize learner well-being than some nebulous one-size-fits-all standard of fairness; your mileage may vary.

So, I tentatively recommend the following learner-centered deadline heuristic: increase the frequency of your deadlines, but decrease their rigidity. The former helps scaffold executive function and time management; the latter recognizes that your class is one among a complicated set of, sometimes serious and unpredictable, demands on learners.

3 Nonideal Pedagogy

I want to close by using deadlines as a case study in what I call *nonideal pedagogy*. Rawls (1999) famously gives an ideal theory of justice—a theory under highly idealized circumstances, such as eliding any previous injustices. He has been criticized by many for not adequately getting round to a nonideal theory of justice: a theory of justice not for some imagined rational idyll, but for our messy, flawed and actual world (e.g., Mills 2005). I worry that when we do learner-centered pedagogy we are at risk of doing ideal pedagogy: pedagogy under conditions of infinite instructor time, patience, and so on.[7] But we instructors—most of us, at any rate—are very much nonideal agents, both in our capacities and in the other demands on our time. Learner-centered pedagogy helps us focus on the nonideal circumstances of *learners*, and in doing so it helps us think about how to make our classes more inclusive (Jacquart et al. 2019). But in discouraging us from casting our pedagogical gaze inward, learner-centeredness sometimes misses the nonideal circumstances of instructors.

Many instructors have very demanding course loads, without grading assistance, on top of research expectations. Many instructors are humans with our own crises and emergencies to handle. For instance, I've had several conversations with instructors with heavy teaching loads who would love to implement some pedagogy they've read about or heard about, but just *cannot*. Perhaps the pedagogy was developed at a small liberal arts college, and it just doesn't scale well to very large classes; or perhaps the pedagogy is hard to implement without TAs, who they just don't have. For instance, I suggested in note 6 that we shouldn't be using deadlines to check in with learners, as that's something we should be doing regularly anyway. But what does adequate checking in look like for large classes and teaching loads? Indeed it's precisely in those circumstances that students are more likely to get lost and need checking in with.[8] I don't have a good answer to this question (more on that below), but one thing worth saying is that a little goes a long way with checking in. If I notice a learner has been absent either for an extended period of time, or uncharacteristically, I shoot a quick email to check on them. I stress that I'm not getting on their case, but am concerned about their well-being. There's no getting around the fact that this takes time and effort, however. But it's something I prioritize in favor of letting other things slide. That's another feature of nonideal pedagogy: things have to give. By being more open about that, perhaps we can make better decisions about what to let slide and what to try and cling onto, even in the face of nonideality.

Deadlines interact with our nonideal teaching contexts in a stark way. Here are two manifestations of that. First, if you have to grade 200 papers, say, you probably need to spread them out over some time. That means your deadline pattern will be in part at the mercy of one's nonideal teaching context, rather than learner-centered considerations or even institutional constraints. To put the point another way, nonideal teaching contexts sometimes force us to give more weight to instructor-centered considerations, such as: in a given time period, given what else is going on in my life, how much grading can I responsibly do (both from the point of view of doing it well, but also from the point of view of doing it in a way that is sensitive to my own well-being)? Second, the very recommendations I made in §2 about deadline frequency and rigidity tend to be harder to implement in nonideal pedagogical contexts.[9] The more deadlines there are, the more there is for the instructor to keep track of. Similarly for rigidity: the softer one's deadlines, the more one has to stay on top of who's work is due when exactly. In short, high-frequency, low-rigidity deadlines are more work for the instructor. And that's often precisely what instructors can't give under nonideal pedagogical conditions.

I don't have a guide for doing nonideal pedagogy without losing one's grip on learner-centeredness.[10] But I do offer three things. First, a name for the problem. Sometimes the first step toward progress is sighting the target. Second, I give permission to instructors in nonideal contexts (which is all of us, at least to some degree) to forgive ourselves for having to make instructor-centered decisions sometimes. Perhaps the problem is not instructor-centeredness per se, but *reasonably avoidable* instructor-centeredness. If a course decision does less well for learners and better for instructors, but could easily be avoided—and the magnitude of instructor taxingness is not too high—we should give way. But there are times when a decision might benefit learners only slightly at great cost to the instructor. Finally, in light of all this, I suggest that we frame the pedagogical enterprise as not only *learner-centered* but also *instructor-sensitive*.

Notes

1. I'm deeply grateful to Joanna Lawson and Brynn Welch, who read and provided extremely helpful comments on a draft of this piece. Thanks are also due to participants of an AAPT Talking Teaching session that I led on this topic: I'm grateful especially to Karl Aho, Claude Gratton, Jerry Green, Yvette Pearson, Renée Smith, and Kimberly Van Orman for thoughtful questions and discussion.
2. I'm grateful to Yvette Pearson for this point.
3. This can vary from deadline to deadline, of course.
4. Learners often admittedly have absorbed very specific ideas about how deadline flexibility works, and overcoming this can be challenging. For instance, in a class where I explicitly allow extension requests *for no reason*, learners are often wary at first of asking for extensions without what they take to be an acceptable reason. This challenge of communication is real, but I hope not insuperable.
5. A worry: this might thwart some learners, who'll just take the end of the grace period to be the real deadline and so not benefit from the scaffolding of the official deadline. This is a tricky empirical issue, but it seems that our best evidence (both anecdotal and from the studies cited earlier) suggests that even very soft deadlines really do help with scaffolding executive function.
6. One thing lost by not having learners ask for extensions is losing out on opportunities to be made aware of problems that they're facing. But I think we should find ways to check in with learners regularly regardless, not least because learners that are struggling the most are least likely to ask for extensions. I revisit this issue in §3.
7. Ideal and nonideal pedagogy likely come in degrees, but we can set that aside for this exploratory discussion.
8. Thanks to Brynn Welch for pressing me on this issue.
9. I owe this point to Joanna Lawson.
10. I also don't mean to suggest that I am the first or only person to notice this problem. For instance, many AAPT events try to be sensitive to what I am calling the nonideal pedagogical contexts of instructors. But it's one thing to flag that in some broad way, and another to keep it at the fore when doing philosophical pedagogy. It's the latter that I'm suggesting we should do more of.

References

D'Agostino, Susan (2023). "'Procrastination-Friendly' Academe Needs More Deadlines." *Inside Higher Ed*, 2023. https://www.insidehighered.com/news/2023/02/10/should-professors-eliminate-deadlines.

Jacquart, Melissa, Rebecca Scott, Kevin Hermberg, and Stephen Bloch-Schulman (2019). "Diversity Is Not Enough: The Importance of Inclusive Pedagogy." *Teaching Philosophy* 42(2): 107–39. https://doi.org/10.5840/teachphil2019417102.

Mills, Charles W. (2005). "'Ideal Theory' as Ideology." *Hypatia* 20(3): 165–84.

Miyake, Akira, and Michael J. Kane (2022). "Toward a Holistic Approach to Reducing Academic Procrastination with Classroom Interventions." *Current Directions in Psychological Science* 31(4): 291–304. https://doi.org/10.1177/09637214211070814.

Rawls, John (1999). *A Theory of Justice*. Rev. ed. Cambridge, MA: Belknap Press of Harvard University Press.

Svartdal, Frode, Tove I. Dahl, Thor Gamst-Klaussen, Markus Koppenborg, and Katrin B. Klingsieck (2020). "How Study Environments Foster Academic Procrastination: Overview and Recommendations." *Frontiers in Psychology* 11. https://doi.org/10.3389/fpsyg.2020.540910.

Warner, John (2019). "Deadlines in the 'Real World.'" *Inside Higher Ed*, 2019. https://www.insidehighered.com/blogs/just-visiting/deadlines-real-world.

5

Philosophy through Spectacle

Meg Wallace

First Impressions

I'll admit: the first day of *PHI 193 Circus and Philosophy* is kind of weird. Students follow narrow steps into an old open gym with plenty of high windows and natural light. Vividly dyed fabrics hang from the ceiling, improbably rigged 20 feet in the air. It is quite a spectacle. As the students come in, there are audible gasps and whispers, leading to jittery chatter. Faces are filled with expressions of awe and wonder. Many are likely thinking "What kind of wacko class *is* this?" There's a *lot* of space—more space than anyone should reasonably expect in a normal college course, and certainly more space than anyone should reasonably expect in a normal philosophy course. It invokes a feeling of being unmistakably small in comparison, yet in a way that is invigorating and inspiring, not defeating. There's an urge to *take this space up* any way possible: to move, to run, to spin, to climb, to swing around on or touch every curious new apparatus or prop. There are odd-shaped objects clearly meant for throwing and (maybe eventually) catching. There's an array of color, an echo of happy claps, occasional woots of encouragement. It's wondrous. Unexpected. And strange.

Circus and Philosophy is an explicit mix of theory and praxis. In roughly half of the class sessions, students learn physical circus skills such as juggling, aerial silks, trapeze, and acro-balancing. In the other half, students learn introductory philosophical topics in ethics, aesthetics, social and political philosophy, metaphysics, and epistemology.[1]

One of my initial attractions to the idea of combining circus and philosophy was the recognition that the circus arts are already fertile

Figure 5.1 *The Circus Lab* at the University of Kentucky. Photo credit: Ayna Lorenzo.

grounds for deep questions about persons, identity, the self, perception, illusion, and magic. This may not be obvious—and it is certainly not obvious if we think of the circus as something we merely *look at* instead of something we *do*. I've been a recreational circuser for nearly a dozen years. In that time, I've realized that one of the best ways to truly understand the value of the circus arts is to actually *do* circus. I've also observed that many of those who *participate* in circus arts—even if only recreationally—are especially attuned to thoughtful reflections on themselves and their place in the world. Moreover, combining circus with philosophy is an innovative way to show students that philosophical theorizing does not have to stay "in the head." Students use first-person circusing *as a way to* philosophical inquiry. They learn philosophy by *moving*, resulting in a truly embodied education.

All of this might sound amazing. (It *is*.) Yet there are a number of significant challenges in implementing a class such as this, each one of which, at one point or another during development, seemed to be a perfectly good reason to give up running this course altogether. In what follows, I describe some of these difficulties, detail how I navigated through them, and explain why teaching philosophy this way is nonetheless worth all the trouble. For those like me who are interested in teaching philosophy in extraordinary ways, perhaps an account of my experiences—including what worked and what didn't—will be helpful.

Challenges

First, there are the logistical challenges. Where could I find a location on campus with enough space for the students to move around? And if I found something, would it be conducive to both students moving around and having substantial philosophical discussions? How can I make sure that the class *meaningfully integrates* physical movement and theory, without it being merely a Frankenstein mash-up of disparate pedagogical parts? Assuming I find a space, how do I equip it? How can I guarantee that it is appropriately rigged and adequately assessed for safety? What about insurance and liability? Does a university waiver cover students flipping upside down on a trapeze? How do I order and fund the circus equipment? And how much will I need? How many students do I expect to enroll in this class? Can I afford 108 juggling balls?

Then there are the pedagogical and organizational challenges. The current philosophical literature on circus and philosophy is nearly nonexistent. How do I teach a class on circus and philosophy if there are no philosophical articles or readings on the topic I'm teaching? How do I convince the students and administration that a course on a topic that currently is not taught anywhere else, *should* be taught? Detail questions: How do I design the syllabus, given that so much of the class will be physical movement and circus skill acquisition? How do I grade the circus portions? Do students get As if they can juggle three balls, but Bs or Cs if they can't? (At one point, after I explained that I was offering an honors option for this course, one of my colleagues jokingly inquired: "Do honors students have to juggle *4 balls*?!") How should I design assignments? Is it appropriate to only require written papers? Or does that run counter to the whole point of the class, combining theory and praxis? Should the students have a performance at the end? Or some kind of creative project that combines circus and philosophy? What does that kind of final creative project look like? And how am I qualified to grade it? Big picture question: How do I show that there is value in teaching philosophy this way?

Logistics

To address the first set of challenges, I tried several approaches. At first, I spliced up the class into two different locations. The physical circus days were in one location—an area where the ROTC folks work out, open to through-traffic and without privacy. The philosophical discussion days were in a different classroom in a separate building. Students *loved* the class. But I was frustrated. The physically separate locations severely undercut the pedagogical cohesiveness I'd envisioned. And the public openness of the movement space was incredibly distracting (although, admittedly, my students and I were quite amused by frequent invitations to a circus vs. army climb-off). Next, I tried having the majority of the class in an on-campus black box studio. This worked well for some of the circus sessions—juggling and acro-balancing, for example. And it was intimate enough that we could have fruitful philosophical discussions there, too. Yet in order to do any sort of aerial arts, I needed to have high ceilings and structurally sound beams to rig *from*. The black box theater was not approved for this; in fact, I hauled a structural engineer on campus and got access to the schematic blueprints of the space to double check. So we had to go back to the ROTC space for this part of the course anyway, making this second iteration of the course only marginally better than the first. Again, the students loved it. But, again, I was frustrated. There simply was no place on campus appropriate for exploring circus arts. And this, I was beginning to realize, was crucial for making the course work.

After taking a break for a year to investigate my options—after many emails, numerous conversations with folks in different areas on campus, and a lot of walking around in random university buildings with unusual classroom spaces—I found an old hidden gym on the backside of an underused building. There were no existing rigging points in this gym, there was no circus equipment, and no one to my knowledge had ever done any circus in this place. But it had potential. *Here* a space for circus arts could be *built*. I brought the structural engineer back to campus to officially inspect it. I checked with facilities and risk management to see what backend permissions would be required, how liability would work, and so on. An aerial rigger was hired. Through various kinds of administrative alchemy that I still don't quite understand (but am incredibly grateful for), and crucial input from numerous individuals who, for whatever reason, thought this wild idea was worth supporting, I somehow secured funding for both the structural build-out and necessary circus equipment. The result was the Circus Lab, a large movement space on campus explicitly designed to encourage interdisciplinary exploration in and cultivation of the circus arts.[2]

The Circus Lab is now (happily) a place where I have everything I need to successfully teach *Circus and Philosophy*. There are six aerial dropline points, making it easy to take down and change out aerial apparatuses such as aerial silks, trapezes, ropes, and aerial hoops (lyra). We have an array of safety mats, juggling equipment (yes, 108 juggling balls, along with 30 rings, and a dozen clubs), two unicycles, and more things on the way. Yet it is also a place where we can close the door, turn off the music, sit in chairs or on mats on the floor, and have a conversation. The Circus Lab is a space intended for trying unusual things, messing up *safely*, a place for fostering creativity and play, and then (if so desired) enough space for sitting around and talking about the experience. There are some upkeep and maintenance issues to coordinate regularly—the drop lines, rigging, and anchor points are frequently inspected by an aerial rigger, for example. Otherwise, the majority of the first kind of logistical concerns have been addressed.

Content and Structure

It is true that there is not a lot of philosophical literature about the circus. (Not yet, anyway.) However, there *is* quite a bit of circus literature connected to philosophy, a significant amount of which is related to my primary area of research: metaphysics and epistemology (M&E). So I initially stuck to what I knew.

In *Contemporary Circus* (2019), for example, the authors discuss philosophical theories of personal identity and philosophy of mind to help elucidate the relationship between a circus artist and their apparatus. This provides an unexpected entry into issues about consciousness and mind-body problems, leading us to Descartes's *Meditations*, Dennett's (1978) "Where Am I?" and Clark and Chalmers's (1989) "The Extended Mind," In *The Ordinary Acrobat* (2013), Duncan Wall recounts his experience as a novice in circus school, integrating discussions of circus history with reflections about how the circus is a strive for human excellence. He emphasizes the importance of habit and practice, the challenges and rewards of having physical limitations (the body) and being bound by laws of nature. This easily blends into discussions of Aristotle's *Nicomachean Ethics*, d'Holbach's arguments for hard determinism in *The Systems of Nature* (1770), and Chisholm on free will in *Human Freedom and the Self* (1964). Many circus high-wire walkers have long been interested in balance as a perceptual sense (in addition to the traditional five) by their many years of cultivating and perfecting their equilibrioception. This makes a fascinating path into Aristotle's *De Anima*, Petit's first-person accounts of wire-walking in *Man on Wire* (2008), Geurtz's analysis of perceptual knowledge in *Culture and the Senses: Bodily Ways of Knowing in an African Community* (2003), and MacPherson's taxonomy of perceptual sense in her introduction to *The Senses: Classical and Contemporary Philosophical Perspectives* (2011).

Sticking to familiar M&E literature and merely using the circus arts as a springboard into such topics worked just fine at first. Yet I realized it was more like using circus as some kind of reverse intellectual pick-pocketing: "Look, juggling balls!" I cry, misdirecting the students' attention while I sneakily slip Aristotle and Descartes into their heads. I'm ordinarily pretty utilitarian about pedagogical methodology: *however* I can get students to learn and love philosophy is fine by me. Yet it seemed that there was a missed opportunity here. I didn't want to discuss philosophical issues that merely *happened* to fall out of circus. Rather, I wanted to discuss philosophical issues that were constitutive of the first-person circus experience. I wanted to discuss issues that the students had unique insight into by way of *doing* circus.

The result has been a natural progression from primarily M&E to an intriguing mix of M&E, ethics, aesthetics, social and political philosophy, with a particular focus on issues of personal identity, self-knowledge, trust, and community. For example, we discuss paradoxes of tragedy, fear, and failure together with lessons on juggling and acro-balancing, supplemented by Hume's *Of Tragedy*, Carroll's (1990) *The Philosophy of Horror*, and Juul's (2016) *The Art of Failure*. By getting students to try an activity that most people are pretty terrible at (juggling), students start to see the value in messing up and failure, despite how paradoxical doing so might seem to be. We discuss C. Thi Nguyen's (2017) "The Aesthetics of Rock Climbing" together with lessons on how to climb, as we physically navigate ourselves through aerial silks and ropes. After lessons on skills that focus on the artistry of practiced, repetitive motion (which most circus skills require), we read Barbara Montero (2017) on flow. We also discuss Alex King (2017) on subtlety vs. heavy-handedness in aesthetic judgments, and Jason Leddington (2016) on magic, impossibility, deception, and trust. This leads us to our acro-balancing sessions, which we connect up with Nick Riggle's (2017) discussions on social openings and community building. As you might imagine, the content for this class is (delightfully) constantly evolving, in a way that aims to significantly integrate the students' personal experiences with various philosophical topics as they bumble about learning circus.

This is a 100-level class. No experience in either circus or philosophy is required. Most of the students have never picked up juggling balls, sat on a trapeze, or read (or heard of) Descartes or Hume. It is typical for many students not to even know what philosophy is, or to know that philosophy is a stand-alone subject that students can major or minor in. So it is important that both the primary philosophical content and the circus skills that are taught are accessible. It is also important to keep the class size manageable—for both the students' physical safety and fostering and maintaining a trusting classroom environment for discussion. With this in mind, I cap the class at thirty-six. (It always fills up; there is always a waiting list.) With six drop lines, this translates to at most six students to each point, which is enough for everyone to have a chance to try everything, but not too many that it makes spotting and physical safety a concern. It also makes discussion sessions intimate enough to give everyone a chance to have their voice heard. In short, the course is a tasting bite of both circus and philosophy for a relatively small group of students, designed to inspire them to want more of each after the class is over. At the end of the semester, if they want more philosophy, they are directed toward the philosophy department's future course offerings. If they want more circus, they are directed to our undergraduate circus club (which, incidentally, was founded in December 2021 by one of my students after taking *Circus and Philosophy*).[3]

As for *teaching* the circus skills, I had a clear vision from the start: I'd get help. Outsourcing the circus portions allowed me to connect with the local circus community and to bring outside guest instructors to campus. It also helped to ensure that anyone—even if they do not have so many years of recreational circus experience as I do—can run a class like this. This course is designed to be passed down to others.

To craft the assignments, I followed examples of courses in the fine and performing arts (in particular, dance and theater), as well as KHP (Kinesiology and Health Promotion), where in-class active participation is crucial. In addition, I applied to have *Circus and Philosophy* qualify as a UK Core Requirement in *Intellectual Inquiry in Arts and Creativity*. This is part of our university's basic general education program, intended to give students exposure to a broad swath of academic disciplines on their way to getting a specialized degree. Once this was approved, I used our university's basic template for implementing a participation-heavy course, which (by design) included opportunities for open-ended projects meant to inspire the students to substantially engage with the relevant artform or creative process. In other words, there was already a fortunate match between what I envisioned for this course and what the University of Kentucky officially encouraged in one branch of their core curriculum.

As a result, participation and attendance count for a higher percentage of the final grade than in my other philosophy classes, and written work and a final creative project comprise the rest of the assignments. I assign three written papers, each of which is similar to paper assignments in my traditional philosophy courses—except that the prompts require that the written discussion include reflections on the students' first-person circus experiences. The final project is open-ended, intended to give them broad creative license to demonstrate circus skills they've learned, to coordinate with other students, and to innovatively incorporate circus with the philosophical ideas we've covered. (One semester, nearly the entire class arranged a large group presentation which gave a broad overview of the entire course. This involved some of the students demonstrating various circus skills, while other students spoke about the relevant philosophical ideas. It culminated in a collective class-wide acro-balancing exercise requiring them to all work together, as they related it to our philosophical discussions of trust and community. It was *amazing*.)

So, in case you were wondering: students do not fail the course if they can't juggle or can't climb to the top of the silks; no one gets an A if they can. And honors students do *not* get credit for juggling more of the things. They have to write longer papers and are held to higher qualitative standards, just as expected in other, more traditional philosophy classes.

One last comment about the final project. The circus is a performing art. As such, it seemed appropriate for a class such as *Circus and Philosophy* to require the students to *perform* the art. The final project should be some kind of in-person event where students *show* what they have learned. At first, I wasn't sure what this kind of assignment might look like. It seemed that it should at least involve an oral presentation, and perhaps also a physical demonstration of the praxis part of the course. However, I was worried that some students would find this terrifying. Indeed, the thought of such a final project would have made an introverted past version of myself nauseous and running for the bathroom. So why make students go through such an ordeal if there was a chance that it would produce so much anxiety?

Many assume that an education in theater and the performing arts is only for those who are already inclined toward performance. If you are outgoing and vivacious and love to be the center of attention, then the performing arts are for you. If you are not, then go take Chemistry or English or Statistics where you can happily stay away from unnecessary public engagements. But this is mistaken. The performing arts are not just eccentric extracurricular activities for those who immediately find them easy and fun. They have real-life skills to teach anyone—*especially* for those of us who do *not* immediately find being in front of others easy or fun. Lessons in theater and dance—and circus!—are different ways of getting us to be comfortable with our bodies in space. They teach us how to speak and move in front of others, how to read body language, use body language, and how to cultivate the ways in which we understand, empathize, and communicate with other fellow human beings. Learning how to exist comfortably within the gaze of another is just one of many crucial life skills that the performing arts can teach. Yet to assume that we must have this skill before it's taught is, of course, to get the causal order of education backward.[4]

With this in mind, I decided to require a final in-person presentation.[5] Many students are initially quite apprehensive about this. Yet most of them soften to the idea as the semester rolls on, as they get more comfortable with themselves and each other. By the end of term, many are still nervous, but they do the assignment anyway—sometimes in a group to make things easier. To my delight, they usually surprise themselves by how much they enjoy it, and inevitably, there are lots of laughs and highfives and cheers on performance day. (If you've ever been to a contemporary circus show or tried recreational circus, you'll know what I mean.) It's still unsettling at the start of each term for me to trust that the students will eventually pull it off at the end of term; I'm always a bit unsure of how it will go. Yet despite the initial uncertainty, the final assignment is now one of my favorite parts of the course—and it is often theirs, too.

Embracing the Spectacle

But why go through all this trouble? What's the point? One reason is simply personal: I love circus, I love philosophy, and I love showing students how these two loves of mine are interestingly combined. Another reason is pedagogical stealth. In my experience, students are incredibly receptive to philosophical content when you come at them sideways with it, distracted with other (non-philosophical) things. Reverse intellectual pick-pocketing *works*. Yet the reason why *circus* makes such a successful diversion is because there's an often unrecognized advantage in getting students to start thinking deeply about the world and our place in it *through* spectacle.

"Spectacle" is often understood as something seen or experienced that invokes a sense of wonder, awe, or curiosity. Overwhelmingly beautiful phenomena in nature—the aurora borealis, the Grand Canyon, a beautiful sunset over the ocean, a double rainbow[6]—are all spectacles in this sense. Man-made examples might include grand architectural feats such as the Great Wall of China, Egyptian pyramids, and the Lloyd's Building in London (Dyckhoff 2018). This gets close to the reaction I have seen in students on their first day of walking into the circus lab. The spectacle *sets the mood*. Once students see the wondrous, unexpected, and strange, they immediately get eager to find more. A taste for the spectacular is *contagious*. Yet "spectacle" is also often used pejoratively. More than merely being a social nuisance, spectacles are sometimes assumed to be aesthetically shallow, devoid of reflective thought or substance.

Yet there is an often-overlooked value in participating in spectacles *with others*. Consider contemporary group spectacles such as flash mobs, public celebrations and parades such as Mardi Gras, festivals such as Ren Faires, Comic Cons, or Burning Man. Whether you love them or hate them or find such events confounding or annoying, it seems clear that, for the participants involved, they foster a very strong sense of community and belonging. There is a playful joy that comes about from finding those who share your weird tastes in fun. When we make spectacles of ourselves *with others*, we often experience aesthetic goods such as the pleasure of moving *cooperatively*, or the satisfaction of successfully collectively creating something worth being seen.

It's clear that there are personal benefits to being part of a community with a shared aesthetic: it just *feels* good to find your people. Yet there are also clearly many social goods that come about from creatively cooperating with others: communication, collaboration, trust, and community. The second time I taught *Circus and Philosophy*, one student commented on the evaluations: "the class made me come out of my comfort zone and become more closely acquainted with people I didn't even know, which contributes to UK feeling more like a community rather than a college of hundreds of strange students." Getting to know people you otherwise wouldn't, forming a community, instilling a sense of trust in yourself and others, cultivating an environment where someone feels comfortable going outside of their comfort zone—*these* are the sorts of goods that teaching philosophy through circus can generate. Moreover, it gives the students an opportunity to *directly experience* these goods for themselves, instead of merely speculating about them as an impersonal intellectual exercise. *This* is why there is value in teaching philosophy this way.

Notes

1. For more, see "Circus and Philosophy: Teaching Aristotle through Juggling": https://aestheticsforbirds.com/2021/12/02/circus-and-philosophy-teaching-aristotle-through-juggling/.
2. For more on the Circus Lab, go here: https://megwallace.org/circus-and-philosophy-193/.
3. "Just Clowning Around," https://kykernel.com/86471/features/just-clowning-around-uk-circus-club.
4. Regrettably, this causal order confusion is quite common. I've frequently heard friends or students say things like "Oh, I could never juggle, I'm too uncoordinated," or "Oh, I can't do yoga, I'm not flexible," or "Oh, I can't take logic, I'm not good at math." In each case, one of the primary reasons to *do the thing* is to *learn to do the thing*. The learning comes *during* and *after* the doing, not before. It's unfortunate that so many of us so often forget this. An indication, perhaps, that more of us need to simmer more seriously over Aristotle (*Nicomachean Ethics*, Book II).
5. To be sure, I also have flexibility in this assignment to make accommodations if needed, just as I would on any assignment in any of my other more traditional philosophy classes. Yet for those that do not need accommodations, a final in-person component is expected.
6. https://www.youtube.com/watch?v=OQSNhk5ICTI.

References

Aristotle (2017). *De Anmia* (The New Hackett Aristotle). Trans. C.D.C Reeve. Indianapolis: Hackett Publishing Company, Inc. Translation Edition (September 2017).

Aristotle (2019). *Nicomachean Ethics*. Third Edition. Trans. Terence Irwin. Indianapolis: Hackett Publishing Company, Inc. (August 2019).

Carroll, Noel (1990). *The Philosophy of Horror: Or Paradoxes of the Heart*. New York: Routledge.

Chisholm, Roderick (1964). *Human Freedom and the Self.* The Lindley Lecture. April 23, 1964. Department of Philosophy. University of Kansas.

Clark, Andy, and David Chalmers (1989). "The Extended Mind." *Analysis* 58(1): 7–19.

Dennett, Daniel (1981). "Where Am I?" in *Brainstorms: Philosophical Essays on Mind and Psychology*, 310–23. Cambridge, MA: MIT Press.

Descartes, René (1641). *Descartes: Meditations of First Philosophy.* Cambridge Texts in the History of Philosophy. Second Edition. Cambridge, TAS, Australia: Cambridge University Press (February 2017).

d'Holbach, Baron (1770). *The System of Nature.* Gloucestershire: Echo Library. January 2007.

Dyckhoff, Tom (2018). *The Age of Spectacle: The Rise and Fall of Iconic Architecture.* London: Windmill Books.

Geurtz, Kathryn Linn (2003). *Culture and the Senses: Bodily Ways of Knowing in an African Community.* Oakland: University of California Press.

Hume, David (1757). "Of Tragedy" in *Four Dissertations and Essays on Suicide and the Immortality of the Soul* Printed for A. Millar, 193–209. South Bend: St. Augustine's Press. April 2001.

Juul, Jesper (2016). *The Art of Failure: An Essay on the Pain of Playing Video Games.* Cambridge, MA: MIT Press.

King, Alex (2017). "The Virtue of Subtlety and the Vice of a Heavy Hand." *British Journal of Aesthetics* 57(2): 119–37.

Lavers, Katie, Louis Patrick Leroux, and Jon Burtt (2019). *Contemporary Circus.* New York: Routledge.

Leddington, Jason (2016). "The Experience of Magic." *The Journal of Aesthetics and Art Criticism* 74(3): 253–64.

MacPherson, Fiona (2011). "Introduction" in Fiona MacPherson (ed.), *The Senses: Classic and Contemporary Philosophical Perspectives*, 3–34. Oxford: Oxford University Press.

Montero, Barbara (2017). "Against Flow" in Sally Davies (ed.), *Aeon.* aeon.co/essays/the-true-expert-does-not-perform-in-a-state-of-effortless-flow.

Montero, Barbara (2018). *Thought in Action: Expertise and the Conscious Mind.* Oxford: Oxford University Press.

Nguyen, C. Thi (2017). "The Aesthetics of Rock Climbing." *Philosophers Magazine* 78: 37–43.

Petit, Philippe (2008). *Man on Wire.* New York: Skyhorse Publishing.

Riggle, Nick (2017). *On Being Awesome: A Unified Theory of How Not to Suck.* New York: Penguin Books.

Wall, Duncan (2013). *The Ordinary Acrobat: A Journey into the Wondrous World of Circus, Past and Present.* New York: Vintage.

Wallace, Meg (2021). "Philosophy through Spectacle." *Aesthetics for Birds.* December 2, 2021. https://aestheticsforbirds.com/2021/12/02/circus-and-philosophy-teaching-aristotle-through-juggling/.

6

Ethics for Everyday Life: Designing a Core Philosophy Course

K. Lindsey Chambers

Students at the University of Kentucky, like many other universities, are required to take a series of core or general education courses. These core courses are aimed at broadening their understanding of themselves and the world they live in and equipping them with the critical thinking and problem-solving skills they need to navigate that world. Core courses create a bridge across disciplines and colleges by building unified criteria of content and assessment. Core requirements can also introduce students to new disciplines by requiring them to take courses outside of their major or college. A student in business or nursing who has not previously considered taking a philosophy course (or even realized there are courses in philosophy) might discover they can fulfill a humanities core requirement by taking a professional ethics course. Or an engineering student might discover that they can fulfill a creative arts core requirement by taking a science fiction and philosophy course.

Most core or general education requirements include a humanities component. Students must take a course that teaches them how to identify and analyze different philosophical, moral, cultural, and/or religious viewpoints. Learning how to analyze and build arguments that tackle different value and belief systems is the bread and butter of moral philosophy courses. An introductory ethics course often does so by introducing students to the basics of the ethics canon, which usually includes some combination of virtue theory, deontology, and consequentialism (and sometimes applied ethics or feminist ethics). This sort of introduction to the canon of moral philosophy does the job: students learn about the major competing moral theories, they examine arguments for and against them, and they practice applying those theories to particular moral problems. For aspiring philosophy majors, an introduction to the big-ticket views in moral philosophy—their strengths, weaknesses, and implications—provides an important foundation for their continuing coursework in philosophy.

For the majority of students taking an introductory ethics course who are not philosophy majors, however, an introductory ethics course taught as a survey of the canon is not all that interesting or, if we're honest, all that useful. Such a course can be made more interesting by selecting cases and thought experiments that make the canonical views more vivid and that highlight the difficult moral problems we face when they conflict. But even so, an introductory course in ethics, billed and taught as an introduction to moral *theories*, is not antecedently appealing to students who aren't already interested in philosophy, nor is it the *only* way to introduce students to moral philosophy.

Dressing up a course designed for budding philosophy majors misses an opportunity: how might we design an introductory ethics course that teaches the essential skills in a core humanities course that better serves the interests and needs of students who may not take another philosophy course? What would such a course look like? I'd wager it wouldn't need to (and we wouldn't want it to!) survey Aristotle, Kant, or Mill. If we want students to connect to material they aren't antecedently interested in and *demonstrate* that it matters for their lives, we could simply teach them how to think about the moral problems that show up *in their actual lives*.[1] What are the familiar (and sometimes unfamiliar) problems that everyone faces? What pressing questions do our students face right now? What issues will they encounter as they leave university and make their way in the world? A course that leads with familiar moral questions, as opposed to canonical moral theories, is primed to catch the attention of students who don't already know or care about what moral theories have to offer.

These questions became the impetus for *The Ethics of a Human Life*, an introductory ethics course that I designed as a core humanities course explicitly for students who would not normally consider taking a philosophy course.[2] It is designed both chronologically and *pessimistically*. The course introduces moral problems that show up as a human life progresses, from coming into existence to what happens after we die. Each topic is introduced as a surprising moral problem or with an argument that some stage of life or life milestone is bad for us. That is, we investigate each stage of a human life by looking at an argument for a counterintuitive or controversial argument about what can go wrong at that stage.[3]

The course begins with the antinatalist challenge to procreation (Benatar 2006). Was it bad for you to come into existence in the first place? Were you wronged by your creators? My students, like most people, typically assume that their life is a gift, or at least, they assume that they should be grateful that they were created in the first place. Starting with the problem of antinatalism sets the tone for the rest of the course: trying to figure out what makes a human life go well becomes a more difficult task when we can't rely on the assumption that it's better to have the chance to live a human life than not at all!

Students are then asked to consider the unique challenges that arise at different stages of a human life. They consider arguments that it is bad to be a child because of one's vulnerability and dependence on others, as well as an argument that being an adolescent or young adult is especially challenging because they are simultaneously held responsible as if they are adults without enjoying the privileges and freedoms of that come with being full adults (Gheaus 2015; Hannan 2018; Munn 2012; Schapiro 2003; Schouten 2017; Thomson 1971). Toward the end of the course, students grapple with arguments about the stigma of aging, the badness of death, why it might be better to die than be immortal, and finally, whether they should care about what happens to others after they die (Jaworska 1999; Nagel 1970; Nussbaum and Levmore 2017; Scheffler and Kolodny 2016; Williams 1973).

In the middle of the course students examine the different kinds of relationships they have with others. When we consider friendship, rather than looking at, say, Aristotle on the value of friendship, we consider an argument that friendship presents a moral danger (Cocking and Kennett 2000), as well as an argument that one can have a moral duty to help one's friend move a body (Koltonski 2016). Though students are not typically faced with the latter dilemma (I hope!), they are familiar with the tensions that arise when they disagree with their friends, especially when those disagreements are about what's right. Students are then able to think about the *value* of friendship, not as something we assume is always morally good, but as a relationship that may be valuable *despite* its moral risks.

In a similar vein, students are often already keenly aware of the ways in which their choices when it comes to sex and romantic relationships can harm or cause pain to themselves and others. For instance, in class we discuss how using swipe-based dating apps to find casual sexual partners might wrongly objectify others, especially when we reject others as sexual partners on the basis of their race, social class, size, or disability. Instead of directly asking what's good about sex, we look at what's fraught about our sexual desires and choices, how those desires can be shaped in ways we ourselves think are objectionable, and then we consider why sexual desire, however problematic, might still be an important component to good sex (MacKinnon 1989; Nussbaum 1995; Srinivasan 2018). Students are then asked to think about whether it's okay that we love some people but not others, and they're challenged to rethink whether it's a good idea to marry the person they love (Brake 2011; Herman 1993; Keller 2000; Velleman 1999).

The final relationship we investigate is the one between parents and their children. Students begin the course with the antinatalist argument that they have been wronged by their (biological) parents by being created, as well as arguments that it was bad for them to be a child and an adolescent. These arguments put pressure on their own choice to become a parent. We ask what moral limits there are on parental choices, and what value there is (if any) in becoming a parent by creating a biologically related child as opposed to, say, adopting (Brennan and Noggle 1997; Brighouse and Swift 2014; Haslanger 2009; Velleman 2005).

By centering pessimistic arguments about what can go wrong at various stages of a human life or in different kinds of human relationships, the course challenges students' preconceived ideas about what's good or right while at the same time demonstrating the value of making and evaluating philosophical arguments. Students may not walk away with changed beliefs or even any firm beliefs about what they think is right in the cases we discuss. But they do gain a better understanding of what's *difficult* about the questions we've considered because they better appreciate their moral stakes. Though the course doesn't directly ask what makes for a good human life, what it is to be a human self, or what obligations they have to other persons, students leave the course having considered these larger questions in the context of the more specific topics we tackled.

By design the course syllabus does not have any canonical figures. All the course readings are written by contemporary philosophers. Each paper advances a discrete argument about one of the topics above, an argument with which the students will likely disagree. This gives students the opportunity to practice evaluating and making philosophical arguments without first siding with a traditional theoretical team or camp. Of course, the arguments we consider may lean toward one camp or another (and that may be more obvious to the philosophy majors in the course), but to most of the students these arguments stand or fall on their own merits, not because they represent the view of some famous historical figure or theory. What's more, because the philosophers we read are not famous (to the students), students tend to be more confident proposing their own take on the arguments and questions at hand.

Offering a core humanities course in philosophy presents a unique opportunity to introduce new students to interesting philosophical questions while equipping them with the tools philosophy offers for addressing those questions. We can make good use of this opportunity by designing core philosophy courses that better serve non-philosophy majors by considering what philosophy can offer *them*.

Notes

1. Many philosophy departments offer a course that covers contemporary moral issues. Though the problems canvased in such a course are relevant to students in a broad sense (e.g., capital punishment, euthanasia, animal rights, etc.), this sort of course often fails to address the sort of small-scale moral issues students regularly face in their day-to-day lives.
2. The course was largely inspired by a bioethics course of the same name developed by Jorah Dannenberg.
3. Dan Korman takes a similar strategy in his introduction to philosophy textbook (Korman 2022). His textbook introduces students to philosophy by way of arguments for surprising or controversial conclusions (e.g., we don't have free will, we don't know anything, God doesn't exist).

References

Benatar, David (2006). *Better Never to Have Been: The Harm of Coming into Existence*. New York: Oxford University Press.
Brake, Elizabeth (2011). "Is Divorce Promise-Breaking?" *Ethical Theory and Moral Practice* 14(1): 23–39. https://doi.org/10.1007/s10677-009-9217-z.
Brennan, Samantha, and Robert Noggle (1997). "The Moral Status of Children: Children's Rights, Parents' Rights, and Family Justice." *Social Theory and Practice* 23(1): 1–26. https://doi.org/10.5840/soctheorpract19972311.

Brighouse, Harry, and Adam Swift (2014). *Family Values: The Ethics of Parent-Child Relationships*. Princeton, Oxford: Princeton University Press.

Cocking, Dean, and Jeanette Kennett (2000). "Friendship and Moral Danger." *Journal of Philosophy* 97(5): 278–96.

Gheaus, Anca (2015). "Unfinished Adults and Defective Children." *Journal of Ethics and Social Philosophy* 9(1): 1–22. https://doi.org/10.26556/jesp.v9i1.85.

Hannan, Sarah (2018). "Why Childhood Is Bad for Children." *Journal of Applied Philosophy* 35(S1): 11–28. https://doi.org/10.1111/japp.12256.

Haslanger, Sally (2009). "Family, Ancestry and Self: What Is the Moral Significance of Biological Ties." *Adoption and Culture* 2(1): 91–122. https://dspace.mit.edu/handle/1721.1/64650.

Herman, Barbara (1993). "Could It Be Worth Thinking about Kant on Sex and Marriage?" in Louise Antony and Charlotte Witt (eds), *A Mind of One's Own: Feminist Essays on Reason and Objectivity*, 49–68. Boulder, CO: Westview Press.

Jaworska, Agnieszka (1999). "Respecting the Margins of Agency: Alzheimer's Patients and the Capacity to Value." *Philosophy and Public Affairs* 28(2): 105–38. https://doi.org/10.1111/j.1088-4963.1999.00105.x.

Keller, Simon (2000). "How Do I Love Thee? Let Me Count the Properties." *American Philosophical Quarterly* 37(2): 163–73.

Koltonski, Daniel (2016). "A Good Friend Will Help You Move a Body: Friendship and the Problem of Moral Disagreement." *Philosophical Review* 125(4): 473–507. https://doi.org/10.1215/00318108-3601037.

Korman, Daniel Z. (2022). *Learning from Arguments*. PhilPapers Open Access.

MacKinnon, Catherine A. (1989). "Sexuality, Pornography, and Method: 'Pleasure under Patriarchy.'" *Ethics* 99(2): 314–46. https://doi.org/10.1086/293068.

Munn, Nicholas John (2012). "Reconciling the Criminal and Participatory Responsibilities of the Youth." *Social Theory and Practice* 38 (1):139–159.

Nagel, Thomas (1970). "Death." *Noûs* 4(1): 73–80. https://doi.org/10.2307/2214297.

Nussbaum, Martha C. (1995). "Objectification." *Philosophy and Public Affairs* 24(4): 249–91. https://doi.org/10.1111/j.1088-4963.1995.tb00032.x.

Nussbaum, Martha C., and Saul Levmore (2017). *Aging Thoughtfully: Conversations about Retirement, Romance, Wrinkles, and Regret*. Oxford, New York: Oxford University Press.

Schapiro, Tamar (2003). "Childhood and Personhood." *Arizona Law Review* 45: 20.

Scheffler, Samuel, and Niko Kolodny (eds) (2016). *Death and the Afterlife*. The Berkeley Tanner Lectures. Oxford, New York: Oxford University Press.

Schouten, Gina (2017). "Fetuses, Orphans, and a Famous Violinist: On the Ethics and Politics of Abortion." *Social Theory and Practice* 43(3): 637–65.

Srinivasan, Amia (2018). "Does Anyone Have the Right to Sex?" *London Review of Books* 40(6).

Thomson, Judith Jarvis (1971). "A Defense of Abortion." *Philosophy & Public Affairs* 1(1): 47–66.

Velleman, J. David (1999). "Love as a Moral Emotion." *Ethics* 109(2): 338–74. https://doi.org/10.1086/233898.

Velleman, J. David (2005). "Family History." *Philosophical Papers* 34(3): 357–78.

Williams, Bernard (ed.) (1973). "The Makropulos Case: Reflections on the Tedium of Immortality" in *Problems of the Self: Philosophical Papers 1956–1972*, 82–100. Cambridge: Cambridge University Press. https://doi.org/10.1017/CBO9780511621253.008.

7

Less Is More: How and Why to Avoid a Content-Driven Class

Heather Anne Phillips

With thousands of years of philosophical work, instructors often feel obliged to cover as much content as they can, especially in core and intro classes. This mentality turns content into a master the instructor must serve, instead of a tool that serves the instructor's goals for her students. While this tendency is understandable—there are just so many interesting topics and articles—indulging it often turns philosophy courses into information dumps when they have the potential to be so much more. In this chapter, we first will explore the reasons why goal-centered course creation and implementation is not only better for your students, but also a better way to teach and do philosophy. Then, we will walk through the practical aspects of embracing a goals-centered approach. Finally, I will answer some questions instructors often raise when attempting to move away from a content-driven class.

You've been asked to teach a new philosophy course or you are wanting to rework a course you have taught before. Allow me to lay out the reasons I contend that your first step should not be thinking about content, but, instead, thinking about outcomes. At a time when students (and administration) wonder what the humanities have to offer, it is important that we not forget ourselves.[1] Even the most basic intro philosophy courses can introduce and develop critical thinking, encourage broadness of thought and charity toward opposing views, and challenge students to have (and expect) good reasons for their beliefs. Depending on the context, courses with smaller enrollment and/or more advanced courses can offer much-needed written and verbal communication instruction and practice.

In addition, goal-centered philosophy courses invite students to be active participants in their learning. Instead of passively listening as the professor explains the key points of a text, students are invited to discover not only the arguments, meaning, and purpose of a specific text, but in so doing, also learn how to uncover the arguments, meaning, and purpose of any text. Of course, this process must happen in stages, where at first the professor takes a more active role modeling in class how to uncover key aspects of a text and then, later, allow students in groups and on their own to take more of a lead in the process. At first, many students will be frustrated, especially if they usually take classes focused on knowledge transfer from professor to student. But as much as professors enjoy the aha moments of our students, students enjoy them even more. In these moments, students begin to recognize learning as something they can do, not just something they receive.

Finally, goal-centered philosophy courses devote time and energy to longer-lasting aims. Except in upper-level major courses and grad courses, which require a focus on content as we train philosophers in the ideas, theories, and texts of our field, students leave most other philosophy courses with very little memory of the specific theories, texts, or authors. Instead, they might remember some interesting thought experiments and the outlines of some moral theories, but mostly they retain whatever broader and bigger ideas were conveyed and any skills they learned through active practice and application. If the course focused mostly on content and most in- and out-of-class time was spent reading texts and hearing lectures on them, students will retain very little long-term. However, if the course used texts to generate interest, introduce new ideas, challenge standard thinking, and/or provide practice in unpacking conclusions, reasons, and objections, then, those students who accepted the invitation to play a starring role in their own learning will likely carry with them an appreciation for the complex and changing nature of knowledge, the importance and reward of not being a passive receptacle of information, and the skills they sharpened.

Of course, all of the above requires careful planning, student-centered instruction, and time. When I start to plan a new class (or rework an old one), I have to consider whatever content is dictated by the course I have been assigned or am creating (i.e., ethics, early modern, epistemology, etc.), but instead of allowing the content to dominate my focus, I think of it as the color palette from which I must paint. I must use those colors (topics/texts), but there is a lot of freedom in how I will use them. Instead, my focus is, first, on the student outcomes I hope the course will achieve and, second, on the strategies and methods (in and out of the classroom) necessary to accomplish those outcomes.[2] For instance, here is how I articulate the learning goals in my biomedical ethics class.

> Students who proactively engage with course content both in and out of class and who seek help when uncertain or confused, will leave this course with:
> 1 The ability to identify, discuss and evaluate moral arguments and the reasons provided (or not) in support of those arguments.
> 2 A better understanding of multiple (and typically) conflicting approaches to various bioethical issues.
> 3 An increased willingness to seek to understand and fruitfully discuss perspectives different from one's own and with which one might disagree.
> 4 The ability to develop, articulate and defend a position on a topic discussed in the class.
> 5 An understanding of key bioethical problems and a general sense of the philosophical approach to moral questions.

These certainly are not the only goals I could have selected, but notice that accomplishing them requires I do more than assign journal articles or textbook chapters covering various bioethical issues and create tests aimed mostly at gauging student comprehension of those texts. Instead, I assign texts at a pace—one text of moderate length per week[3]—that leaves room for students to reflect on the reading before class[4] and move beyond merely coming to understand the text during class. In particular, as outlined above, there must be time to help students learn how to not just read a text, but unpack the arguments, consider objections, identify strengths and weakness, and begin to form their own responses.

In assigning any text, my aim is never for the students to gain maximal understanding of the text itself.[5] Of course, we cover key elements, but in doing so the aim is always to further the above learning goals. In the beginning, I actively guide students through the process of identifying main arguments—conclusions and reasons—and, then, help them understand how to evaluate an argument's strengths and weaknesses and how the argument could be improved. By allowing room for students to gain understanding of and practice in the above process, I am increasingly able not only to allow, but also expect students to take the lead in unpacking the arguments we encounter. This process is aided by in-class activities such as reflection exercises, guided large-group and small-group discussion, argument reconstruction,[6] and debate, just to name a few. When an instructor assigns either too many or too long texts per week and/or focuses on ensuring that students gain a complete and thorough knowledge of the texts as texts, there typically is limited time to have students engage with, seek to understand, and evaluate arguments within the text. It's like walking through an art museum listening to a recorded audio guide. Sure, you are told interesting information about each of the paintings, but you rarely are encouraged to seek to understand the paintings and form your own thoughts about them. Similarly, content-directed classrooms typically are structured to impart one-way information and expert-mediated understanding of distinct texts. There is a time for such instruction, but in order for philosophy classes to have long-term impact we must not only help students develop the ability to seek to understand and analyze the varied arguments that surround them, but also allow them to experience first-hand the rewarding aha moments that result from the effort they put in.

Thus far I have made my case for abandoning the content-centered philosophy class and move toward goal-centered classes in which we invite students to take an active role in their learning by learning and practicing attitudes and skills philosophy is excellent at teaching: critical thinking, charitable reading, curiosity, seeking to understand, identifying, forming and analyzing arguments, written and verbal communication, to name a few. In the space that remains, I will attempt to answer common concerns and questions I hear from instructors about adopting such an approach to teaching.

My teaching/research load is too heavy to have time to rework my classes.

This is a common and very real concern. In fact, every time I learn about a powerful new pedagogical idea or technology I want to figure out a way to incorporate it into my classes. However, I have had to learn that doing so is not feasible. Instead, I have learned to make small, but impactful changes each semester with the goal of building toward the course I ideally would like to teach. For instance, you might begin by reviewing your reading list and consider one or two texts you could remove in order to free up time for more student engagement with the text so as to learn and practice argument identification and evaluation skills. Or you might consider your desired student outcomes for your class, rework them as needed, and then choose one to focus on next semester. Make a few changes that would help better accomplish that goal. Changes to our classes are like repairing a boat at sea. Unless you are creating a new class from the ground up, you can never fully dismantle your class. Instead you make strategic changes over time.

I am convinced about the benefits of goal-centered courses, but these require a lot of pedagogical skills and activities with which I have no experience.

You are not alone. Very few of us received meaningful pedagogical instruction during our Ph.D. programs, so we have to muddle together what we can through reading teaching books, taking trainings, or learning from our colleagues. My advice here is much like what I said above. Don't undervalue baby steps. Once you have identified a change you want to make in your course, seek out instruction and ideas on how to implement that change. If your course currently has few opportunities for students to actively engage during class, spend some time learning about active learning activities. If you are worried that allowing for more student engagement might take your class off-course, learn a bit about cultivating and facilitating discussion. It might take you a while to move your course the full distance you want to take it, but starting is the most important step. As you become more comfortable with a change, start thinking about the next step you would like to take and how to get there.

The course I teach is a prerequisite for upper-level philosophy classes so I have to cover as much material as possible.

This can be tricky. Of course, you want to cover anything that a future instructor will assume students have learned in prerequisite courses. However, we must also remember that doing philosophy is not primarily about knowing a lot of philosophy. Doing philosophy requires certain attitudes (curiosity, openness to new ideas, seeking to understand, etc.) and skills (critical thinking, argument identification, creation, and evaluation, verbal and written communication, etc.). Our students will thrive in other philosophy courses if they have developed these attitudes and skills. In fact, the reason that upper-level major and grad courses can be content-heavy is because we hope that these students have already learned and developed the skills necessary to fruitfully engage with and integrate the new material they are exposed to. Our intro and lower-level courses must cultivate philosophers or at least philosophical thinking. Then, those who want to gain further knowledge of philosophical content will have the skills needed to do so.

Many of my students are non-humanities majors and they are accustomed to content-centered courses. Won't they dislike having to be more active in the classroom?[7]

A key element to the success of an active-learning classroom is cultivating an environment in which mistakes and wrong answers are expected as a normal part of the learning process. If we remind our students that they are in our class to learn and, therefore, by definition don't already know everything, then there shouldn't be any surprise that they get confused, offer a wrong answer, or don't understand. Unfortunately, this is not the usual attitude that students (and many faculty) have, but with constant explicit reinforcement, you can help lower the expectation that every answer or contribution must be 100 percent on target. This, then, allows students to be more willing to contribute because they are being appreciated for their effort, not necessarily on its content. In fact, I find that students enjoy answering questions, engaging in discussion, and offering their perspectives when they don't worry that every word will be parsed and judged. Further, most students (both those who contribute and those who observe) find classes in which students are regularly invited to participate much more interesting.

I am ready to begin moving my courses away from a content-centered approach. Where do I begin?

I think the most productive place to start is to familiarize yourself with backward course design. The internet is overflowing with information, tutorials, and worksheets that do a wonderful job of helping one understand both the theory and the practice. Begin to think of your classes in terms of the student-centered goals you aim to accomplish. Then think about how your particular course content can be used to facilitate those goals. Reimagine your in-class time and your assignments as opportunities to learn, practice, and demonstrate the knowledge and skills necessary for your students to attain your course goals. For some it will be a radically new way of creating and carrying out their classes, but as you adopt and incorporate these ideas, either in baby steps or in the creation of a new course, I am confident you will appreciate the impact this approach can have on your students and on your enjoyment of teaching.

There is much that couldn't be said or covered here, but I hope I have at least convinced you to consider the possibilities of a goal-centered approach to philosophy classes. I would like to end, however, with one caveat. The success of this approach rests not only on the instructor, but also on the students. Goals-centered instruction only works when students are willing to take some ownership of their learning by rejecting passivity and embracing active learning. While the instructor must make the case for this form of learning, create an environment conducive to student engagement, and provide opportunities for it, students must step up and contribute.[8] Student buy-in and engagement will vary from class to class for a variety of reasons. While we must always be willing to evaluate our approach when we encounter resistance, we must also recognize that the attainment of the goals we seek is not fully within our control.

Notes

1. The approach I advocate here is not motivated as some way to turn philosophy into a college-to-career darling at your university. However, we do ourselves and our students a disservice when we don't focus on the real benefits philosophy has always had to offer.
2. Many readers will recognize that I am advocating for a backward-design model of course creation. The literature and guides for backward course design is vast and important. It is not my intent (nor within my ability) to attempt to replicate this literature or replace one's need to consult it to fully carry out such a design of one's course. I merely want to argue that such an approach not only benefits our students, but also maximizes the best that philosophy has to offer.
3. The pace you use will depend on the aims and level of the course you are teaching.
4. I use Perusall—an online social annotations tool—to assign readings because it encourages interaction both with the text and with fellow classmates.
5. Again, I am referring to intro and lower-level, non-major courses.
6. I find argument mapping particularly effective for this; though other methods can work as well.
7. This is in no way a critique of non-humanities courses. Expert-mediated transfer of knowledge is entirely appropriate for some classes.
8. By this I do not mean that every student must regularly talk in class. Rather, they must play an active part in their learning both in and out of class by carefully and thoughtfully engaging course content and exercises, remain attentive and curious during class, contribute to small group discussion and activities, seek help when confused, and plan for and carefully complete course assignments.

8

The (Un)Political Classroom: How Content and Positionality Intersect to Encourage Students to Be Agents of Change

John R. Torrey

Philosophy classrooms are unique spaces for educational and even personal development. In my experience, both in pre-college and in college classrooms, students receive a different educational experience because the focus is often on the development of student abilities to, at least, interpret the world they live in. What is allowed inside these spaces because of the encouragement of criticality is the freedom of thought that students get to experience when parsing out philosophical issues in their own world, however messy those issues may seem. That this freedom is available inside philosophy classrooms is something to be celebrated in its own right—it is laudable to be able to impact how young minds engage and develop their own worldviews. We do not, however, teach in a vacuum, and this suggests that we should be considerate of what issues we choose to navigate inside of our courses because of the world that we live in and the various institutions we work at. There will be questions that are pressing for some communities that are not necessarily even on the intellectual radar of other communities; issues that bear directly onto the experiences of some people in our classrooms and only affect others tangentially; and worldviews that can be offensive to some and seen as justifiable for others. Inside of this space, it is our job as professors to assist our students with their skill development in creating arguments to support their worldviews and abilities to critique and receive critique for the worldviews they hold.

In many universities across the country, the choices of which worldviews that professors can engage, critique, or educate their students about has been taken out of our hands. Recently, states such as Florida and Texas have passed legislation that bans Critical Race Theory (CRT) and diversity, equity, and inclusion training at state universities under the guise of protecting students from harmful content. This type of legislation directly affects the abilities of professors to develop their course content because of the threat of potential penalties, including being fired. As a result, more philosophy professors will find themselves asking a different question—"what *can* I teach that won't impact my career prospects while still being an effective philosophy professor?"

My goal here is to provide a method to try to answer that question for professors, one focused on recognizing one's positionality inside of three spaces: the values that we wish to impart to our students, our personal positionality, and our professional positionality. Through these lenses, we can start to find answers that assist each of us with providing our students with the educational experiences we desire, specifically the sorts of experiences that encourage our students to be change agents in the world.

1 Values in the Classroom

As a professor, I find nothing more exciting than seeing the proverbial light bulb pop up when a student is engaging with an issue and comes to a realization or conclusion that they had not considered or makes a connection that helps the world make sense to them. Part of what makes that so exciting for me is that student has taken on an important role in developing their own worldview. I take it as a central goal in my classroom to provide students with the skills and information needed to continue developing their sense of the good, how they want their world to exist, and how to advocate for that world through philosophical argument. This approach directly informs perhaps not what I teach, but certainly *how* I teach. This includes encouraging conversations over lectures and using a philosophy-for-children inspired model of the community of learners.

There is a wide range of skills we might wish to impart on our students—punctuality, strong writing and research skills, and an ability to charitably engage with opposing views are a few that come to mind. A central focus on the goal of our classroom experience should begin with an examination of the values we want students to gain, not merely the skills, because the values we wish to inculcate will be the primary lens through which students will engage our courses and when they leave our classrooms. The kinds of values that would empower people to create change, on my view, include (but are not limited to) having respect for others, having a strong sense of justice, a sense of anger toward injustice in their communities, and perhaps most importantly that they recognize the power of their own agency and the agency of others to develop their own notion of the Good. Having that awareness allows us to move forward to assessing how we want to transmit those values, whether through in-class experiences or readings and assignments, and how we can do that with the backgrounds and experiences that we possess.

2 Personal Positionality

Inside the classroom is a group of people with a shared goal—gaining new information. That said, people are extraordinarily different, something that makes teaching both difficult and exhilarating! To that end, when we think about how who we are affects making our choices about what and how we teach, it may be important to remember that both students and professors have personal positionality inside the classroom. Let's start by considering the concerns about diversifying the canon (or decolonizing the canon, another approach to shift the context in which we offer a diverse representation of what philosophy looks like). Shifting the basic understanding of who participates in the canon and what questions are canonical is in large part due to changes in our student populations who wish to see more of themselves and the relevant philosophical questions for themselves and their communities, one notable group being Black women who have been increasing their attendance and graduation from college. Even if the institution has more of a traditional population, broadening our students' understanding of the canon through diversifying our content is a proper response to a historical problem of excluding important voices in philosophy. The current trend toward the diversification of syllabi suggests that we should recognize that our students wish to see themselves and others in their community reflected inside their classroom experiences. In many instances, this means recognizing that we may be quite differently positioned from our students. It is here that the political nature of the classroom begins to show itself quite nakedly—our students frequently want to know what *we* think, especially about meaningful issues, and we have to make a choice regarding how open we want to be with our social and political views. That said, it behooves us to notice that the kind of people we are impacts how course content is received by our student communities and impacts our ability to connect with our students.

Since the Covid-19 pandemic transitioned us from online back to in-person learning, I make a statement at the beginning of class each term: "Your professors are not machines." We are people with unique research interests, diverse backgrounds, and different characteristics that define each of us as the people that we are. We cannot ignore that *who* we are plays a role in how the course is received. For example, I'm a Black man who frequently teaches moral and political philosophy in my introductory classes. I recognize that students may have assumptions about my moral or political leanings because of my racial and gender combination (to say nothing about other aspects of my identity that students may have assumptions about!) and that I can opt to be explicit about my leanings as part of how I teach or purposefully leave students in the dark as a pedagogical practice. These are political choices on what kind of connection I take to be desired to help my students utilize the values mentioned above and more importantly, become change agents. Another example is to consider that certain conversations in the classroom about issues connected to racism and racial justice are ones that may be received differently because I am a Black man (one needn't have to imagine similar situations for a variety of people, including professors who identify as women teaching about sexism having assumptions about them and their political positions) and a similar set of choices exists in this example— lean into whatever perceived personal expertise I have, purposefully leave my experiences out of the pedagogical framework of the class, or provide my actual views on the presence of racism in society. In both examples, my person provides me a chance to add to the classroom experience, regardless of which choice I make, provided my choice is in the service of providing a critical lens of student agency and generating a different context for my students.

3 Professional Considerations

While last, this is perhaps the most important lens to evaluate one's choices by—how secure is my job going to be based on my curricular and classroom choices? Some states have stronger unions, other states have fewer legal protections, but there is a current trend by some states to shut down attempts to increase diversity in their educational experiences that are funded by the state, impacting many public institutions and plenty of private ones. Connected with that is how this might impact tenure applications for junior professors who work at teaching colleges or small liberal arts colleges in these states. Simply put, there is no replacement for the comparative safety afforded tenured professors and the kind of pedagogical choices they can make. This has changed significantly in recent years, as legislation passed in Florida and Tennessee can threaten the jobs of those who violate their anti-CRT laws. I would not be able to teach at least two of my preferred classes at a public, state-funded institution in those states because it would violate the legislation. My research might violate the same legislation! For both junior and senior faculty, the tenure protection does not necessarily have the same strength that it would have otherwise. As a result, let's split this into two scenarios—states without anti-CRT legislation, and states with those laws in place. For those who are in states without CRT legislation, then the professional considerations are primarily satisfying the needs of the institution and the department and generating a student population that wants to change how the world sees them and how they see the world. For those who do have their job security in question, I cannot in good conscience suggest that they jeopardize their job! I can, however, suggest that they find space to continue to provide accurate information to their students, a goal that all professors share as part of their commitment to education.

Conclusion

What can you teach? It truly depends on where you are, who are, and what you want to accomplish inside your classroom. While the job security lens is the most acute of the three to help gain insight, there is no doubt that who you are plays an important role in how we transmit skills and information. Our ability to be effective teachers improves when we recognize the relationship that we have, as people, with our students in the classroom. Teaching, in my mind, is a mutual endeavor to become better scholars and stronger learners in an environment that we help to create alongside our students. Crafting that environment requires being intentional about the choices that we make with our pedagogy, and those choices are not made in a vacuum. Let's continue to inspire our students by meeting them as the people that we are, while recognizing that there are places (from departments, to institutions, to local and state governments) that have created obstacles for that task. Thankfully, these obstacles are not insurmountable (yet!) and our young people continue to have an unshakeable spirit of change that we must foment and nurture.

9

A Student's Reflections

Zyaire Hadrian Agee

During one of the very first philosophy classes that I attended at the University of Alabama at Birmingham, I quickly realized that there was something fundamentally different about the way that I understood philosophy (and the world) in comparison to those around me.

When issues were presented and we, the students, were tasked with working through solutions and establishing stances of our own, each time I spoke and my peers followed, something was off. It wasn't that we were constantly at philosophical odds, it was more that our inherent understandings of the issues being presented were clashing. We didn't just come to different conclusions; we identified the root causes differently. This sort of cyclical conflict made it feel impossible to ever get anywhere during discussion because we hadn't established an agreed-upon baseline to argue from. I couldn't argue for or against Issue A because neither I nor my peers fully agreed on what Issue A actually was. We were vaguely aware of the concept we were talking about, but when it came down to the act of actually *doing philosophy,* there was no objective starting point. It felt like the most watered-down, unintentional case of a strawman fallacy I ever encountered but on constant repeat. I could never articulate why I felt like this, and the frustration that came along with not having the language to communicate this was incredibly annoying.

It took a while for me to identify that this was just a case of conflicting defaults. Maybe our cultural backgrounds contributed to our differences in social beliefs. Maybe our life experiences made us disagree on what even constituted a problem that needed to be solved. I specifically remember a conversation that took place in class about the process of unlearning defaults and temporarily thinking, "This is it! This is the reason things are weird!"

While all of these likely have a hand in the makeup of our ideals, what I eventually came to realize was that this was not just a difference in opinion or understanding. It was an opposition of our worldviews entirely. The reason that it always felt as though we were comparing apples to oranges is because that's exactly what was going on. But what was even more polarizing was that it felt that the purposes of our discussions were coming from different places, as well. Most of the points felt unsolvable whereas I believed and was taught that philosophy should be a tool to find answers. We would learn about an argument made by people much more experienced, seasoned, and who were smarter than we were, and we're left with no thoughts other than, "Well, this all makes sense to me. How could anyone disagree with these points? It seems obvious!"

(Spoiler Alert: things are rarely ever obvious when philosophy is involved.)

Those "obvious" arguments were always soundly trounced by some other equally as experienced, seasoned, and smart individual who would pull each student over to their side. And this sort of thing continued. This endless sort of tug of war. Back and forth like dogs on leashes, we were yanked between stances and arguments that always made perfect sense alone but fell apart when put up against one another. Was this fun? Absolutely. Picking apart every little argument made and driving my classmates crazy by challenging their reflective equilibrium gave me a lot of joy and allowed me to remain deeply engaged with every single lesson. Did I also wonder what the point of it was? 100 percent. I enjoyed provoking existential crises as much as the next undergraduate philosophy major, but many of these pressing issues seemed inherently impossible to actually solve with any degree of certainty. To me, that was a major problem. It wasn't just *a* problem; it was *the* problem.

Western philosophy generally feels detached in the academic sense, whereas philosophy as I knew it was more of a tool to be applied for the betterment of the community in daily practice. Up until my freshman year of college, the majority of my interactions with philosophy were through the lens of the African diaspora. I was originally committed to attending Howard University, and it was through existing philosophy students and summer opportunities that I was able to see the history of philosophy outside of Plato, Aristotle, and Socrates. Most of my self-study centered around the works of Angela Davis, James Baldwin, bell hooks, and W.E.B Du Bois—all of whom were prominent, Black intellectuals focused primarily on issues concerning racism, systemic oppression, and a myriad of other urgent social matters that had a real, material impact on our community. The sort of philosophy that we were doing in class, though, was more abstract, in a sense.

There is an "outside looking in" element to academia in which things are talked about because they're interesting versus important. But because there's no skin in the game for these topics, there's also no sense of urgency or true need to resolve them. There is thinking just for the sake of thinking and then thinking with a purpose beyond that. Of course, thinking for the sake of thinking has a use. Sharpening critical thinking skills has many applications outside of the scope of the classroom; however, I'm not sure that this alone justifies the lack of solution-oriented work. Why can the purpose not jointly take care of improving critical thinking whilst *also* solving a real problem? And how can looking beyond the hope of developing that skill change the way that we engage in the act of philosophy? Books, journal articles, etc., are all full of academic jargon that would go over the heads of the common person, but these are the very people that philosophy itself is meant to help— at least from my perspective. The end result is a classroom full of students with the ability to think critically in circles, but the potential for something greater is *right there*. I found myself thinking critically, alright. I thought *very* critically about why I should only care about critical thinking.

Despite this purpose, many Western ideals focus on the individual and promoting self-interest. This isn't *bad*, though. It's just different from what I know, and that's perfectly okay. But in separation from a community-minded goal, it can feel very stark, unmovable, and (I say this very reluctantly) pointless. This is where I landed on day two of Contemporary Moral Issues. I felt out of place and very nervous about what I could contribute to the class in addition to wondering how the class could benefit me and what I even wanted to gain from it. But rather than dropping the class, I took a risk and actually communicated these internal struggles with my professor, and I was genuinely *encouraged* to bring that difference in paradigm into the class discussions and homework responses. Who would have thought that effectively communicating your struggles with those capable of fixing them would have a positive outcome?

That outcome is what I think all philosophy courses could benefit from, the opening of the space for other schools of thought. And not just a utilitarianism versus Kantianism debate or moral objectivism versus cultural relativism argument. I mean a true tolerance and whole acceptance of the various philosophies and disciplines of the world. One has to understand that the motivations of each person are vast and colorful and that a one-size-fits-all approach is very limiting and even off-putting. A changing point in my education was acknowledging that my "why" for doing philosophy did not align with the common "selling points" of academic philosophy such as improving my critical thinking skills, becoming a better writer, or being able to articulate my arguments in an intellectual way. While these are nice by-products of what I do, they don't push me to become better, nor do they drive my passion for doing philosophy. Identifying this difference in purpose is what led to the realization that personal values matter, and creating space for these varying values creates a more enriched experience for all involved. Students have hundreds of personally relevant reasons for doing philosophy, and professors have an easier time of showing how learning philosophy can benefit a wider variety of students rather than just those who want to make their family members dread arguing with them.

Philosophy did not originate in the West. Various aspects of it did, of course, but the diverse and evolving field of philosophy itself has its roots from all around the world. Many philosophy professors engage with their students by presenting arguments and poking holes in student responses, but not engaging with alternative defaults can leave several un-poked holes in the reasoning of the professor. And because you can't task yourself with repairing invisible holes, this is a mutually beneficial arrangement in that growth is promoted on both ends. Suppressing these disciplines and failing to incorporate more varied lines of thinking could unintentionally make a number of students feel as though they're running into a brick wall without the resources to scale it. When student and teacher alike are jointly working to bridge the gap, the need to scale that wall disappears. Instead, both work on either side to create a door, giving each the opportunity to step over into the other's worldview.

Part II

The Philosophy Classroom

10

Save the 1001 Cats! Lecture as a Performance Art

Jimmy Goodrich

Something's gone wrong. You assigned David Lewis's "Many, but almost one" for class tomorrow, but the pre-class homework reveals mass confusion about the Paradox of 1001 Cats. What do you do? You don't really want to lecture ... Students should be active in their learning! And lecturing impedes that. But some lecturing seems necessary to make the discussion productive. How do you avoid reducing your students to passive recipients of your chalkboard scribbles? How do you engage them while you drone on about the Paradox of the 1001 Cats?

Students are accustomed to sitting through two hours or more of other people talking. They do it all the time. They sit, say nothing, and remain highly engaged. I'm referring to movies, theater, stand-up comedy, and other performance art forms. I think we can learn something from these art forms that will improve our lectures.

I'm not saying, "Film, theater, and stand-up are entertaining. We should try to be entertaining." I doubt Michelle Yeoh's approach to acting, Jordan Peele's approach to writing, or Suzy Izzard's approach to stand-up comedy involves all and only the thought, "I should now try to be entertaining." They each have their own set of ideas and techniques that guide their respective approaches. And it's these ideas and techniques—ideas about and techniques for writing good stories, getting into character, and live performance—that might improve our lectures.

Skeptical? There's a proof of concept. YouTube channels, ContraPoints, and PhilosophyTube have millions of views on philosophy-driven video essays lasting over an hour and a half. (That's certainly longer than I ever lecture.) These videos present nuanced philosophical ideas with characters and a narrative arc. Of course, Natalie Wynn and Abigail Thorn, the creators behind these YouTube channels, are immensely talented, have a greater aesthetic flare than I could hope for, and often spend a month or more writing scripts and producing these video essays. So, lectures like their video essays may be beyond us mere mortals. But let's not let the best be the enemy of the good: Our lectures can still be improved.

Here's an example from my teaching. A few years back, I taught a course on "Capitalism and its Critics." (According to the registrar, it was called "Business Ethics.") Often, well over half the class spoke without provocation. But sometimes, it was like pulling teeth. I could tell from some pre-class assignments that our session on Marx's Theory of Exploitation was going to be a tooth-puller. I needed to explain Marx's motivations to the students. But here's a principle of good story writing: Show, don't tell. If I just told the students about Marx's context and concerns, that may have helped. They may have been able to "get it" well enough to parrot the ideas back to me in an exam. But would it have helped them really *engage* with Marx's ideas? Would it help them see why so many have been attracted to the way Marx thinks about exploitation? I doubt it.

A couple of weeks earlier, I had listened to a podcast of comedians discussing Dan Harmon's Circle. It's a way of breaking a story down into distinct conceptual parts. Harmon uses it to guide his writing. Here it is:

1. You: A character in their normal situation.
2. Need: Something isn't quite right for the character—they need something.
3. Go: The character enters an uncomfortable situation.
4. Search: The character adapts to the situation.
5. Find: The character gets what they needed.
6. Take: The character pays the price for what they've found.
7. Return: The character returns to their familiar situation.
8. Change: The character has changed.

These eight parts of a compelling story aren't necessarily distinct chronological steps of a good story. Instead, they are conceptually distinct parts that should somehow be clear to your audience. It's easy to find blog posts and videos explaining Harmon's Circle further, including a video by Harmon himself.

If I need to show the students what Marx's motivations are, maybe I could use Harmon's Circle. I tried it. I designed my lecture around playing a character. This character begins as a kind of classical liberal that cares, not unlike John Locke, about the connections between individual property rights and labor. (The students were familiar with these ideas from earlier in the course.) This classical liberal's desire was just to see what her theory says about what a worker should be paid. The situation becomes uncomfortable when she has trouble squaring some of her views with the idea that business owners should make a profit from owning the means by which workers' labor becomes more productive. If we're following Locke, then surely we have property rights over the product of our labor! But then how could it be that there are profits for the company if that's just more of what was produced by the workers' labor? Private ownership of capital seems to get in the way of giving laborer's the product of their labor! The classical liberal *adapts*: She accepts that the best way to resolve the tension in his views is to deny that the means of production can be privately owned. The classical liberal now realizes, however, that she's not much of a classical liberal anymore. And this itself is a cost. It makes her uncomfortable. But she has returned to the comfort of consistency, though changed in her views.

From what I can tell, it was a success. The students had more than a few ideas about where my character went wrong: "You were misunderstanding Locke!" "The owner of capital actually puts in more labor than the workers!" But these ideas weren't rooted in a failure to see Marx's motivations. Some seemed more impressed by the motivation than they did in their pre-class assignments. It's hard to say, of course, what would have happened had I run that class as I normally did. It seemed better than other sessions where the pre-class assignments raised similar red flags.

I should stress something. I didn't just organize my lecture around a narrative structure. I was playing a character. I wasn't just presenting a puzzle as premises on the board, detailing the various consistent ways to reject the premises of that puzzle, and then assessing the few ways that are most plausible. I wasn't giving a lecture on Marx's place in history, comparing his views with Locke's to pinpoint the heart of their disagreement. I was attempting to act as genuinely concerned and confused about "my" own views as I could. It all involved a kind of physicality. I was pacing around the room. Sometimes I was quiet and contemplative. Sometimes I was loud and gesticulated wildly. I didn't plan most of it. Once I outlined the character, their story, and committed to the bit, the "physicality of the performance" came naturally. You hear actors say that sort of thing. And, of course, actors are mocked for taking it overboard. I certainly couldn't bear to see a video of that day of class.

Anecdotally, there's one success of trying to make a lecture more performative. Do I now organize all my lectures in this way? No. I only rarely do. It's a lot of extra work. It takes a lot of energy during class. It seems like an inappropriate approach for certain topics, like when teaching on the ethics of abortion. And it requires trust in your students. I lost the nerve to attempt my performance of Marx's Theory of Exploitation with a recent batch of students. I had failed to engage the students in other ways earlier in the course and the fear of being met with blank stares won out. I regret it.

But let's again not let the best be the enemy of the good. My hope is to slowly add more and more performances to my lecture repertoire. Or at least, I hope to get more comfortable introducing ideas and techniques from various performance arts into my lecture style. One step, therefore, is to learn more about storytelling and performance. Harmon's Circle is just one tool. It may not be helpful in every case or for everyone. There are countless other ideas and techniques we might draw on. I've begun glancing at two books for beginners. The first is the *Upright Citizen's Brigade's Comedy Improvisation Manual*. The second is a book about screenwriting called *Save the Cat* by Blake Snyder. So far, I've found at least a couple of things in them useful. Maybe you will too. Or perhaps you'll find an acting, writing, or improv class helpful. I'd be curious to know.

Improving as a teacher is hard work. And there's obviously a lot more to teaching than lecturing. One benefit of my suggestion, I hope, is that trying to get better at lecturing by improving one's knowledge of ideas and techniques for storytelling and performance is that it's often good fun.

References

Harmon, Dan (2020). "Dan Harmon's Story Circle." *YouTube*, uploaded by Adult Swim. https://www.youtube.com/watch?v=RG4WcRAgm7Y.

Snyder, Blake (2005). *Save the Cat: The Last Book on Screenwriting You'll Ever Need*. Studio City: Michael Weise Productions.

Walsh, Matt, Ian Roberts, and Matt Besser (2013). *Upright Citizen's Brigade's Comedy Improvisation Manual*. New York: Comedy Council of Nicea LLC.

11

Flatten That Hierarchy: Everyone Wins When We All Teach (and Learn) Together

W. John Koolage

Introduction

One central idea to learner-centered pedagogy is, unsurprisingly, that learners should be foregrounded in the classroom and course-related learning activities. There are many ways to express the idea of foregrounding the learner. For instance, we find it among the central ideas of pedagogic paradigms, such as Ungrading, and in conceptual metaphors for teachers, such as facilitators or guides on the side (to be contrasted with sage on the stage). While the idea is common in teaching and learning circles, and has a number of conceptualizations, it does not get enough airtime in casual conversations about teaching. Generally, I think centering the learner does not get its due because it sounds scary or maybe even simply wrongheaded. Further, I think, as an idea to bring to practice, it just is not very clear. I think it is simply hard to see what it would take to foreground learners. Most of us were not taught in this way, or when we were, we did not recognize it as such.

In what follows, I briefly explore the idea of foregrounding learners along the lines of my favorite frame for this sort of pedagogic move: flattening the hierarchy. On this frame, foregrounding learners by flattening the hierarchy is mostly about adopting a handful of ideas about teaching and learning spaces and participants. In my experience, an effort to flatten the hierarchy starts as simply as making new observations about one's classes, assignments, and students, in light of these ideas. Eventually small changes and new observations lead to new learning activities and syllabi for courses. These changes can produce benefits for students, but, equally importantly, for faculty. While changing one's dispositions can take some time, there are a few reasonably simple things you can do to get started.

I teach both at the introductory level and the upper and graduate level. At the lower levels, I tell students that the classes are learner-centered and that this means the class is about their learning and about them. At the upper level, I welcome students to the research team. While "telling" is only so effective as a teaching and learning tool, it serves to get us started on the right foot. If you are genuine in these first "tellings," students are easily recruited to partner in making your classroom hierarchy flatter. Beyond this, have fun and embrace your curiosity. Try out letting students lead each other to an understanding of some argument, or spontaneously let them complete an in-class assignment as a class instead of as individuals. Enjoy the learning that your learners offer you. Not every attempt to flatten the hierarchy is an unmitigated success, but flatter is better.

Flattening the Hierarchy

In his 2013 book, *Creating Significant Learning Experiences,* L. Dee Fink says this provocative thing: power dynamics in the classroom should move away from faculty, as distributors of knowledge, to "empowered students sharing with each other and faculty." He also suggests that faculty's role should be to develop students, rather than classify and sort them. These suggestions nicely summarize the idea of flattening the hierarchy, but require some unpacking.

Content knowledge is not *transferred to* students, rather it is *co-constructed with* students. The idea that faculty are to distribute knowledge to students was famously critiqued by Paulo Freire, who called this "the banking concept of education" (Freire 1970). In addition to the horrors of the commodification of knowledge, a conception of knowledge as something to be bestowed on students fails to properly describe the process by which learners develop an understanding of course material, find its relevance in application to their lives, integrate it to their various identities, and build new knowledge. In short, not only is the idea that knowledge is to be merely distributed to students a tool of oppression, it fails to describe learning in any useful way at all.

In *Teaching to Transgress*, bell hooks calls for a dramatic change in power dynamics and the roles of faculty and students (1994). hooks observes that academic institutions play a role in entrenching racism and sexism, and if we are to empower change in these structures, we must at least (1) validate (and teach for) boundary transgression, and (2) diminish racism and sexism, and their scaffolds, in our classrooms. She notes a number of ways we should transform our pedagogy, including a call to re-conceptualize knowledge, link theory to practice, and empower students. Further, hooks argues that implicit and explicit divisions between students and faculty, whether by race, class, gender, professional standing, and so on, prevent the validation of boundary transgressions and enforce traditional (read: racist and sexist, at minimum) standards. In short, hooks contends that genuine teaching requires that students and faculty allow for environments where hierarchies are diminished, put on display, or simply flattened. Describing the idea of foregrounding learners as a project of flattening the hierarchy is to adopt hooks's frame, and I think we should be all right with that.

The combination of a reconceptualization of knowledge in learning, an anti-racist and anti-sexist agenda, and taking on the role of developing students, rather than classifying or judging them, makes up the core of the idea of flattening the hierarchy and foregrounding learners.

Reconceptualizing Knowledge

The reconceptualization of knowledge that is required for learner-centered teaching is complex, but I will highlight one important component that serves to help flatten the hierarchy. We need to abandon the idea that knowledge is a fixed set of facts that is transmitted from expert knowers (faculty) to students. The idea of co-construction replaces this idea. Students are participants in building knowledge together with faculty. There are many ways to understand the new conception but one mundane version is this: students assemble their own knowledge by fitting what is offered to their prior learning and concerns, and how faculty offer those ideas and tailor them to students is also of relevance to the construction. A more radical version is more like this: we must abandon the idea that there is some target knowledge that faculty help students move toward, and instead we should hold that even the knowledge faculty and students are building together is aimed at approaching a fallible and moving target. One could go even further and suggest that knowledge exists as it is enacted, meaning that theory becomes knowledge only when it is put into practice. I think the mundane version of co-construction is enough to begin a journey toward flattening the hierarchy. The more radical your view on this reconceptualization the more readily one will flatten the hierarchy.

Given the breadth of possibility in learning activity design and variation in preferences about such design among faculty, and the goal of foregrounding students by flattening the hierarchy, of empowering learners to transgress boundaries, it seems only right to suggest some heuristic guidelines rather than concrete rules. I propose that there are three sets of ideas that faculty, as learning activity designers, could keep in mind for hierarchy flattening purposes. These sets of ideas are as follows: (1) mattering and partnership, (2) the fluidity and dynamics of the teacher-student distinction, and (3) social procedural objectivity and the epistemic landscape of the classroom.

Partnership and Mattering

The ideas of mattering and partnership have been examined in the teaching and learning literature, and the idea of mattering is enjoying a resurgence as a component of belonging.

Taking on the idea of partnerships in the classroom can help you empower students. The kind of partnership I have in mind can be summarized as follows: partners collaborate to achieve agreed upon goals. Further, they do so without a pre-set division of labor or leadership structure. Faculty who think of themselves as partners in learning endeavors will find that this language for teaching and learning is pretty different from the traditional vernacular, and it frees us up to consider new ways of engaging in the teaching and learning process. One common view is to consider students as experts in their experience of teaching, but this attitude, while helpful, is limiting relative to the partnership language. Partners can take the lead, direct the flow of learning, and bring knowledge and expertise from many domains. Experts on their own experience have a very particular thing to offer, so I find it more useful to focus on the partnership idea than the expertise idea.

There are at least two advantages to partnering with students to build knowledge around course content. First, students are much more engaged when they know the class is about their learning and they are a part of the learning team. Put slightly differently, when students are partners in knowledge production, and are thus responsible for teaching and learning in the classroom, they bring more to the table. Students learn more and take preparation much more seriously when they are asked to teach something as compared to being asked to answer some questions or take a test. Since one cannot develop students who aren't engaged, this is a pretty significant advantage. Second, in my experience, preparation time for class goes way down when students are partners in the teaching and learning of the material. In fact, aside from being a content expert, your role in the class becomes more like pointing students at important curiosities in the material and enjoying where the class goes from there. Letting class go where it may, providing redirections and summaries takes a bit of practice, but is richly rewarding.

A compliment to the partnership idea is a conception of mattering. Students have to matter in order to flatten the hierarchy and foreground learners. On the one hand it might seem silly to say this, since there is no teaching without learners. On the other hand, how faculty convey to students that their voices, ideas, and learning matter is not captured by simply reporting on the necessity of learners. To foreground learners, to develop students, and to flatten the hierarchy, learners need to matter in broader and deeper ways than merely being necessary for a teaching and learning interaction. This comes in degrees; so, adjusting a due date or providing an opportunity to redo an assignment are ways of demonstrating that learners, and learning, matters. Further along the continuum we find things like designing activities that permit students to relate course content to their identities or communities. You are enacting this concept of mattering when your course activities are responsive to the learners you do have, rather than some abstract, idealized, or, worse, fictional learner. When learners matter, their voice is heard, their ideas are considered, and their experience (not just of learning) shapes what and the way in which they are taught. The benefits of adopting this conception of mattering are not as obvious as partnerships, but without this conception it is difficult to see how one could be seriously flattening the hierarchy.

The Dynamic Nature of Teacher and Learner

The next idea that serves flattening the hierarchy is sometimes summarized by the phrase, "teacher-student, student-teacher." In familiar learning activities, such as large group discussion, whether one is learning or teaching can turn on a dime. At any given moment in a discussion, one may find themselves clarifying content, offering examples, making connections between ideas, or tinkering at the edges of some theory. This can happen whether you began the class as a teacher or a learner, a faculty member or student. Further, one might find themselves asking clarification questions, offering a counter argument, or being skeptical of some conclusion. This too can happen regardless of one's institutional role (faculty or student) and regardless of whether one was teaching or learning at the start of some particular investigation. In short, the teacher-learner distinction is fluid, or dynamic and enacted. In this way, faculty can serve to flatten the hierarchy by permitting this fluid movement between roles as teacher or learner for all members of the class, regardless of institutional role, in most, if not all, classroom interactions.

Learning is fun. I think many of us deprive ourselves of the opportunity to be a learner in our own classroom. Taking onboard the idea that we are in the role of learner frequently, even as we assume the responsibility of "faculty member" in our classrooms, can bring a lot of joy to your classroom. Since the role of learner intersects with lots of other roles, including those handed to us by race, gender, and so on, how to demonstrate and enact this fluidity can vary greatly from one faculty member to the next. Taking the roles of teacher and learner to be dynamic or fluid certainly serves to foreground students, but it can also reduce stress associated with thinking of teaching as a kind of performance, an enaction of expertise, or, worse, a "thing we must do."

Social Procedural Objectivity and the Classroom as Research Program Avenue

Helen Longino's conception of science as a social endeavor provides her an opportunity to highlight some previously unappreciated epistemic norms. When a science takes seriously diversity, equity, and inclusion, theories and hypotheses are opened to novel transformative critique—serving to reduce bias in hypothesis creation. A diverse community of knowers is more likely to identify sexist or racist experimental designs, or research programs that embed systematic bias, and so on. Further, such a group is more likely to move a research program away from the traditional interests of powerful, white men. Increasing the objectivity of a particular research program is about increasing the possibility of transformative critique. Longino identifies four pillars that play important roles in increasing the possibility of transformative critique: shared standards, recognized avenues for critique, community uptake of critique, and equality (or tempered equality) of intellectual authority.

This idea of social procedural objectivity requires only a few transformations to benefit our classrooms, both for teachers and learners, and to flatten the hierarchy. If we treat our classroom as filled with research associates, with whom we are working to build knowledge, students become epistemic partners in identifying bias and generating potentially transformative critique. In lower-level courses, they may serve to transform examples, explications, and applications of philosophical content. The classroom is an avenue for sharing of philosophical ideas, complete with a set of co-researchers (students) to engage in the critique of engagements between philosophical ideas and (currently) outsiders to philosophy. At the very least, students transform how we share philosophical research programs with other students. Further, in developing students to engage philosophy's shared standards for critique, we can also discover new questions about those standards. In these ways, students can impact the objectivity of philosophical research programs, indirectly, by way of their faculty teachers. Lower-level classes are also opportunities to bring a greater number and diversity of researchers into disciplinary research programs. Upper-level and graduate classes offer even greater opportunities for our new researchers (students) to engage in transforming disciplinary research programs, often as partners or independent researchers, not just indirectly. Thus, I find that conceptualizing students as co-researchers, or at least partners in research, and conceptualizing classrooms as avenues for critique, both serves the disposition to flatten the hierarchy, but also serves to improve the objectivity of disciplinary research programs.

One way this might be characterized is as an asset-based, rather than deficit-based, approach to philosophy teaching. Rather than thinking of students as lacking something, philosophical skill or knowledge, we think of them as having a great deal to offer to philosophic research programs—or at least to the objectivity of our research programs. On this account, the faculty member, and our own disciplinary research programs, has much to gain from treating students as co-researchers.

Some Final Thoughts

Flattening the hierarchy is one way to think about foregrounding learners in our teaching and learning. It is called for by scholars, such as L. Dee Fink and bell hooks, who believe that decreasing the distance between faculty and students is critical to achieve both quality learning and important social goals. I suggested a very small set of ideas can serve to transform one's view of teaching and learning. Those ideas include reconceptualizing knowledge, partnering with students and ensuring they matter, recognizing the dynamic nature of the teacher-learner distinction, and finally considering the classroom as another avenue for the possibility of transformative critique in disciplinary research programs. Taking on these dispositions and enacting changes to teaching in light of them serves to flatten the hierarchy. More interestingly, though, enacting these ideas has benefits for faculty. These benefits include the joy of learning, lessening the burden of performing the expert role, sharing of classroom responsibilities for learning, greater student engagement, and an opportunity to engage students in philosophical research programs as partners (or at least important potential critics). Put slightly differently, a reconceptualization of the faculty role *qua* teacher can really serve the faculty member.

I am curious whether these tools for flattening the hierarchy can also serve to lessen the worry that greater student engagement comes at some cost. If our classrooms become avenues for transformative critique, and learners (including faculty) engage in well-chosen efforts to co-construct knowledge, teaching becomes an opportunity to improve the research programs to which these classes are connected. Put a little differently, I am skeptical that foregrounding learners in the classroom really comes at some cost to the discipline, as is sometimes suggested. Further, I believe I have shown it doesn't have to come at the cost of the teacher.

Giving up the authority of the classic conception of teacher can feel scary. I think that fear comes from a particular conceptualization of the classroom and of the roles of teachers and students. I hope I have offered some ways of thinking about the teaching endeavor that make flattening the hierarchy not just less frightening, but downright rewarding.

References

Fink, L. Dee (2013). *Creating Significant Learning Experiences: An Integrated Approach to Designing College Courses*. San Francisco, CA: John Wiley & Sons.
Freire, Paulo (1970). *Pedagogy of the Oppressed*. New York: Continuum.
hooks, bell (1994). *Teaching to Transgress*. New York: Routledge.
Longino, Helen (1990). *Science as Social Knowledge*. Princeton, NJ: Princeton University Press.

12

Trust in the Classroom

Barrett Emerick

In *Pedagogy of the Oppressed*, Paulo Freire argued that trust is essential to good teaching (2012). Indeed, it is partly constitutive of what he called the "problem-posing" model of education, which we should embrace, rather than the "banking model," which we should reject. I have come to believe that he is right—deeply so—and that trust is operative at just about every level of good teaching. In this chapter, I will briefly review Freire's view before exploring three different ways that trust takes shape, why it is so important, and how it can be cultivated practically. Although what it will take to build such trust will vary in different contexts (affected by things like classroom size, student population, and political climate), it is my hope that this account will prove useful to a wide range of learning environments.

1 Liberatory Education

Freire was concerned with the way that education can be a method of liberation from oppression, both in that it could help students to challenge oppressive social structures, and insofar as education is itself a method of liberation. One outcome of oppression is that people are dehumanized, reduced to tools that can be used to maintain exploitative social arrangements. This is due to the ways that exploitative ideologies can constrain someone's understanding not only of the world, but also of their own place in it, leading to what Sandra

---

Many thanks to Chris Blocher, Ariana Peruzzi, Sara Protasi, Rosa Terlazzo, and Brynn Welch for their valuable feedback and insight.

Bartky called "psychological oppression" (1990: 22–32) which involves what she called "internalized intimations of inferiority" in which someone buys in to the story that the world has told about them as "less than" (1990: 22).

Bartky's work helps me to understand that, for Freire, the aim of education was no less than to help students to become more fully human (2012: 44). I take him to mean that the aim of education should be to help students to become more complete people—more able to exercise agency, to think critically, and to be better equipped to self-determine and indeed to self-create. The liberatory potential of education thus plays out in the lives of individual students who would come to throw off such oppressive, internalized narratives, and could lead to a liberated group consciousness as well. In that way, true education is a project of worldmaking (or remaking).

Such goals can only be accomplished in community with others and must themselves be nonhierarchical; the type of learning community for which Freire advocated was not one where the teacher saved the students from their own internalized oppression or false beliefs. "Attempting to liberate the oppressed without their reflective participation in the act of liberation is to treat them as objects which must be saved from a burning building; it is to lead them into the populist pitfall and transform them into masses which can be manipulated" (Freire 2012: 65). Instead, the teacher should treat their students like *people*, as having agency, who are able to exercise reason, and who can choose for themselves (at least partly) who they will be and what projects they will pursue.

The way that the liberatory, rehumanizing project plays out is by rejecting what Freire called the "banking" model of education in which the teacher understands their task to be to "fill" students with the contents of their lectures.

> Narration (with the teacher as narrator) leads the students to memorize mechanically the narrated content. Worse yet, it turns them into "containers," into "receptacles" to be "filled" by the teacher. The more completely she fills the receptacles, the better of a teacher she is. The more meekly the receptacles permit themselves to be filled, the better students they are. Education thus becomes an act of depositing … In the banking concept of education, knowledge is a gift bestowed by those who consider themselves knowledgeable upon those whom they consider to know nothing.
> (Freire 2012: 71–2)

The alternative is what Freire called the "problem-posing" model of education which rejects vertical hierarchy in the classroom and embraces a type of collaborative solidarity among everyone involved—students and teachers alike. The result is a mixed identity:

> Through dialogue, the teacher-of-the-students and the students-of-the-teacher cease to exist and a new term emerges: teacher-student with student-teachers. The teacher is no longer merely the-one-who-teaches, but one who is himself [sic] taught in dialogue with the students, who in turn while being taught also teach. They become jointly responsible for a process in which all grow ... The students—no longer docile listeners—are now critical co-investigators in dialogue with the teacher.
>
> (Freire 2012: 80–1)

Approaching students this way recognizes that people can grow and change, both over the course of their lives and within the course of a semester. "Problem-posing education affirms men and women as beings in the process of *becoming*—as unfinished, uncompleted beings in and with a likewise unfinished reality" (Freire 2012: 84). The alternative, to treat students as things—as static and unchanging, whose identities are fixed and determined—certainly serves to make them more compliant workers, less likely to fight for their own rights and the rights of others, but is not the liberatory aim of the ethical (much less revolutionary) teacher.

Instead, Freire argued that the revolutionary educator's "efforts must be imbued with a profound trust in people and their creative power" (2012: 75), that "it is necessary to trust in the oppressed and their ability to reason," and that falling short of such trust will be a type of superficial, slogan-style activism that doesn't actually do any real liberatory work (2012: 66). Indeed, "trusting the people is the indispensable precondition for revolutionary change" (Freire 2012: 60). As I understand what Freire meant there are at least three different forms that such trust takes.

2 Trusting My Students

The first type of trust is from teacher to student—trusting that my students will show up prepared and ready to do good work together, trusting that our collaborative efforts will bear fruit, and trusting that they have something to say about the difficult topics with which we will collectively grapple.

Part of trusting my students (and adopting the problem-posing model) means giving up control over how each class will go. Static lecturing (as recommended by the banking model) is appealing because if I go in to class with a thoroughly scripted talk to deliver, in which I convey information which my students write down, memorize, and will be tested on, then I already know much of how the semester will go before it has even begun, since I have left no room for variation. Of course, students might do better or worse at memorizing but that's the only real surprise that could emerge from a tightly orchestrated, top-down pedagogy.

That doesn't mean that there's no place for lecture in a liberatory classroom; different levels and types of classes might call for different pedagogical strategies. What I mean to emphasize is that part of what can sometimes make lecturing compelling to a teacher is that it allows them to retain control and avoid the risk that comes from trusting their students to join them in the act of building the class together. Most of the time for me that means leading seminar-style discussions in which I have particular topics, questions, or concepts I want to be sure to explore, but the route by which we get there remains mostly unmapped. I'll often start class with a few minutes to "free write," asking students simply to reflect on the text (what did they find helpful or frustrating, with what did they agree or disagree, about what do they have questions or want further clarity) and to share what they thought. We then have a free-flowing conversation, engaging dynamically with the things that I had on my list, along with lots of things that I didn't. All of that can be scary! Open conversations can sometimes go off the rails and head in unanticipated directions that are at best unproductive and a waste of time, or worse, that can be harmful (by causing offense and undermining the community I was trying to build). Giving up control means accepting vulnerability to the risk that things won't go well. Moreover, if things don't go well they might require correction or repair in future class meetings as we grapple as a community with where things went awry and work to get back on track (or on track for the first time!) together.

Part of what enables such community is the attitudinal orientation I bear toward my students. I do my best to view them as minds in the room— as active, critical thinkers who are able to grapple with and understand difficult concepts and to form their own views in response. There are many different ways of doing this but for me that means regarding them as being engaged in the same project that I am as a professional philosopher and that the differences between us are mainly that I've been doing it longer and with a more demanding audience. In other words, I simply think of them *as* philosophers from the very first day. They might not initially be especially good philosophers (though many are), but that's ok, it often takes time to become good at something and philosophy is no different. They might not take other philosophy classes, but that's ok, too, since I take many of the questions that we ask to be essential to human life, and so they'll have the chance to continue practicing philosophy in lots of ways, even outside the classroom. They might not love philosophy the way I do (they might even dislike it or hate it!), but that's also ok, since you don't have to like the thing that you do in order to be good at it (and, as it turns out, I rarely have students who would say that they hate philosophy by the end of the semester, a fact that I think is at least partly born from having treated them as if they were themselves capable of doing good philosophy).

The point throughout is that being oriented toward my students as if they are capable of good work assumes that I am expecting them to do that work in the first place; I am trusting that they are up to the challenge, that they will put in the effort and time to meet that challenge, and that when they try to develop their own view they will be able to do so. It also means expecting that I will learn from my students—that they have something to say that I have never thought of, that even a well-trod point or argumentative move will find new meaning for me in light of a personal anecdote they share, or that their own way of combining concepts will bring new life to an old argument. In short, I aim to be the teacher-student and to help them to be the student-teachers that Freire calls on us all to be. Note the loss of control and the trust that such collaborative transformation requires. It is much less predictable (and so manageable) to be open to what my students might teach me than to assume that I am there to pour out wisdom but not to receive any myself.

3 Earning My Students' Trust

The second type of trust is from student to teacher—trusting that the method and design of the course (from the assignment structure to story arc of the topics and texts) will be meaningful and worthwhile. If I ask students to read difficult texts and to grapple with challenging topics (both in terms of technical difficulty and emotional vulnerability) it had better be worth their time and effort, or I'll lose them. If they don't see the point they won't in fact do what I'm expecting them to do. If their assignments are busywork, if they are pointlessly tedious or if they can't recognize the underlying meaning and value behind those assignments, then my students won't see the point in doing it and will devote time and resources to other projects (both academic and non-academic) that *do* have such meaning and value. And, it turns out that's exactly what I should want! Choosing not to devote time and energy to a project in which they don't recognize the value is an appropriate response from people who aren't simply doing what they're told, who aren't simply cogs in a machine who follow orders without reflecting on them. Indeed, I follow Freire in thinking that part of the role of education is to help students to question why they are being asked to do what they are being asked to do so that they can then choose whether to do it. That means being careful in my syllabus design and revision to make sure that our topics and texts are worthwhile—and listening to my students (via course evaluations, their papers, and our in-class conversations) to help make sure I'm hitting the mark. That also means trusting my students to be honest with me, to be thoughtful in their reflection, and to be genuine in dispensing advice, so that I can revise the course appropriately. And, it means being transparent and communicative about all of this, helping them to know that the reason I'm asking for such feedback is that I genuinely value what they think and their experience of the class.

4 Trusting Together

The third type of trust is that which emerges holistically, for the class as a whole, when we work to build what I call a trustful epistemic community together. It's not just that I need to trust my students, and it's not just that they need to trust me, but that we all need to trust each other as we enter in to ongoing conversation together. I do this by asking students what makes for good discussions and how we should conduct ourselves to be sure to be able to work well together over the course of the semester. Although their answers usually include some constants (be active listeners, be respectful of each other, come in having done the reading) the form that those answers take are often specific to particular a class. So, what does it mean *for us* to be respectful of each other? What does it mean *for us* to be active listeners? And, even if the answers *are* the same as those I've gotten in other classes, even other classes with the same students, it is still important to come up with those rules together again at the start of each new semester. Doing so says, "We are all of us engaged in a shared project to which we will dedicate time and energy for the next 15 weeks. Here is how we will pursue that project, together." Then, about one third of the way in to the semester I give out an informal and anonymous course evaluation, asking questions like whether students are learning and finding the course to be valuable, whether they feel like they can contribute, what they would like me to do differently, and what they would like each other to do differently. We then work through those answers and adjust course together in light of that insight. Again, note the loss of control and the importance of trust: instead of telling students how it will be I ask them to help decide together how we will collaborate (how we will co-labor). This creates not only motivation but space for students to be the minds in the room that I trust them to be, and to manifest some of the person-making traits which Freire argued can emerge from liberatory education.

5 Making a Wager

What about students who aren't interested in the problem-posing model of education but who seem to prefer the banking model? I'm thinking here of students who come to office hours to ask what they need to do to earn a good grade and who don't show much interest in the class material. It's tempting to dismiss such students and become frustrated with them for focusing on the wrong things—for only caring about their GPA and not caring about learning, much less becoming more complete people. Even though such conversations can be disheartening, I think it's a mistake to judge students too harshly in light of them. After all, most students in the United States today have been raised in a culture that portrays the value of education as simply a method of credentialing—checking boxes that allow you to access different types of jobs and different levels of income. That valuation is enforced and incentivized by standardized testing that determines whether students can advance to the next grade or get in to college. It is understandable to me, then, when students express initial confusion (and sometimes frustration) at being asked to deviate from the banking model—to think for themselves and not just memorize and recite what they have been told.

Despite encountering students who express an initial preference for the banking model, I still think it's crucial that I regard them in the ways I have described throughout: as people who have agency and who can think for themselves; as minds in the room who are capable of grappling with and understanding hard concepts; as philosophers. That sometimes feels like a bit of a wager; I'm betting that if I expect such things from my students they will meet or exceed that expectation. It's not a bet that always wins—sometimes I am disappointed—but most of the time I have found that students get on board by the end of the semester. One of the ways I know that's the case is that they tell me so. On the last day in all of my classes I attempt to get some closure on the semester. I ask my students what topics they liked or disliked, what they changed their mind about or which starting beliefs had deepened over the course of the semester. Most importantly I ask them to share the ways that others' comments had affected them (to give each other shout outs for their helpful contributions to discussion). On many occasions during this closure exercise students have volunteered that ours was the first class they had ever taken where they had been asked to think for themselves, often accompanied by head nods from others in the room. I have always felt quite ambivalent about that comment. On one hand, it is heartbreaking that they could have taken so many classes and never felt like they had the opportunity to argue for their own view. On the other, it's a profound honor for me to get to be a part of creating the opportunity for them to do so. Either way, I will continue to make the wager that my students want to be treated as people, and I will trust that when given the opportunity to think for themselves and to be a part of a community where we can all do good work together, they will take it.

References

Bartky, Sandra Lee (1990). *Femininity and Domination: Studies in the Phenomenology of Oppression*. New York: Routledge, 22–32.
Freire, Paulo (2012). *Pedagogy of the Oppressed*. New York: Bloomsbury Academic.

13

What to Do When Students Don't Do Course Readings

Alida Liberman

1 Framing the Problem

This scenario is probably familiar to most college teachers: you ask your class a specific, simple question about the content of an assigned reading. No one volunteers an answer. You ask a more open-ended question about the general theme of the reading—still crickets. It soon becomes clear that your students aren't just shy, but unprepared: they haven't done the reading. What can you do to prevent this, and what can you do in the moment when it happens? To address this question, we first need to identify why student failure to read is a problem.

One concern is that you might feel frustrated, sad, angry, demoralized, or even disrespected when students don't read. Such emotions are understandable. But while some of these reactions are fitting—it is appropriate to feel disappointed if class does not go well because students are unprepared—others are not. After all, students fail to read for a wide range of reasons, many of which have nothing to do with you: they may be working many hours per week to pay their bills, or focusing on family or caregiving duties, or devoting a lot of time to a sport or extracurricular activity. Students may also be triaging a high academic workload by skipping your reading to make time to read for a class in their major or to meet a crucial paper deadline. Whatever their reasons for not reading, it is unhelpful to take it personally or to treat it as an insult. More importantly, an instructor's negative emotional reactions do not address how failure to read is bad for the nonreading student.

A more pressing problem is that class discussion flounders when students are unprepared. Course readings provide a basis for shared conversation, and it can be hard to do productive or creative philosophical work together if most students lack this basis—which is bad not only for the nonreaders, but also for their classmates who miss out on a more engaged and robust discussion. Nonreaders also miss out on the benefits of practicing their skills of comprehension and analysis as they grapple with a text, which likely makes their papers and arguments weaker. And they are deprived of the intrinsically valuable experience of engaging with an interesting, exciting, beautiful, or challenging piece of writing.

I think these problems demand a multi-pronged response. In Section 2, I offer strategies for increasing students' intrinsic motivation to read. In a world of overburdened students taking general education philosophy courses with high-stakes GPAs, intrinsic motivation is not always sufficient, and we need to instrumentally motivate reading via the use of graded reading assignments. I offer examples of such assignments in Section 3. Finally, in Section 4 I consider how we might help students attain the instrumental and intrinsic goods achieved by reading even when they do not read before class. Each section offers a general discussion of an underlying pedagogical goal or value followed by concrete tips and suggestions.

2 Intrinsically Incentivizing Reading

As Renée Smith notes, students will fail to read when they are not given any guidance for reading well, cannot see the value or relevance of doing the reading, or when the reading is "too technical, too obtuse, or simply too much" (2011: 178). The most essential question to ask yourself is why reading matters—not in general, but in your particular situation. How does reading this text at this time in the semester help achieve your course learning goals? This is a very basic question, but it is easy to be unreflective about it; many of us assign canonical authors or the same texts we read as undergraduates without too much thought. If you cannot explain how a reading supports your specific course goals, you should not expect students to be engaged with it (and should probably not be assigning it). Whether a text is useful will depend on your teaching context; traditional and canonical texts will help in achieving some goals but not others.[1]

A mismatch between your learning goals and the texts you've chosen is likely to disincentivize student reading. For example, I used to make my intro ethics students slog through selections from Kant's *Groundwork for the Metaphysics of Morals* when I introduced Kantian ethics. Students hated it; most quickly gave up attempting to read it, and those who didn't were confused and frustrated. There is value in grappling with complex primary sources, and in another context it would be worthwhile to give students the tools to do this. But my goal was for students to understand the core content of Kant's moral theory. And this goal is better served by assigning a textbook chapter that clearly summarizes, applies, and critiques the categorical imperative.[2]

I haven't switched out all of my primary sources because some of them serve my learning goals. For example, I want students who read Mill's *Utilitarianism* to trace Mill's process of raising and responding to objections to his own theory.[3] A secondary source wouldn't serve this goal as well, so I assign the primary text (selections from which we then review in class). Thinking about what my learning goals are and whether a text serves them has also led me to make other changes, such as assigning an excerpt instead of a full essay, subbing out a journal article for a piece of accessible public philosophy by the same author, using a short story to illustrate a philosophical point, or replacing a traditional reading with a philosophical podcast or YouTube video.

Texts that align well with your learning goals can still be challenging for students. Some who struggle assume that the text is overly complicated or needlessly confusing—and if they're correct about this, the text should probably be replaced with a more straightforward one. More insidiously, many struggling readers assume the problem is not with the text but with themselves: that they are too "stupid" to grasp it or must not be philosophically minded. And it is very hard to find the intrinsic motivation to read philosophy if you believe you're not cut out for it. One strategy for combatting this attitude is encouraging students to adopt a growth mindset, or the belief that intelligence, skills, and capacities are not fixed but can improve with time and practice.[4] For example, on the first day of classes I have students identify a non-academic activity they excel at. I ask them to reflect on what they were like when they first started and what they did to improve since then. We discuss how athletic, musical, artistic, and other skills improve with structured practice over time. I explain how growth mindset research shows that academic skills are similar and remind students to adopt growth mindsets throughout the class, especially before assigning tough readings. Crucially, encouraging a growth mindset about reading must be paired with giving students the support they need to practice reading in a productive way—for example, by giving them explicit instruction in how to read philosophy and practicing reading together as a class.[5]

Another way to discourage demotivating and negative self-assessment is to help students appreciate how reading difficulties often stem not from the reader's lack of ability or the complexity of a text but from missing background knowledge.[6] I use the following exercise to illustrate this. First, I display a short newspaper excerpt recapping a popular sport; in Dallas, I use a Cowboys football game. I survey students to see who understands all of the passage, most of it, or at least some of it; many students easily grasp every nuance, and most comprehend at least the basics. I then feign total ignorance of the rules of football and have students explain the passage to me, asking clarification question after clarification question about their responses. It quickly becomes clear that massive amounts of background knowledge are built into the passage, from the names of the famous players on each team to the basic rules of football to presumptions about what counts as an impressive play.

I then show students a second passage from a similar newspaper recapping a sport that is much less popular; in Texas, I choose cricket. I sometimes have one or two cricket fans who grasp everything. But most do not understand the passage well, and some cannot even identify what sport it is about. We discuss why the second passage feels so much more challenging: after all, both are written in a simple, straightforward way with a low degree of complexity. Students realize that their existing background knowledge determines whether the passage is easy or incomprehensible, and that this background knowledge depends not on their skill or intelligence but their previous exposure and experiences (e.g., whether football or cricket is popular in their home region). As the semester progresses, I encourage students to identify what background knowledge they are missing and try to fill this in or ask me questions about it.

The aim of these exercises is normalizing and destigmatizing the feelings of confusion that arise when reading philosophy. If you're a Texan reading about cricket for the first time, you're probably going to find it hard to comprehend. But this difficulty says nothing about your current intelligence or reading ability or about what reading skills you may be able to develop in the future. Understanding this can help generate intrinsic motivation to read even when doing so is challenging.

3 Instrumentally Incentivizing Reading

An obvious way to encourage student reading is to put grades on the line. One common method is giving reading quizzes before or during class. However, as David Sackris notes, while true/false or multiple-choice reading quizzes "prod students to at least pass their eyes over the text, such methods fail to produce engaged, critical readings" (2020: 72). If quizzes ask superficial questions about the content, they will not encourage close or careful reading. But if quizzes ask more in-depth or sophisticated questions, they will be very demotivating for students who do the reading but do not understand it, and thus give incorrect answers despite trying their best. Why would you bother attempting to read a challenging text if you're likely to fail the quiz anyway?

I find that it better serves my learning goals to give students reading assignments that encourage a wide range of engagement and are graded for completion rather than accuracy.[7] I require students to complete regular reading reflections that are collectively worth 10 percent of their grade.[8] In each reflection, students engage with the texts they read in any three ways chosen from a list of different kinds of engagement sorted into six categories. Students label which category each reflection is from. Submitting three on-topic engagements results in full credit, even if what the student says about the reading is incorrect.[9]

The categories I use are:

1 **Comprehension:** identifying the author's thesis; summarizing a portion of the author's argument in your own words.
2 **Queries:** identifying missing background information; asking a question and attempting to answer it (including clarification questions about what you don't understand, curiosity questions about what you'd like to learn more about, and critical questions about the argument's presuppositions or implications).
3 **Connections:** making connections between what you're reading and what you already know; applying concepts or theories to new contexts.

4 **Criticism:** constructively criticizing the author's argument; attempting to reply to criticisms on the author's behalf.
5 **Epiphanies:** describing something you changed your mind about or a realization you had while reading; describing how the reading made you feel and trying to explain why you felt this way.
6 **Other:** engaging with the text in any other creative or constructive way, including: drawing a picture; paraphrasing a key idea as a tweet; making an original meme related to the reading; creating a discussion question or essay prompt about the reading; offering a "hot take" gut reaction to the reading, etc.

To be transparent with students, I include the following in the assignment instructions:

> If you don't completely understand the reading, that's okay! You're doing reflections instead of quizzes because I don't expect that everyone will fully comprehend every single reading on the first try. What I do expect is that you will make a serious effort to try to understand each reading and engage productively with it—for example, by raising good questions about it, making an educated guess about the author's thesis, looking up words or concepts you don't know, or articulating why you found the reading challenging.

These guided but open-ended reflections encourage students to engage with texts in whatever ways they find interesting and valuable, which can increase their intrinsic motivation to read throughout the semester.

Making reading a communal experience is another way to provide students with both intrinsic motivation (since they enjoy working together and do not want to let their classmates down by being unprepared) and instrumental incentives (since communal activities can be graded for completion). Sasha Biro (2021) describes using the online tool Perusall to have students collaboratively annotate texts in a course that suddenly went online during the Covid-19 pandemic. While Biro's aim was creating an asynchronous online substitute for in-class discussions, digital annotation platforms like Perusall also incentivize reading for in-person classes. Clair Morrissey and Kelsey Palghat (2014) explain a scaffolded method that moves from giving students readings annotated by the instructor to having students annotate readings on their own to having a collective class Google Doc that "served as a digital annotation of the course as a whole, to which every member was encouraged to contribute" and for which students received participation credit (2014: 42). What kind of graded reading assignment makes most sense for your class will depend on what your learning goals are and what kind of student reading activities best serve them.

4 When Students Still Haven't Read ...

Increasing students' intrinsic and instrumental motivation to read can only take you so far; there will always be some (perhaps many) students who do not complete the reading for a given class. Accordingly, it's worth strategizing about how to create productive discussions even when students haven't read. What information is essential for students to know to discuss the topic? You may be able to present that information in a way that helpfully reinforces it for those who have read and introduces it to those who haven't—for example, by showing a short YouTube video about the topic, asking the students who are prepared to summarize the main idea in their own words, or illustrating an author's idea with an example that wasn't in the text. What discussion questions can you ask or thought experiments can you raise that are relevant to the topic at hand but do not require the background knowledge of having read the text? Students who have not read will not be able to answer questions about the content or evaluation of a text, but they should be able to reflect on their personal experiences, moral intuitions, or pre-theoretical beliefs in a helpful way.

Students can also practice applying philosophical skills to texts in the classroom. This can be as simple as displaying a key quotation in class and having students use a "think/pair/share" approach to reflect on the passage, share these reflections with a partner, and then discuss them as a large group. A more in-depth activity is using a "think aloud" method to respond to a quotation.[10] Think alouds—which can be done in pairs, small groups, or with a single student talking through a passage in front of the class—involve reading a passage out loud and pausing as you read to narrate your thought process (e.g., by raising questions you have, mentioning what the passage makes you think of, explaining what you do not understand, etc.). Students who have done the reading will have richer resources to draw on while thinking aloud, but the practice is accessible to anyone.

Class time can also be used for collaborative philosophical analysis of texts. For example, Daniel Silvermintz (2006) outlines a method for structured in-class student reading groups, during which students respond to specific questions about a text and turn in a one-sentence gloss of each paragraph that receives a participation grade. While Silvermintz assumes that "students have already attempted the day's assigned reading and bring to their group work some level of familiarity" (241), even those who have not read in advance can benefit from closely reading a short passage in a group.

Some may worry that structuring classroom discussions and activities to make them accessible to nonreaders is "giving in" to student non-engagement or letting students off the hook. I think this worry is misguided. Students who read will gain intrinsic benefits from working through assigned texts and completing reading activities, for which they will also receive the reward of a completion grade. Offering a bit of flexibility and grace to those who have not done the reading—for whatever reason, justifiable or not—enables everyone to fully participate in class sessions and helps create a learning environment that is better for all and more conducive to achieving your course goals.[11]

Notes

1. See Liberman (2022) for discussion of how the readings we choose may reflect harmful and limiting presumptions about prestige and perfection in philosophy.
2. I upload the selections from the *Groundwork* as an optional supplementary reading, framing it as a good stretch for those students who are feeling "philosophically hardcore."
3. This is feasible in part because Mill (while challenging) is more accessible than Kant. I also find Mill's writing quite beautiful, and I have a secondary learning goal of fostering aesthetic appreciation for lovely philosophical prose.
4. See Dweck (2006). For discussion of fostering growth mindsets in philosophy classrooms, see Jacquart et al. (2019: 111–13) and Green (2015: 51). For discussion of grading practices that promote growth mindsets in ethics classes, see Gaudet (2020).
5. See Concepción (2004) for discussion of the importance of explicitly teaching reading skills and for a helpful "How to Read Philosophy" handout for use in the classroom.
6. See Concepción (2004) for discussion of the importance of background knowledge for reading comprehension. Concepción explains that it is essential to provide students with missing background knowledge

not only about course content but also about the "idiosyncrasies of philosophy" (353).

7. Other philosophers have described different kinds of graded reading assignments that effectively provide instrumental motivation to read before class. For example, David Sackris (2020), Reneé Smith (2011), and Anne-Marie Bower and Michael Beaty (1999) each offer examples of structured, guided reading assignments that target specific skills. Paul G. Neiman and Linda V. Neiman (2015) outline several kinds of reading assignments that use novelty to increase student engagement. And Jessica Gosnell (2012) describes a process of having students identify important quotations before class and translate them into contemporary language in groups during class.

8. How often students should complete reflections depends on your teaching context: how many readings do you assign, how many students are you teaching in a semester, and how burdened or burned out are you and your students? I usually create an assignment in my course LMS page for each reading then let students skip a set number of them (usually between two and ten) determined by that semester's context.

9. I review the reflections before class starts; if students make major errors, I'll leave a comment noting that they've misunderstood something that we'll review in class. The grading process for these reflections is fairly fast and painless. It's also fun to see what students come up with, and it gives me an opportunity to connect with them about a range of topics that they bring up and to incorporate their questions and criticisms into lecture and class discussion.

10. I was introduced to the think aloud method at a workshop led by Stephen Bloch-Schulman, who uses comparative think alouds (performed by undergraduates and professional philosophers) to "focus on how our students' approach to the texts and tasks, as revealed in the think alouds (and in the difference between their responses and those of philosophers) can and ought to inform the goals we set in our teaching and the agenda we set in our pedagogical research" (2016: 92). The paper contains helpful illustrations of what think alouds look like.

11. Thanks to Joshua Crabill and Brynn Welch for helpful feedback on this draft. Thanks also to the participants in my session about student reading reflections during the AAPT virtual conference in July 2021 for discussion of these ideas.

References

Biro, Sasha (2021). "Reading in a Time of Crisis: Using Perusall to Facilitate Close Reading and Active Discussion in the Remote Philosophy Classroom." *Teaching Philosophy* 44(3): 241–54.

Bloch-Schulman, Stephen (2016). "A Critique of Methods in the Scholarship of Teaching and Learning in Philosophy." *Teaching and Learning Inquiry* 4(1): 80–94.

Bower, Anne-Marie, and Michael Beaty (1999). "The Use of Reading Questions as a Pedagogical Tool: Fostering an Interrogative, Narrative Approach to Philosophy." *Teaching Philosophy* 22(1): 17–40.

Concepción, David (2004). "Reading Philosophy with Background Knowledge and Metacognition." *Teaching Philosophy* 27(4): 351–68.

Dweck, Carol (2006). *Mindset: The New Psychology of Success*. New York: Random House.

Gaudet, Matthew (2020). "The Two Types of Grades and Why They Matter to Ethics Education." *Teaching Ethics* 20(1–2): 75–90.

Gosnell, Jessica (2012). "Integrating Quotations into the Classroom." *Teaching Philosophy* 35(1): 19–27.

Green, Paul (2015). "How to Motivate Students: A Primer for Learner-Centered Teachers." *AAPT Studies in Pedagogy* 1: Practices in Pedagogy: 47–60.

Jacquart, Melissa, Rebecca Scott, Kevin Hermberg, and Stephen Bloch-Schulman (2019). "Diversity Is Not Enough: The Importance of Inclusive Pedagogy." *Teaching Philosophy* 42(2): 107–39.

Liberman, Alida (2022). "In Defense of Doing Philosophy 'Badly,' or: How I Learned to Stop Worrying and Love Imperfection." *AAPT Studies in Pedagogy* 7: Who and What Is Philosophy For? 1–21. https://www.pdcnet.org/aaptstudies/content/aaptstudies_2023_0999_5_1_58.

Morrissey, Clair, and Kelsey Palghat (2014). "Engaging Reading." *Teaching Philosophy* 37(1): 37–55.

Neiman, Paul G., and Linda V. Neiman (2015). "Engaging Students in Philosophy Texts." *AAPT Studies in Pedagogy* 1: Practices in Pedagogy: 157–68.

Sackris, David (2020). "How to Encourage Reading and Learning in the College Classroom." *Teaching Philosophy* 43(1): 71–92.

Silvermintz, Daniel (2006). "Reading Philosophy with Friends: Introducing Reading Groups into the Philosophy Classroom." *Teaching Philosophy* 29(3): 237–43.

Smith, Renée (2011). "Reading to Learn to Read Philosophy." *Discourse: Learning and Teaching in Philosophical and Religious Studies* 10(2): 175–94.

14

When Conversation Goes Wrong: Managing Student Errors

*Russell Marcus and
Alessandro Moscarítolo Palacio*

Introduction

In traditional philosophy lectures, students typically assume that the instructor believes what they tell the class. Students may even safely assume that many of their lecturer's claims are true—for example, that Plato believed in the theory of forms or that Thomson believes that a right to life does not entail a right to use someone else's body. Still, many claims that we assert in class are open to discussion. We often frame them as such: while Descartes argues that there are minds and bodies, Hobbes argues that there are only bodies and we are trying to figure out who is right.

Many philosophy teachers now reject traditional classroom structures. Our reasons may be, roughly, forward-looking or backward-looking. We might use active learning in light of research that shows that students learn better what they do than what they hear or read.[1] We might seek greater student empowerment and voice, allowing students to determine the direction of conversation or class content.[2]

Whatever our motivations—and we might be motivated by both kinds of considerations—a student in a non-traditional class is likely to hear many claims, made by their peers, that are neither believed by their instructor nor true. They may be working in small groups, out of earshot. They may be engaged in a seminar conversation in which the instructor allows students to explore without interference. They may be working on collaborative projects outside of the classroom.

In a traditional classroom, when a student makes a misleading or false claim, the instructor typically confronts the claim—perhaps in Socratic fashion—helping the student and the rest of the class rid themselves of errors and misinterpretations. Students learn to be skeptical of claims from other students, looking to the instructor for guidance. Such faith in the instructor is grounded in the instructor's authority and expertise: unlike their peers, instructors have the degrees, the job, the experience, and the gradebook.

In student-centered classrooms, by contrast, the situation is stickier. Instructors cannot correct every problematic claim made in the context of a class. Moreover, we might be wary of correcting students for at least two kinds of reasons. Looking forward, we might want our students to learn to listen to each other critically, to have them learn to help themselves. Such skills are part of what studying philosophy can teach well. Looking backward, we might decenter ourselves to take student empowerment seriously, avoiding asserting epistemic authority that can undermine at least some aspects of student autonomy.

Two Models

We present two models for managing student errors, imagining them as poles between which lie various defensible positions. The first model is the *faculty expertise model* (FEM), according to which it is paramount to maximize the number of true or reasonable claims made in a classroom, even in active-learning or student-centered contexts, so that participants in the class are not misled. FEM is informed by a broadly pragmatist metaphilosophical and pedagogical framework, according to which philosophy is an activity, one main function of which is to empower students to shape their own learning and lives. FEM posits that if students fail to correct themselves or one another, instructors are prima facie obligated to correct them. In most actual classroom settings, some degree of heteronomy is the only viable way to foster student autonomy: in order for philosophers-in-training to become autonomous philosophers, they need to heed the prescriptions, in the form of corrections, made by those with more expertise. Doing philosophy requires some type of practical expertise, which we could oversimplify as the ability to reason properly, i.e., the ability to argue for a thesis by making adequate inferential moves and to diagnose flawed inferences supporting competing theses.

As any professional philosopher knows, it is not easy for philosophers-in-training to master this elusive skill unless someone with the requisite practical expertise shows them in practice, in the course of examining actual philosophical arguments, why the inferences supporting a given thesis are adequate or fallacious. Moreover, instructor corrections need not undermine student autonomy: instructor corrections can bolster student autonomy by providing them with skills without which they will not be able to ascertain the merits of competing theses or arguments. In other words, instructor corrections empower students to appreciate why in philosophy anything goes but not everything works.

To clarify, consider similarities between the practical knowledge that students can acquire in a philosophy class with the practical knowledge in whose acquisition learners rely on those with epistemic authority, such as the use of a new language. As anyone can attest who reflects on the process by which they have mastered a language, the role of the expert is absolutely critical: mere peer correction will almost always prove insufficient.

An instructor who deploys FEM is only *prima facie* obligated to correct student errors. Students may correct themselves or one another instead. The model bolsters student autonomy if certain conditions are met: namely, that the instructor should prioritize empowering students themselves to diagnose and correct errors, serving merely as a last resort. Naturally, the extent to which the instructor intervenes is also determined by factors such as the class level.

FEM is compatible with active-learning and skill-oriented classes. The model does not posit that the instructor is the gatekeeper of the truth, but that correcting content-related errors is a means to correcting skill-related errors. The primary goal of an instructor who deploys the philosophical expertise model is not to teach content—the correct interpretation of a text or the correct answer to a philosophical question—but to teach skills. The model rests on the generally uncontroversial assumption that the instructor has more experience in reasoning philosophically, which does not guarantee that the instructor is in possession of the correct interpretation of a text or argument.

The second model is the *student empowerment model* (SEM), on which it is more important to let students converse and explore than it is for them to assert claims of high epistemic value. On SEM, the importance of student autonomy entails that instructors should be wary of correcting students who make errant claims. Such corrections emphasize instructor authority at the possible expense of student engagement.

Consider a classroom using a floating-chair policy for classroom conversation. On typical models of classroom conversation, student comments tend to go through the instructor: The instructor calls on a student who asks a question or makes a comment. The instructor responds. The instructor then calls on another student, and the pattern repeats. In contrast, in a floating chair structure, after a student speaks, that student calls on the next speaker, typically another student. The instructor refrains from inserting themself in the conversation unless a student requests input. Instructors thus de-center themselves, empowering students to lead conversation and listen to each other.

Now, imagine a class on moral theory, using a floating chair to discuss the contrast between utilitarianism and Kantian deontology. In the course of discussion, a student says, "The utilitarian would say that affirmative action is unjust because it is a violation of individual rights." The instructor might be sorely tempted to jump in, perceiving various problems in the student's claim. "For the utilitarian," the instructor might reasonably say, invoking their expertise, "Rights are at best a derivative concept. The utilitarian should primarily appeal to the consequences of a policy."

In contrast, on SEM, the instructor lays low. Inserting one's voice as a corrective communicates that the student has violated a rule or expectation. The student who makes the errant claim may have their views about utility and rights corrected. All students also receive a message that they do not have free reign to make mistakes. To avoid these outcomes, on SEM, the instructor waits for other students to address the problem. With practice, students learn that making errors is part of the process of doing philosophy and that they can do so without violating classroom norms. Instructors may still raise questions about particular comments without asserting authority. "What do we think about the claim that utilitarians reject policies because of rights considerations?"

Even without explicit corrections or assertions of authority, students often quickly infer an instructor's views, especially when we disagree with them. Our body language can speak volumes, often in ways that are imperceptible to ourselves, even when we are trying to keep straight faces. There are power structures in any classroom and students are often aware of their places in classroom hierarchies. The instructor who is truly committed to student-directed conversations may need not only to allow student errors, but resist judging student comments at all. Such an approach can be a challenging exercise in humility for an instructor, to resist our no-buts and embrace our yes-ands. Moreover, the proponent of the SEM has to be willing to allow students to walk away from class potentially misinformed. On SEM, we are concerned less with the truth of student beliefs and more with their active engagement with course material and finding their own ways through it.

Of course, every instructor has limits to the kinds of errors we allow since we all hold classroom norms. On even the most extreme SEM, instructors may consider some views unacceptable even to state. For example, an instructor might believe that there is no legitimate philosophical debate about the humanity of people in certain racial or ethnic categories. Following the SEM, instructors will typically involve students in conversation about such norms early in the term, so that the students can learn to self-regulate.

The central goal of the SEM is to help students to develop skills for effective philosophical conversation that they can take into contexts that do not include instructors. The SEM helps them to practice those skills. The instructor takes as light a touch as possible, framing or summarizing, adding comments only on request.

Applications

Instructors rightly have varying preferred positions between these extreme poles. Differences may emerge from considering different claims in different contexts. Consider, for example, the following problematic claims:

- Clear Factual Error, e.g. "7+5=11."
- Philosophical Error, e.g. "Hume's arguments for the problem of induction are terrible."
- Moral Error, e.g. "Trans women are, of course, really men."

Various contexts might also lead to different kinds of responses. We briefly consider each of these three types of claims in a few representative contexts.

Large Classes

SEM is typically unavailable in large lectures and difficult to manage even in classes of thirty or forty. Indeed, the question hardly arises, since both models are constructed to apply to active-learning classrooms. Instructors may implement active-learning strategies in large classes by using small-group work, but such conversations are rarely regulated by instructors. Conversations in large classrooms typically require strong instructor leadership.

Moral errors and other violations of classroom norms require correction as a matter of course.[3] A clear factual error might be too unimportant to merit comment, or corrections may be handled gently without being problematic assertion of authority (e.g., "I think you mean twelve"). In response to a less clear factual or philosophical error, the instructor can approach a SEM by reflecting questions to the class rather than correcting the errant claim.

While FEM seems ideally suited for large classes, its application to these settings in fact poses challenges very similar to those faced by SEM: namely, finding feasible ways of correcting student errors by means of active-learning strategies that do not undermine student autonomy. While addressing these challenges in large classes proves difficult regardless of which model one subscribes to, an instructor who subscribes to FEM can manage student errors by asking the students questions which empower them to diagnose and address the error in question; in other words, an instructor who subscribes to FEM strives to serve as a last resort in correcting errors. Still, on the FEM, factual and philosophical errors must be addressed, to avoid propagating misunderstanding, whereas the proponent of the SEM is more comfortable allowing students to remain misinformed.

Small Classes

In small classes, say seminars of fifteen students, the contrast between an FEM and an SEM is more obvious. Again, the minor factual error may not merit attention. Violations of accepted norms and moral errors are again essential to address; in both large and small classes, we must avoid normalizing bad behavior.

There is a world of room between these extremes of simple factual errors and violations of norms. Here an instructor's pedagogical style is defined. On SEM in introductory classes, students are less familiar with norms of philosophical discussion and more likely to seek an instructor's expertise and the FEM may be more natural. In upper-level classes, when students are more eager for free rein and more stunted in their development by frequent correction, the SEM is most at home.

While the contrast between FEM and SEM becomes most obvious in small classes, so do the similarities. Since both FEM and SEM share the goal of student autonomy, instructors on both models will hope that students themselves address errors. Given that the main difference between FEM and SEM is the emphasis placed on the value of heteronomy as a route to intellectual autonomy, an instructor who subscribes to FEM will not especially worry about making assertions of authority, even in small classes, in hopes of bolstering, not undermining, student autonomy.

Introductory or Gen Ed Classes

Faculty expertise can be of special importance in introductory classes, because of both our greater knowledge of concepts and our experience in critical conversations. It's important to model good philosophical discussion and to get students started with a firm foundation. Students new to philosophy typically make a lot of errors. The FEM might be a better approach at the introductory level.

Concomitantly, the importance of supporting student engagement and inclusion entails that we must be wary of asserting our authority heavy-handedly. Most students come to philosophy tentatively. As a discipline, we have struggled especially to welcome members of under-represented identity groups. It may be more important to encourage engagement than to correct the factual or philosophical error. Even the moral error might be handled more gently in introductory classrooms, though instructors must be wary of normalizing dangerous language or views.

Various Institutional Contexts

SEM seems more likely to work with small classes, whereas large class sizes can be seen as the natural home for FEM. We might thus expect institutions with more small classes to see more SEM and larger institutions, with larger classes, to see more FEM. One might go on to assume that SEM is likely to work best at selective institutions, where students tend to come well prepared to autonomously steer their college classroom experience. We must be careful here, though, as general preparedness for college-level courses does not necessarily equate to preparedness for doing philosophy. Indeed, the former may engender attitudes—such as arrogance or entitlement—which are inconsistent with the latter. In these settings, SEM may simply validate these attitudes, instead of challenging them. Therefore, FEM alone, or a combination of both models, might be better suited to (some) selective institutions.

Conversely, one might go on to assume that FEM works best at institutions serving student populations that, for various reasons, are somehow lacking in their ability to actively participate in college-level class conversations. But we must be careful here, too. After all, these student populations, which often include students from disadvantaged backgrounds, tend to be lacking in traits such as self-confidence (*qua* learners), and it is precisely these deficits that SEM is ideally equipped to address. Therefore, a combination of SEM and FEM that (at least at the early stages of the process) gives more centrality to SEM might be better suited to (some) institutions that serve these student populations.

Summary: Between the Poles

Teachers must find their own voices. In determining how and when to correct student errors, instructors committed to student development, as we imagine proponents of both poles, must consider both the kind of error and the classroom context. Does the error violate norms, so that it must be swiftly addressed? If not, we should weigh the consequences of correction. Is instructor intervention likely to produce a better result, both long term and short term? Are we respecting the development of long-term autonomy by empowering students to avoid blunders? Are we asserting authority in ways that will turn students away from further philosophy? Cultural differences, both of student backgrounds and institutional context, may be relevant. An instructor's pedagogical style or identity may dictate a pole of preference, too. The co-authors of this chapter have discrepant approaches. Whichever way you lean, and however far, it is important to recognize the effects of intervention in conversation, both on learning philosophical content and on empowering students to lead and listen in conversation.[4]

Notes

1. Active learning helps students to proceed to higher levels of cognition, for example in Bloom's taxonomy or Fink's taxonomy of significant learning (Fink 2013). On Bloom: See Anderson et al. 2001 for the revised Bloom's taxonomy; Bloom 1956 for the original; Armstrong 2010 for an effective overview. For evidence of the effectiveness of active learning strategies,

see Johnson, Johnson, and Smith 1998; Freeman et al 2014 and Johnson, Johnson, and Smith 2014.
2. See Freire 1968 for the ur-text on student empowerment. See Whiteside 1980 for an example of a student-designed introductory philosophy course.
3. See Van Orman 2019 for some suggestions for how to do so.
4. Thanks to the editor and to audiences at the 2022 Biennial Workshop Conference of the American Association of Philosophy Teachers at Otterbein University and at the Panel of the Association for the Philosophy of Education at the 2023 APA Pacific Division Meeting in San Francisco. Thanks also to Ann Cahill (Elon University) for useful conversation about the floating chair model of classroom conversation.

References

Anderson, Lorin, David Krathwohl, Peter Airasian, Kathleen Cruikshank, Richard Mayer, Paul Pintrich, James Raths, and Merlin Wittrock (2001). *A Taxonomy for Learning, Teaching, and Assessing A Revision of Bloom's Taxonomy of Educational Objectives*. New York: Addison Wesley Longman, Inc.

Armstrong, Patricia (2010). "Bloom's Taxonomy." Vanderbilt University Center for Teaching. https://cft.vanderbilt.edu/guides-sub-pages/blooms-taxonomy. Retrieved February 13, 2023.

Bloom, Benjamin S. (1956). *Taxonomy of Educational Objectives*. New York: Longman.

Fink, L. Dee (2013). *Creating Significant Learning Experiences: An Integrated Approach to Designing College Courses* (Revised and updated). San Francisco: Jossey-Bass.

Freeman, Scott, et al. (2014). "Active Learning Increases Student Performance in Science, Engineering, and Mathematics." *Proceedings of the National Academy of Sciences* 111(23): 8410–15. www.pnas.org/cgi/doi/10.1073/pnas.1319030111.

Freire, Paulo (1968). *Pedagogy of the Oppressed*. Trans. Myra Bergman Ramos. New York: The Seabury Press.

Johnson, David W., Roger T. Johnson, and Karl A. Smith (1998). "Cooperative Learning Returns to College: What Evidence Is There That It Works?" *Change* 30(4): 26–35.

Johnson, David W., Roger T. Johnson, and Karl A. Smith (2014). "Cooperative Learning: Improving University Instruction by Basing Practice on Validated Theory." *Journal on Excellence in College Teaching* 25(3&4): 85–118.

Van Orman, Kimberly (2019). "Working with Diverse Student Perspectives: When Discussions Get Difficult." Presentation at the Hamilton College Summer Program in Philosophy Conference on Pedagogy, July 8, 2019. https://digitalcommons.hamilton.edu/presentations/22/.

Whiteside, David E. (1980). "A Student-Planned Course for Introductory Philosophy." *Teaching Philosophy* 3(3): 283–99.

15

Gender Dynamics in the Philosophy Classroom

Harry Brighouse

Let's start with a famous *The Onion* headline: "Guy in Philosophy Class Needs to Shut the Fuck Up." The story continues: "According to students enrolled in Professor Michael Rosenthal's Philosophy 101 course at Dartmouth College, that guy, Darrin Floen, the one who sits at the back of the class and acts like he's Aristotle, seriously needs to shut the fuck up."

Some suspect that people—well, specifically *young men*—like Darrin are among the reasons that women continue past their first, and past their second, course in philosophy at a lower rate than men do. Brian Leiter quotes an unnamed senior female philosopher: "My assessment of the undergrad women in philosophy thing: undergrad women get sick of being talked over and strawmanned by their peers in and out of the classroom, and get sick of classes where the male students endlessly hold forth about their own thoughts" (2016). Leiter himself says: "I will say that over two decades of teaching, it has seemed to me that the students who speak out of proportion to what they have to say are overwhelmingly male" (2016).

My experience is exactly the same as Leiter's. And I've heard from countless women that they just got tired of being ignored, both by professors and male students, and also tired of trying to get a word in among the ramblings of men who think that they are really smart. One exceptionally philosophically capable young woman (who has, in fact, continued in Philosophy) complained to me at graduation that during her first two years of Philosophy classes she felt stupid in comparison with the young men whose endless talk she couldn't understand. She exhibited genuine anger when telling me that, later, she realized that the reason she didn't understand what they were saying was because they hadn't bothered to do the reading and what they said didn't actually make sense. Her rage was not only for them, but for the teachers who rewarded their behavior.

This happens even in classes taught by women. And it has happened, I'm embarrassed to say, in classes I've taught (though, according to observers, not in recent years). To make things worse I think that the behavior I've described can be a very good strategy for learning—it gets the attention of the professor, who will correct or argue with the student. Even if the professor is extremely irritated, this can be quite valuable for the frequent talker.

Leiter goes on: "Maintaining control of the classroom, and creating a welcoming environment for all student contributions, can probably go some distance to rectifying this—but that, of course, supposes levels of pedagogical talent and sensitivity that many philosophy faculty probably lack" (2016).

I'm not sure that it's *talent* that philosophy faculty lack. And *The Onion*'s comment, perhaps, implies too harsh a judgment of Darrin Floen. Faculty members typically could do *many* difficult things if they devoted some time and energy to learning how to do them. My suspicion is that what most faculty lack is just the *skill*: they were not trained in ways that would develop whatever talents they possess into pedagogical skills, and have not compensated for that lack of training. The obvious contrast is with research: we focus considerable effort on developing our talent as researchers, consuming the research of others, discussing their research, our research, and other people's research in a community of learner/researchers, putting our research out for comments from friends and, ultimately, for review and publication. Whatever your talents with respect to research, if you apply yourself in this environment, they're liable to turn into skills. We ought to become pretty good at research. But, as David Concepción and colleagues show, we receive *hardly any* training in instruction (2016: 1–24). Once we become teachers we might *try*, and perhaps try *very hard*, but we invest very little in the kinds of processes that would enable us to learn from experts, as opposed to improving through trial-and-error. Someone might naturally have the *talent* to become a good violinist, but trying to become a good violin player without anyone ever listening to them, and without ever listening to anyone who plays it well is hardly a recipe for becoming skilled.

So, from my own trial and error (combined with some watching of experts, and employing observers to coach me) here are some things that I have learned how to do which seem to make the classroom one in which women participate at a similar rate to men and seem to reduce the problem of particular male students dominating the room.

1. Deliberately wait till women raise their hands, and do not call on the guy who always talks, even if he has his hand up. In my current class there is a lovely, smart, guy (who is not at all like Darrin Floen) who sits at the front and always has something to say before anyone else. I just say, "I'm going to go for someone who doesn't usually talk/hasn't talked recently."
2. When someone strawmans someone else's argument you always either point it out yourself, or, much preferably, get someone in the classroom to point it out. Always.
3. If your students write weekly online memos (as they should), you can immediately see which women (and men, for that matter) who are not talking in class have interesting things to say. Call them out in class when the point they made is immediately relevant to the matter at hand: "Well, Hannah, you said X. Could you elaborate on that for us?" One of my teaching assistants would bring print-outs of students' weekly memos to class and deploy his (startling) ability to recall all the comments to orchestrate discussions which put hesitant talkers at the center.
4. You can email a student about a comment they made in class. This can be very encouraging. A graduate student subbing for me a while ago commented to me that A and B (both capable, and very reserved-in-class, women) had said particularly insightful things.[1] He emailed them saying so, and it was like gold dust. Both were more participatory afterwards, and after the following class, as I was leaving I heard one of them telling a classmate with great excitement (but no pride) that he had emailed her about how interesting what she had said was. I do the same thing now (and not only to women, but more generally to students who are reserved in class).
5. Here's a trick I have been criticized for (because it knowingly deploys sexist norms, albeit for nonsexist ends). In my large lecture classes, I break students into groups to address particular questions or think through thought experiments. I tell them to appoint a note taker. When they report out, I ask the note taker to report. Naturally, the note taker is almost always female, and usually, even if not female, a nontalker. They get the experience of talking and, bizarrely, seem not to notice the patterns.
6. Warm calling. This is the term I use for cold calling done with sensitivity. You are not trying to put people on the spot, so you warn the class ahead of time, and tell them that it is fine to wait a moment

while they gather their thoughts, and also fine to say that they don't have anything to say right now. Students may not like it when you start doing it. (Something I've been told more than once: "After the first time you called on me, I called my mom after class and told her that I hated you.") It is more effective if cold calling someone is not the first time you have talked to them—always get to class several minutes early and have casual boring conversations with particular students who don't talk much (or at all) in class, so they are more relaxed when you call on them.[2]

7 If you have a serious problem, directly tell a student (obviously, not in class, but in a private conversation) that they are talking too much, and that you want them to talk less. I can't give firm general criteria for what constitutes a serious problem, but the main things that prompt me to talk directly to a student are (i) consistent evidence that they are oblivious to the interests and concerns of their classmates and (ii) the sense that I am expending so much energy on trying to control their behavior that I am neglecting the interests of other students. A strategy I once used was to tell a student I did not want him to raise his hand until at least four people had spoken after he had spoken. Compliance was imperfect but he told me, later, that he learned more in class because he started listening to what other people were saying rather than thinking about what *he* was going to say all the time.

8 Conversely, talk to a student about why they *don't* talk. Several years ago, I taught a (small) class which was 50/50 M/F, and about 25 percent freshmen, 25 percent sophomore, etc. Early on one female student was not talking in class, and looking very embarrassed when I would warm call her, despite writing consistently excellent weekly comments online. I got the impression she was a senior who was moderately hostile to the class, so felt bad when, after I asked her what her major was, she told me she didn't have one because she was a freshman. I worked on getting her and another reticent girl to talk more in class. At the end of the semester, I told her that I felt I had not really succeeded in my mission of making her talk more and she said, "Well, I'm the kind of person who only talks if I think that what I have to say is really worth saying." This made me laugh, and I told her that she needed to lower her standards a bit so that the rest of us could hear things that were really worth hearing even if she didn't think they were really worth saying. By her junior year she seemed to have a much better handle on the value of what she had to say, which benefited not just her, but her classmates.

9 In smaller classes you can find out which students are good at drawing other students out pretty quickly, by observing what happens in small group discussions. Once in only the second class of the semester I observed a group of five in which four students were participating enthusiastically and one woman was, for quite some time, silent. After eight minutes I noticed a male student, who knew she had been listening intently, unobtrusively draw her into their conversation, after which point she was just as talkative as the rest of her group. Another student who (luckily for me) took several of my classes quite deliberately sat by quieter students whose online comments she found interesting in order to draw them out. Deploy people like them purposefully. Sometimes this might involve telling them directly that you see they do this sort of thing and encouraging them to do it more. Sometimes it might just involve calculating in which small group discussion they are most likely to do good.

10 And, of course, you can quickly see who does, and who doesn't, talk a lot. Be purposeful about your construction of small groups—in particular, at least occasionally, place reserved students together, so that they are not dominated by more talkative students in their small groups.

What I *don't* do is alert the class to the fact that men are talking a lot and women are talking less, and ask women to talk more (or men to talk less). There's a case for being quite explicit with the students about various aspects of pedagogy, and it's quite possible that it would be better to be explicit. My reticence is based on reports from many women that when this is done to them in other classes (which it sometimes is) they feel self-conscious and put on the spot, and that it doesn't help them become confident talkers. The women I talk to may be atypical of course, and even if they are typical, their self-reporting of their feelings may belie the actual effects. I don't know of any science on this question (and, as with most questions about pedagogy, I have asked people who work on the science of teaching and learning whether there is any reliable science on it). So I genuinely don't know whether it would be better to be explicit. Given the apparent success of various combinations of the above strategies, conservatism leads me not to try a method that, while it might improve things, might make things worse.

Of course, it is not *only* men that dominate classrooms, and not *only* women who are reticent to share their ideas. Working class and poor students are, on average, more reticent, as are students for whom English is not their first language and, of course, students who are shy or anxious. Most of the above strategies are worth a try with those students too.

Darrin Floen does, indeed, need to shut the fuck up. But what I mean by saying that Leiter may be implying unduly harsh judgment of him is this: in classrooms managed by skilled teachers he *would* shut the fuck up, indeed he might never have become excessively loquacious in the first place. His habitual rambling has been facilitated and rewarded by his teachers. With more skillful teachers he might have become an entirely considerate and cooperative discussant. He might be one of the many, if admittedly one of the less sympathetic, victims of suboptimal pedagogy in higher education.[3]

Notes

1. This was the same person as the TA mentioned in the previous paragraph.
2. For (much) more on warm calling see "Cold Calling. Or Warm Calling" at https://crookedtimber.org/2022/12/02/cold-calling-or-warm-calling/ (accessed May 15, 2023).
3. Thanks to Britta Clark, Gina Schouten, Tim Brighouse, Bob Moon, Allyson Janowski and various Crooked Timber readers for comments.

References

Concepción, David W., Melinda Messineo, Sarah Wieten, and Catherine Homan (2016). "The State of Teacher Training in Philosophy." *Teaching Philosophy* 39(1): 1–24.

Leiter, Brian (2016). "Why Do Undergraduate Women Give up on Philosophy?" *Leiter Reports: A Philosophy Blog*, April 5. https://leiterreports.typepad.com/blog/2016/04/why-do-undergraduate-women-give-up-on-philosophy.html. Accessed June 21, 2023.

16

Cultivating Playfulness for Unlearning in the Philosophy Classroom

Rebecca G. Scott

In his influential work, *Homo Ludens*, Johan Huizenga defines play as a voluntary activity wherein the norms and rules of ordinary life are temporarily suspended. This voluntary suspension of reality creates a space for the creation of new ways of being and being together by allowing us to try out new norms, values, and beliefs (Huizenga 1950).

Specifically in the context of teaching philosophy, Thi Nguyen has argued for the value of cultivating an attitude of playfulness as an intellectual virtue that helps us to avoid epistemic traps (2022). Nguyen argues that an attitude of playfulness allows us to take a distance from new views in order to temporarily entertain them. Entering what Huizenga calls the "magic circle" of playfulness loosens us up from our sedimented beliefs and values in a way that Nguyen argues is enjoyable and less risky than giving up our beliefs in "real life." In this way, we can try out new ideas that might otherwise feel too threatening to our understanding of ourselves and the world.

In addition to helping us avoid or escape from epistemic traps, I contend that a playful attitude in the classroom is even more broadly valuable. In particular, it can help to facilitate an important form of "unlearning." When the learning environment becomes a playful "magic circle," we open up possibilities for engaging with academic work in new ways. In this space, we can say, what if school is fun? What if you're good at it? What if you like it? What if learning doesn't have to involve shame and self-doubt? What if "failing" can be fun and useful? What if your teacher trusts you and is on your side? What if?

The Case for Unlearning

In order to learn, we often need to unlearn. Students come into our courses with all kinds of ideas about what school is, what teachers care about, how to be successful, how to write a paper, how to play the education "game," whether or not they are "good" at school, and so on. Sometimes students' preexisting understandings of themselves and education are beneficial for what we hope to accomplish in our classes, but we often need students to engage in productive unlearning.

For example, in my own classes, I have found that I need to help students unlearn their approach to writing a paper. When I have asked students to do something in writing that they haven't been asked to do before (like analyze a question instead of answering it), I have been surprised when some of them submit work that seems to have completely ignored my detailed and carefully written instructions.

One of the problems, I have come to realize, is not that students don't care about my instructions or are "too lazy" to read them, but that they have come to equate "writing a paper" with "writing a research paper" or "writing a persuasive essay." And so, when I ask them to engage in a different kind of philosophical writing, they often fall back on what they have been taught about how to write. Their past learning overrides my own instructions, no matter how detailed I am. In order to do the kind of thinking and writing that I am asking them to do, they need to unlearn what it means to "write a paper."

It is important to note that this unlearning is not a mere conceptual transformation in their understanding of writing whereby new genres of academic writing are simply added to their repertoire. To do the kind of philosophical thinking and writing that I hope they will engage in, students also often need to unlearn whether writing is something that can feel meaningful or even enjoyable, whether they can be "good" at it, why professors might ask them to write, and so on.

In particular, one of the important things that I find it necessary for students to unlearn is their relationship to me as an authority figure. I find that in my current teaching context, students often have an oppositional understanding of the relationship between teachers and students. They tend to view teachers as obstacles to their goals, not as human beings who care deeply about both the material and their students.

In this way, unlearning in higher education can involve the transformation of complex attitudes, beliefs, and dispositions concerning the nature of schoolwork, the role of the teacher as an authority figure, and one's self-conception as a learner. These attitudes, beliefs, and dispositions have often been sedimented from an early age, making them extremely difficult to change.

There is, of course, no single quick and easy pedagogical strategy that we can employ to immediately bring about the many and complicated kinds of unlearning that we might hope students will undergo in our classes, but cultivating an attitude of playfulness is one strategy that I have found can lay the groundwork for this kind of productive unlearning in philosophy.

Creating the Magic Circle of Play in the Classroom

One way to cultivate an attitude of playfulness is to mark the classroom as a different kind of space. In my own teaching context, I am lucky to teach in classrooms designated as "philosophy learning labs." These rooms have shared round tables instead of individual desks, books and games, softer lighting, plants, and philosophy posters on the wall.[1] As soon as students walk into the room, they encounter a different kind of learning environment that helps them to suspend their assumptions about what learning looks and feels like. The physical environment helps to mark the classroom as a "magic circle" where the usual way of things has been suspended and we can try out new ways of being and learning together.

Of course, not everyone has the option of designing their own classroom, but even in a traditional higher education classroom, there are ways of marking the space as different that can contribute to the cultivation of playful engagement. Instructors can play music, arrange the room in unexpected ways, have coloring books and art supplies for students to doodle with as they come in, have students volunteer to bring snacks, or even bring props or costumes.[2] What an individual teacher chooses to do will vary depending on the course, the students, and the teacher's own personality, but physically and visually marking the space of the classroom as different, as a place where students are invited to bring different parts of themselves to their learning, can unsettle old norms and habits to create the space for new ways of learning together.

Philosophical games are another way to cultivate playfulness. These games can range from the simple to the complex. For example, in my ethics classes, we play a role-playing game that spans several weeks of class in which students enact the various ethical theories we have covered.[3] But games can also be used quickly for reinforcing content knowledge. For example, I often use pub-style trivia for review. Students are divided into teams. They create a team name and then compete in several rounds of trivia including picture rounds, matching, fill in the blank, and so on. Charades or *Pictionary* are also simple games that are especially helpful for reviewing content.

In a similar vein, group work can easily be turned into a game with the introduction of a point system and some light-hearted competition. To keep things playful, it's important for the stakes to be low. I like to offer baked goods, a very minimal amount of extra credit, or just the glory of victory. Having students create team names goes a long way toward creating the spirit of playful competition for these kinds of exercises.

Lightly competitive team games are, in my experience, especially helpful when students need to make mistakes in order to learn. One of the benefits of the playfulness of games is that it creates a space where "failure" can be experienced more productively. While sometimes in philosophy classes, we want to encourage students to explore their own ideas and find ways to affirm even the most tangential contributions to a class discussion, there are times when we need to tell students that they are wrong—that they have misunderstood a reading or have not quite mastered a skill or concept. Telling students they are wrong without causing them to shut down or think that they are unable to do philosophy can be difficult. In games, however, failure is the norm. If we won a game the first time or every time we played, we would quickly lose interest in playing it. We expect that we will lose and face setbacks in games, and so failure can be more easily taken in stride.

I have found, for example, that using argument mapping games in critical thinking is especially useful for creating space for productive failure. I divide students into teams (always with team names!) and give them an argument map template and a set of claims that they work together to place in the right spot on the template.[4] If teams place the claims correctly, they get a point for the round. At the end of the class session, the team with the most points wins. Since I have started turning this activity into a game, I have found that students are less distraught by getting the wrong answers. Rather than giving up and disengaging from the activity, students groan and rally, ready for the next round. The context of the game, the fact that the failure happens within the "magic circle" of playfulness, allows students to take a certain amount of emotional distance from the mistake and not see it as a reflection of their intelligence or ability.

Another easy way to incorporate a playful element into an activity is by using dice. For example, if students are practicing exercises from a logic or critical thinking text, you can roll dice to assign each group a particular exercise. Or you can have students roll dice to choose from a list of possible discussion prompts in a small group conversation. I find that introducing an element of randomness offers a spontaneity that supports a playful attitude. When we roll dice, we give up, to a degree, control of what happens next in the classroom. Ceding this control publicly, letting the dice "decide," introduces an openness into the activity that opens us up to receive novelty.[5]

Finally, discussion itself can also be made playful with the introduction of a meta-cognitive approach. We can think about academic conversations as a series of "moves" that one can make, not unlike moves in a game. For example, someone can propose a thought experiment, request additional evidence, present a counterexample, make a connection to another thinker/text, and so on. Identifying and making these moves can help students to improve their ability to participate in academic conversations and become more aware of what it is they are learning from a class discussion. You can turn this into an actual game,[6] or you can simply use the game-analogy to support student understanding and engagement.

Beyond Gimmicks

Playfulness and fun in learning are sometimes viewed derisively as gimmicks or tricks whereby we manipulate students into "real" learning. This is often the line taken by those who want to "gamify" learning. In my own experience, however, playfulness is not a gimmick or trick to manipulate students but contributes to both student learning and my own ability to be myself in the classroom. I became a philosopher because I find joy in wrestling with difficult questions alongside others. One of the great delights of teaching is being able to share this joy with students.

A playful attitude in philosophy, however, is, of course, not always appropriate, and playfulness can be risky. When a playful attitude is encouraged, students may feel more comfortable making jokes that push boundaries, and they may be harder to rein in when you need to get their attention. Classes can be loud and chaotic, and students (or even colleagues and administrators) can sometimes fall into the mistaken idea that because we are being playful, we are not being serious. It is also important to note that cultivating playfulness lands differently for different instructors for many reasons, including the credibility gap that many marginalized faculty face.[7]

As with all teaching advice, context is everything, and there are many ways to be an excellent teacher. What I hope to have briefly shown here, however, is that being the "fun" teacher does not need to come at the expense of student learning. In fact, cultivating a playful attitude in the classroom can help students bring new parts of themselves to the learning environment. Entering the "magic circle" of playfulness can help students suspend their normal ways of "being a student" and open all of us up to new ways of being in relation to one another and to philosophy.

Notes

1. The philosophy learning lab initiative at Harper College was initially conceived of by Brett Fulkerson-Smith and implemented by our department in the Spring of 2020, ironically just before the Covid-19 pandemic hit. The key to our success was first working with our Liberal Arts division operations manager to shift our course schedule so that only philosophy classes met in the rooms designated as learning labs. Our first lab was furnished using tables and chairs that were in storage and a modest budget for plants and posters. We were then able to provide data showing that students found that the labs enhanced their relationships with their peers, their sense of belonging, and their overall experience of learning. This promising data allowed us to expand the project with the support of our Dean and Provost. We now have three learning labs and almost all of our philosophy classes occur in the labs.
2. For examples of how to implement these strategies, see Weston, Anthony. 2018. *Teaching as the Art of Staging: A Scenario-Based College Pedagogy in Action*. Sterling, VA: Stylus.

3. For more details on how I run this game, see my blog posts: *Aesthetics for Birds*. 2020. "Why I Use Dungeons & Dragons to Teach Ethics." https://aestheticsforbirds.com/2020/08/03/why-i-use-dnd-to-teach-ethics/; *Blog of the APA*. 2020. "Teaching Ethics with Dungeons & Dragons." https://blog.apaonline.org/2020/03/11/teaching-ethics-with-dungeons-dragons/.
4. The website Thinker Analytix (https://thinkeranalytix.org) has many examples of this kind of argument mapping game.
5. My thinking on the importance of spontaneity for cultivating a playful attitude has been influenced by a conversation with Kinley Gillette about using role-playing games in the philosophy classroom.
6. I initially encountered the idea of implementing discussion moves in a game-based way from Ann Cahill. Claire Lockard, Ann Cahill, and I worked together to further develop this idea for the APA Teaching Hub Poster Session at the 2020 Central Division Meeting. For more on using discussion moves in the philosophy classroom, see Kaija Mortenson's blog post: *Blog of the APA*. 2021. "Using Discussion Moves to Balance Philosophical Conversations." https://blog.apaonline.org/2021/01/13/using-discussion-cards-to-balance-philosophical-conversations/.
7. For teaching strategies to mitigate some of these challenges, see Neuhaus, Jessamyn, ed. 2022. *Picture a Professor: Interrupting Biases about Faculty and Increasing Student Learning*, Morgantown: West Virginia University Press.

References

Huizenga, Johan (1950). *Homo Ludens: A Study of the Play-Element in Culture*. New York: Roy Publishers.

Mortenson, Kaija (2021). "Using Discussion Moves to Balance Philosophical Conversations." *Blog of the APA*. https://blog.apaonline.org/2021/01/13/using-discussion-cards-to-balance-philosophical-conversations/.

Neuhaus, Jessamyn (ed.) (2022). *Picture a Professor: Interrupting Biases about Faculty and Increasing Student Learning*. Morgantown: West Virginia University Press.

Nguyen, C. Thi (2022). "Playfulness vs. Epistemic Traps" in Mark Alfano, Colin Klein, and Jeroen de Ridder (eds), *Social Virtue Epistemology*, 269–90. New York: Routledge.

Scott, Rebecca (2020a). "Why I Use Dungeons & Dragons to Teach Ethics." *Aesthetics for Birds*. https://aestheticsforbirds.com/2020/08/03/why-i-use-dnd-to-teach-ethics/.

Scott, Rebecca (2020b). "Teaching Ethics with Dungeons & Dragons." *Blog of the APA*. https://blog.apaonline.org/2020/03/11/teaching-ethics-with-dungeons-dragons/.

Weston, Anthony (2018). *Teaching as the Art of Staging: A Scenario-Based College Pedagogy in Action*. Sterling, VA: Stylus.

17

When Crito and Plato Came to Class: Gameful Learning in the Philosophy Classroom

Greta LaFore

"Dr. L, I spent the weekend researching the Socratics. Did you know some of his students supported the 30 Tyrants who killed my sons? I'm going to make them pay." I smile just a bit. Keeping a poker face is now one of the most challenging parts of my job. "I'd heard rumors about that, Cassie."[1] Cassie's sons are, of course, Athenian men who lived and died roughly 1600 years ago. But in 2022, my first-year students sprawl in front of me at 9 a.m. on a Monday in a class required of all students at Gonzaga. I remember pulling teeth some years ago to get these students to do the required reading in Plato's *Republic* set before us today.

But today is not like those days. I open the book and give some cursory background to Plato's view of the soul and the city. And then I ask for questions. Cassie raises her hand. "Excuse me, but how can you write about justice, here, Plato, when your teacher and his followers participated in the killing of my sons?" "There's points for that Cassie!" remarks her desk mate. A cavalcade of snaps, oohs, ahhs, and boos from her classmates attends her accusation. Joanna, my student who is Plato this semester, looks nervously at her team leader, Cameron, known in my classroom by his Athenian persona of Crito. Cameron leans back and smiles, "Your justice, Athenian democrat, sounds a lot like whoever is most popular having control of our government. Surely that's not really what justice is." And more boos and snaps and questions and accusations and fifty minutes of raucous discussion of the nature of justice and Socrates's hopes for a new Athens in the *Republic* go by in a blink.

Cassie's research over the weekend and Cameron's careful preparation to defend his teacher Socrates in our discussion of the *Republic* were never prompted by me. They are evidence of the power of the gameful structure and role-playing content my classes are built on. In this chapter, I'll first explicate gameful pedagogy and then role-playing learning in hopes of showing why they form together an irresistible structure of support for student learning in the philosophy classroom.

But first, the why. Why mess with a traditional grading and class structure that was meeting my course outcomes? Before adopting these new pedagogies, I often had the sense that the goals I set for my students to achieve through course assessment and assignments were one size fits all. This was especially concerning to me since my courses are in our university's core, taken almost exclusively by non-philosophy majors to fulfill a universal requirement for the bachelor's degree. I felt tension for students who struggled to write the two required papers in the course that together made up a large portion of their grade. I struggled to support students who weren't confident in their abilities to raise probing questions of the text in front of their classmates for their participation grade. And often, walking through difficult philosophical texts in core courses for non-majors felt more like a weighty double burden for me. I had to simultaneously make the meaning of difficult texts clear to students while motivating them to care about the readings, to see why the texts mattered to them.

Beneath all of this, I felt a nagging guilt around the college student I'd been myself. In college, I was freshly exited from the cultural system of my childhood where women were discouraged from expressing disagreement in front of men. In the male-dominant philosophy classroom, this meant that my need to achieve a good participation grade was in direct conflict with every personal impulse I had. My grades in those early courses were a reflection of who I was when I entered college, a reflection of what I'd left, not of the confident thinker who I wanted to become. When a friend asked me if I would enjoy my own courses as a student a few years ago, I felt the only honest answer was no.

Gameful Pedagogy

Gameful pedagogy removes this tension for me because it gives much of the choice in assignments leading to course completion to my students. A newer innovation in pedagogical structure, Gameful pedagogy, according to its architects, reorients course design to channel students' "intrinsic motivation" to master course material (Hayward and Fishman 2020: 1007). Barry Fishman, Cait Hayward, and their collaborators have identified principles by which well-made games motivate players to win. These include having an identified, uncomplicated goal to be met, "giving learners meaningful choices about the work they do, enabling multiple pathways to success, and fostering a sense of purpose and mutual respect" (Fishman and Hayward 2022: 3).

In my gameful courses, I provide students a direct goal to achieve by laying out a points threshold for each grade at the beginning of the semester. To earn an A, let's say they need 300 points. Every student can articulate this goal by the end of Day 1 of my course. But how those 300 points are earned is largely up to student choice, giving them the opportunity to identify their own path to the grade they want. To meet course outcomes for the university, all my courses feature required writing assignments. But scoring less than perfectly on those assignments no longer dooms a student's final grade. Students must complete those assignments to pass. But they can also earn points by asking a question in class, asking me a question privately in office hours, attending an on-campus event with a classmate, responding to a classmate's contribution, or even creating memes or social media posts summarizing what we discussed in class. The menu of ways to achieve points is long. Some students earn high grades without ever raising a question in class and others do so without meeting with me in office hours. But the opportunity to choose how they earn their grades has allowed students to dare themselves to engage the parts of the class they might once have been reluctant to. Students resembling my former self who are less eager to jump into philosophical debate have begun participating, not out of fear of what might happen to their grade if they didn't, but out of self-determined desire to earn points.

To foster a sense of purpose and mutual respect, students are organized into teams that persist through the semester. They can earn points for spending time working on class projects with their teams. In some of my courses, I hold biweekly team championships in which the team with the highest current point total is rewarded with an extra ten points for each teammate. Gameful learning has shifted my students' identity in my courses. Now instead of individually rabidly pursuing a grade, hoping their classmates don't impede their achievement of that goal, students spur each other on to growth and mutual success. It's a frequent occurrence, entirely unprompted by me, for students to ask each other for feedback on their writing assignments to increase the likelihood they score well on their paper assignments. I've watched teammates clap loudly when one of their members asks a question and logs it for points in our class times. I see them spending time with each other on campus organically. They are supporting each other in their growth and gameful learning allows them to chart their own unique, collaborative path toward success in the course.

Now I want to acknowledge that this sounds like a lot of extra work to already overworked instructors. But the surprising fruit of the initial labor to shift my grade structure to gameful has been that it has been far less work for me in the end. Hayward and Fishman have developed a minimal-cost learning management system available to instructors and supported by the University of Michigan that tracks the gameful learning journey of each student in my class and allows students to log their own completion of assignments. My students report initial skepticism of this learning management system, GradeCraft, but I've yet to receive anything but enthusiasm about it by the course's end. Even second semester seniors are getting excited about seeing their point totals increase online. Nearly every student I speak with about GradeCraft expresses relief that the gameful system takes away the stress and mystery of the grading process. They know what their final grade is for my course long before it shows up on their transcript because they built it step by step themselves in GradeCraft.

Role-Playing Pedagogy

While gameful pedagogy provides the structure that allows me to give students ownership of their own learning, role-playing pedagogy transforms the content of my courses to allow students to motivate their own learning. In the role-playing pedagogies I use, students are assigned to play a specific person, usually deceased long before present time, at a crucial moment of intellectual turmoil from the past. Some of my courses take place in Athens in 403 BCE, others in 1864 London. Games are authored by professors across disciplines and published through the Reacting to the Past Consortium based at Barnard College. A lively Facebook group, Reacting Faculty Lounge, supports faculty new to the pedagogy. New faculty are given access to extensively helpful instructor's manuals and are invited to twice yearly summits where seasoned instructors run Athens and other games so that faculty can first experience the pedagogy as a participant before they support students through the games run on their home campuses.

My textbook for Philosophy 101 looks much like an anthology of major philosophical works from the ancient world at first glance. It has swaths of annotated sections from *The Republic*, discussions of the historical events just preceding the times of Plato, Aristotle, and Socrates, and maps of the Greek world. But instead of broad questions for philosophical contemplation, it asks students to consider how their particular character might feel about these historical events, and whether Socrates's satire and utopic visions would have felt hopeful or disillusioning given their character's hopes and fears. Our campus bookstore guides them to purchase this book, published by the Reacting to the Past Consortium, as the primary textbook for my class.

One student plays a farmer whose livelihood was recently decimated by war with the Spartans. Another plays a veteran of the war with Sparta, willing to die for the sake of Athenian democracy. I hand them their character sheets in envelopes marked "confidential" at the beginning of the semester so that they and they only know their character's secrets. The discussions about *The Republic* are seamless because, as students have told me repeatedly, they feel confident advocating for intellectual positions "in character," far more so than they do as their twenty-first-century selves. In my classroom, everyone knows Cameron is arguing as Crito, not as Cameron, that Joanna's passionate defense of the rights of foreigners to play a role in Athenian politics is motivated by her commitment to her characters' way of thinking. Their characters give them a mask from which to try on bravery in intellectual discussion.

Too often in philosophy classrooms, we struggle to show students how adopting differing philosophical approaches to the world impacts the way human history actually turns out. But students in role-playing pedagogy learn this lesson firsthand by advocating for intellectual viewpoints that transform how history re-unfolds in the classroom. The Athens game seldom ends the same each time and I tell my students the first week that who wins and who loses is entirely up to who can argue and speak best from their character's intellectual perspective, that ahistorical outcomes created only by them are far more common than those which follow the story of Athens they have been told before. As almost a bonus, role-playing pedagogy has been repeatedly shown to demonstrably increase students' skills in rhetoric, argumentation, public speaking, writing, and empathy for others (Carnes 2014; Hagood et al. 2018; Joyce et al. 2018).

The gameful structure and role-playing content of my courses have fundamentally transformed my teaching. I hope Crito and Plato would be pleased with the robust intellectual discussions that happen organically within the walls of my classroom, or at the very least, pleased that a high grade is well within their reaches on a cold winter day in 2023.[2]

Resources

Introduction to Gameful Learning: https://www.gamefulpedagogy.com/

GradeCraft Gameful Learning Management System: https://gradecraft.com/

Reacting to the Past Role-Playing Pedagogy: https://reacting.barnard.edu/

Notes

1. All student names in this chapter have been changed to protect student privacy.
2. Thanks to Barry Fishman and Cait Hayward for their clear articulation of the principles of gameful learning and eager, steady help in every moment of my transition to it. I owe many thanks as well to the entire team at Michigan who makes gameful learning possible. To the Reacting Faculty community who have seen me through many an unanticipated military coup in my classroom and taught me to embrace the method, I couldn't do any of this without you. To my interdisciplinary collaborators John Orcutt, Amy Pistone, and Julie Weiskopf, the Gonzaga University Philosophy Department, the Gonzaga Honors Program, the amazing staff at the Campus Printing Center, and the Center for Teaching and Advising at Gonzaga, who have helped my students and I write new history every semester, my students and I owe you thanks in every century. And most of all to the students whose experiences filled this chapter; I owe so much of the joy in my life to you. Avery Kain (the ever-generous and mischievous Diognetus and Joseph Dalton Hooker) and Charlie Barr (forever one step ahead of us Lithicles), your tireless, cheerful work as peer educators make every adventure in my classroom possible.

References

Carnes, Mark C. (2014). *Minds on Fire: How Role-Immersion Games Transform College*. Cambridge, MA: Harvard University Press.

Fishman, Barry and Caitlin Hayward (2022). "Gameful Learning: Leveraging the Learning Sciences to Improve the 'Game of Learning.'" *Rapid Community Report Series*, Digital Promise and the International Society of the Learning Sciences, https://repository.isls.org//handle/1/7663.

Hagood, Thomas Chase, Naomi J. Norman, Hyeri Park, and Brittany N. Williams (2018). "Playing with Learning and Teaching in Higher Education: How Does Reacting to the Past Empower Students and Faculty?" in C. Edward Watson and Thomas Chase Hagood (eds), *Playing to Learn with Reacting to the Past*, 159–92. London: Palgrave Macmillan.

Hayward, Caitlin and Barry Fishman (2020). "Gameful Learning: Designing with Motivation in Mind." *Proceedings of the International Society of the Learning Sciences* 2: 1007–14. https://repository.isls.org//handle/1/6287.

Joyce, K. E., A. Lamey, and N. Martin (2018). "Teaching Philosophy through a Role-Immersion Game: Reacting to the Past." *Teaching Philosophy* 41(2): 175–98.

18

Not Just for the Kids: Using Children's Literature and P4C Methods in the College Classroom

Karen S. Emmerman

As a professor at a university and a philosophy for children (P4C) practitioner, I have the rare good fortune to think philosophically with students in kindergarten, graduate school, and most stages in between. Like many university-level philosophy instructors, I began teaching in graduate school—first as a teaching assistant and then with my own classes. I was fortunate to be doing my graduate work at the University of Washington where Jana Mohr Lone, the Executive Director of PLATO (Philosophy Learning and Teaching Organization) was affiliated. Through Jana I was introduced to the theory, methodology, and joys of doing philosophy with young people in grades K-12. It was a few years before I realized that as much as my philosophical training helped me in thinking along with young students, the central tenets of P4C praxis would have a lasting and important influence on my approach to teaching my college students. Utilizing the theoretical and practical commitments of P4C in the college classroom can facilitate learning and philosophical reflection. Focusing my attention on wonder, curiosity, community, and epistemic humility—all vital for communities of philosophical inquiry with young people—has forever changed not only my teaching methods but my attitude as I head into the college classroom.

One of the central tenets of P4C is the community of philosophical inquiry (CPI). In a CPI, students come together to think critically and collectively about philosophical questions in a discussion that is driven by the values of mutual respect, curiosity, and epistemic humility. The latter is particularly important on the part of the adult facilitator. In a CPI, the teacher is a co-inquirer who thinks along with the students, offering questions or suggestions that drive their discussion deeper and hone their critical thinking, but never putting themselves forward as the possessor of the answers.[1] For most P4C practitioners, philosophical exploration with young people is guided by a desire to decenter the role of the teacher in the classroom, a profound respect for the epistemic authority of young people, and an emphasis on wonder.

P4C sessions typically involve using a prompt to generate philosophical questions and discussion. Prompts can include children's literature, poems, music, animated short videos, art, and sometimes just a question a student posed at the start of the session that the group took up and wanted to think about together. For example, a few weeks ago I had an extensive discussion with a group of second graders about whether it is problematic to call Sesame Street's Cookie Monster a "monster" after one student wondered aloud about the permissibility of using "monster" as a descriptor.[2] With the exception of some high school classrooms, absent from our prompts are philosophical texts or lessons on what philosopher X said about topic Y. Indeed, historical and professional philosophers and their arguments are rarely if ever discussed in P4C sessions for students younger than high school. Students' questions, ideas, and wonderings direct the philosophical exploration and what is discussed is determined entirely by them.

Long-time P4C practitioner and college instructor, David Shapiro, has written about how doing philosophy with pre-college students informed and changed his teaching practice with his college students (2013). In particular, when Shapiro started using the flow of P4C sessions (reading→reflection→question-gathering in small groups→discussion of students' questions as a whole class), he experienced a transformation in his classroom. Students' investment in discussions increased. They asked engaged and engaging questions, and dialogue flowed far more easily. I, too, have found both the theoretical and methodological commitments of P4C to be transformative for my college-level teaching.[3]

The first, and perhaps most important, shift arrived in the form of reconsidering my intention as I walk into my undergraduate and graduate classrooms. Previously, I had a fairly singular mission in mind, namely, to ensure that I articulated the positions of the philosophers we were reading as clearly and effectively as possible and then provided ample space for "discussion" of what I took to be the most important elements of the theory or argument under consideration. In itself, there is nothing wrong with wanting to be a clear and effective educator who values discussion about the crucial elements of what we are studying together. After doing P4C for a number of years, however, I found that intention to be rather a killjoy. P4C connects us to the joy of wondering and curiosity and to the excitement of hearing what others find most pressing or worthy of discussing. It connects us to the "togetherness" of thinking, to the idea that we are a communal brain wondering together. While I still value being a clear and effective articulator of complex ideas and theories, my intention as I walk in the door is no longer so singular in focus. Instead of "it's crucial I explain these ideas and show them what is important and interesting," I think "it's crucial that we have a space where we can all think together about this very complicated matter in a way that prioritizes what the students feel curious about." It sets a different tone for everyone when I arrive in that frame of mind and results in a more collaborative and engaged learning space.

I have also come to see the value of using children's literature in the college classroom. I often start my upper-division animal ethics class with the first chapter of E.B. White's *Charlotte's Web*, for example. Students read about Fern Arable's campaign to save the runt who will become Wilbur from her father's axe. They share thoughts and questions in small groups and then we use those questions as the basis for a discussion. Without fail, the students' questions cover numerous themes we will think about during the term—how we value animals' lives differently than humans' lives, how perceptions of ability and capacity influence our understanding of a being's value, how justice and care perspectives differ from one another, and how attachments to animals radically shift our sense of how we ought to interact with them.

Beginning a course or a class session with a children's story is powerful for several reasons: (i) it provides an accessible entry point for most students, (ii) it offers a low-stakes opportunity to think together about the questions that will drive their reflections for the term or that class, and (iii) it centers the importance of *their* questions to our philosophical reflection, something that can become lost when thinking about the arguments and answers provided by academic philosophers. By recreating the CPI method of individual thinking time followed by small group sharing followed by gathering students' questions, it is made clear that what these students think matters, that while I may have read more in a particular philosophical area, they are knowers and thinkers in their own right. In my undergraduate course on philosophy for children we use only prompts appropriate for young people to generate discussions and wondering about the prominent areas of philosophy. The ensuing discussions are rich, textured, and profound. Students regularly report that it is the first (at times the only) opportunity they have in college to reflect with other students about questions of central importance in their lives.

I have also discovered the power of another P4C tool in the college classroom: the warm-up exercise. In P4C sessions, I often spend a few minutes warming up the students to get them ready to do philosophy together. I don't assume they are in the right headspace for philosophy simply because I walked in the door. In pre-college classrooms, the warm-up also serves as a time for us to build our community a bit, getting to know one another through sharing simple thoughts or a fun exercise. I might ask "What's something good about being a 5th grader?" or "What is something beautiful you saw today?"[4] The warm-up takes mere moments, but it changes the energy in the room and brings us together in common purpose. In the past, I have made the mistake of thinking my undergraduate and graduate students arrive ready and willing to be in a philosophical space. It is unclear how I arrived at such an incorrect presumption, but there it is. Just like my young students, older students enter class in different emotional, psychological, spiritual, and logistical states. Some have sprinted across campus to arrive on time, others had a difficult therapy session that morning, others just saw something upsetting or heartening in the news or on social media. The warm-up, I now think, is just as necessary for undergraduates and graduate students as it is for first graders. It brings us together, reminds us of our communal endeavor, and provides an opportunity for us to get a brief and important glimpse into the mental lives of others in the room.

More than anything else, doing P4C has driven home for me that the things I often worry are "wasting time" or "not as valuable as getting through all the material" in the college classroom are indeed absolutely vital to both who I am as an educator and how I want to model philosophical engagement for my students. Philosophy is so much more than understanding what so-and-so said and what we think about that. It is about taking joy in wonder, curiosity, and uncertainty. Time spent warming up is valuable because we all need to be present and ready to think together about life's most challenging and important questions. We can read one fewer essay by an academic philosopher in favor of the words of E.B. White so that students can arrive in their own way at the questions they find most pressing about our topic.

Though I always valued discussion in the college classroom, P4C has driven home for me that I also value providing opportunities for students to think together about the questions *they* find most pressing and worthy of discussion without influence from my determination of what is interesting or important. Engaging in philosophical dialogue with young people has taught me to trust that we can get at what is truly important in university-level teaching through multiple entry points, not all of them grounded in academic readings and my guidance. Indeed, it has shown me that I can trust college students' questions and ideas to generate philosophical discussion just as much as I can trust those of kindergarteners.

Notes

1. For more information about the CPI and P4C praxis generally, see Lipman 2003; McCall 2009; Lone 2011; Goering et al 2013; Lone and Burroughs 2016.
2. Several students felt that since Cookie Monster self-identifies as a monster then it is perfectly appropriate to use "monster" when discussing him. Others felt that since Cookie Monster has shockingly poor manners he warrants the monster description. Still others remained uncomfortable with the use of a word with such negative connotations for someone so loveable and fundamentally kind.
3. For a helpful discussion of how P4C methods can help college teachers incorporate Critical Race Pedagogy insights into their classrooms, see Fitzpatrick and Reed-Sandoval 2018.
4. PLATO's website has a list of warm-ups put together by David Shapiro and Jana Mohr Lone that is organized by area of philosophy: https://www.plato-philosophy.org/teachertoolkit/range-warm-activities-philosophy-sessions/.

References

Fitzpatrick, Melissa, and Amy Reed-Sandoval (2018). "Race, Pre-College Philosophy, and the Pursuit of Critical Race Pedagogy for Higher Education." *Ethics and Education* 13(1): 105–22.

Goering, Sara, Nicholas J. Shudak, and Thomas E. Wartenburg (eds) (2013). *Philosophy in Schools: An Introduction for Philosophers and Teachers*. New York: Routledge.

Lipman, Matthew (2003). *Thinking in Education*. Cambridge: Cambridge University Press.

McCall, Catherine S. (2009). *Transforming Thinking: Philosophical Inquiry in the Primary and Secondary Classroom*. New York: Routledge.

Mohr Lone, Jana (2011). "Questions and the Community of Philosophical Inquiry." *Childhood & Philosophy* 7(13): 75–89.

Mohr Lone, Jana, and Michael D. Burroughs (2016). *Philosophy in Education: Questioning and Dialogue in Schools*. Lanham, MD: Rowman & Littlefield.

Shapiro, David (2013). "Engaging Students—of Any Age—in Philosophical Inquiry: How Doing Philosophy for Children Changed the Way I Teach Philosophy to College Students" in Sarah Goering, Nicholas J. Shudak and Thomas E. Wartenburg (eds), *Philosophy in Schools: An Introduction for Philosophers and Teachers*, 168–76. New York: Routledge.

19

Participation as Gratitude Practice

Stephen Bloch-Schulman

For the first fourteen years at my current institution, I did not grade participation in class because I found it counterproductive. In the classes I teach and at the school I teach at, I do not have a problem with students wanting to participate. I understand this may be different elsewhere and so my suggestions may need to be rethought in different contexts with different students and a different faculty member.

But I find typical participation grades counterproductive, almost anywhere. I believe that we either should teach a skill or not grade work that requires that skill, as much as possible. And I believe that teaching a skill means, at the very least, a reiterative process wherein there is an explicit discussion of the skill, how to use it and why; practice for the students; feedback on that practice; and chances to practice again. As far as I can tell, most faculty who include a participation grade do not do these things. They do not explain the what and why of participation, what good participation looks like and how to distinguish good participation from bloviating. Faculty who grade participation typically do not offer substantive feedback throughout the semester so students know how they are doing in relation to the what and why of participation. They do not, for example, scaffold different skills of participating as they would (and should) with other work, for example, with written assignments. Many of us recognize that "write

---

I would like to thank Claire Lockard and Ann J. Cahill for their exceptionally helpful comments and Brynn Welch for her vision and flexibility.

a high-quality paper" isn't useful advice because writing a paper requires so many subtasks and subskills (and sub-subtasks and sub-subskills), and so we often know to teach toward the subtasks and subskills (e.g., for this assignment, you will write an annotated bibliography. Next you will work on how to craft an effective thesis. Then …..). That is to say, participating well is no less (and often more!) complicated than writing well and we know (or I hope we know) that we need to break down the tasks of writing well; likewise, we ought to break down the tasks of participating well. (Note: if one does want to really teach participation, I strongly recommend Stephen Brookfield and Stephen Preskill's excellent *Discussion as a Way of Teaching: Tools and Techniques for Democratic Classrooms*; I recommend it even if one doesn't want to grade participation.)

I would highlight one additional way that participating well is hidden to students and the analogy to writing instruction is helpful. Whereas it is typically clear who the written assignments are for, it is not typically clear for whom one is participating. Is it for the faculty member (because lecturing without student input is miserable)? Is it for the student themself who makes the comment (they are learning how to say things, to offer things)? Or, it is for other students? That is, we are rarely clear to students what the point of class discussion is. We may not even really know, ourselves.

I think of the class very much in line with how Iris Marion Young thinks about democratic decision-making, as forms and fora of collective intelligence. I don't mean anything mystical by that (though that would be cool!). I mean that a group of people who are sharing and listening responsibly to each other, responding to each other, taking each other seriously will be able to learn things, self-correct when things go wrong, and come to better thinking (even as the people in that conversation do not agree, often, at any time during the conversation) (Young 2000: 21–33). I certainly have had those experiences in classes I have been a student in, in political spaces, and in classes where I have taught.

Put another way, I think the goal of teaching through dialogue is to think better and that that requires that lots of people say different things and that people listen to each other; it follows that participation (at least, the speaking side of it) should be directed primarily toward other students and their thinking—or at least, not any more to me than to others, and likely more to them than to me. That is not to say that I don't learn from students. I do. A lot! Nor do I mean to say that they don't learn by formulating their thoughts and speaking them. They do! But that the sign of an excellent student contribution is that it shows up *for other students* as having been helpful for the thinking of those other students.

I have been developing student-focused participation practices, graded and ungraded, that center the role of student-dialogue as being *for* the benefit of other students (rather than for me as the instructor). And I have now developed participation grades that follow this student-centered understanding of classroom dialogue and collective intelligence.

I now use several different ways of appreciating and assessing student participation, mixing and matching based on how many students are in the class and the particular structure of each course. Here are some:

> *1a.* I ask students at least twice (sometimes three times) during the semester to publicly thank other students in the class. When I do this, I want to be clear that the goal is for students to address and thank other students. Because they are inclined to think that whatever goes well in class (and poorly, of course) is my doing (because they believe it is "Stephen's class"), I start with something like this:
>
>> "So, it is important—in a class where we talk with each other so much and where you are doing so much of the sharing and where so much of the learning happens by listening to other students—to appreciate the hard work and contributions of your classmates. I would like you to take some time to think, and then to publicly, out loud, in class, *thank* other students for how they have helped you learn in this class. I understand that you might want to thank me for something that has gone well (if anything has). So I will preempt that by saying: … " [I say this in an intentionally ridiculous voice, totally over the top] "wow, Stephen, you are the best professor ever. In all of human history …." [Returning to a my normal voice]: "Okay, now that I have been thanked, you don't need to thank me; you can take some time to thank other students in class. And I encourage you to thank someone who might not even know you or someone who might not be expecting it. Certainly it is great to thank your small group partners if they have been good partners. But there are likely others in the class who have said something, done something, that helped you learn, and this is the chance to thank them. I will give you 4 minutes and 12 seconds to think about who you might want to thank, and then I will open the floor for thank yous and appreciations."

There are no grades associated with these thank-yous, and often, they are quite lovely. One excellent and, to me, surprising theme for the thank-yous in the middle of the semester is the number of students who thank people and explain how much they disagree with the person they are thanking, but how much that person they disagree with has led to their learning. Young would be pleased, I believe (Young 2000: 21–33). And, in a gesture of deep care, I often see students noticing who is being thanked and going out of their way to make sure everyone is recognized. (I bring thank yous of my own to add if I am worried that this will not happen, though I always prefer to have any thank you come from a classmate.)

> *1b.* Sometimes for the final "thank yous" I assign them as the last small assignment for the semester (note: I have something small due almost every class meeting; often very short so I can keep up with it; e.g., explain the difference between anti-patriarchal and anti-capitalist feminisms for Srinivasan in fewer than 132 words). I then use the final assignment to have students write thank-yous, which has led to some beautiful moments of acknowledgment and recognition. After reading their thank you, they hand a copy to the student (or students) they have thanked (and everyone who completes the assignment gets full credit for it).

> 2. I have begun to offer students the chance to give other students participation points when they recognize the value another student's comments had for them. In my recent classes, I have been focused on the value, structures and understanding of questions. In those classes, I have given each student two "thank you" notes that say "dear fellow student, thank you for asking such a good question. Here is my thanks, and 0.5 points as an appreciation." I printed these with sweet pictures (drawn by my daughter) and gave two to each student. The way they worked is this: each student could interrupt anything we were doing, any time, to thank another student for asking a good question. To do so, they stop the class or their small group work (raising their hand is fine, though a more forceful interruption is fine too) to walk over to another student and physically hand them the thank you note in the middle of whatever we are doing.

I believe by focusing the appreciation and recognition of student contributions on how students impact other students, I have found a way to have student contributions appreciated, to show students the importance of public appreciation of these contributions and avoided the encouragement for some people to simply say more words in class. And because the class has lots of small group work, which is work that I cannot see all of, these student-led participation acknowledgments foster collaborative spaces.

References

Brookfield, Stephen, and Stephen Preskill (2005). *Discussion as a Way of Teaching: Tools and Techniques for Democratic Classrooms*. 2nd edition. San Francisco: Jossey-Bass.

Young, Iris Marion (2000). *Inclusion and Democracy*. Oxford: Oxford University Press.

20

In Conclusion, I Don't Know: Humility as the Beginning and End of Every Class

Brynn F. Welch

In graduate school, I was observed by a few professors during my time as a Teaching Assistant. Two of those professors gave me exactly the same feedback: wrap up the content of the discussion by telling the students what they should take away from the conversation. Huh. I confess I found this advice puzzling. I definitely wanted to keep my supervising faculty happy, but I honestly didn't know how to do what they were suggesting I do. The reason was quite simple: *I* didn't know what I thought the take-away from the class discussion was. I could certainly summarize lectures, but *discussion sections*? I felt as though they wanted me to put a tidy bow on the messiest of ethical puzzles and send students on their way. I wish I could say that my concern about this advice was a deeply entrenched commitment to a lofty ideal about resisting imposing my own views in the classroom. Nope. My concern was that these very puzzles troubled me deeply, and I had no way to fill in the blank if my sentence began, "So, to sum up: _____." Do arguments about Deaf culture show that cochlear implants ought not to be available, or at least not funded? And if they are still available and/or funded, does consistency in reasoning demand that surgical deafening of children also be available and/or funded? I had—and still have—absolutely no idea. I felt unable to offer students a summary of discussion sections because I had no clear picture of how this all could or should be resolved; instead, I was in the maze with them.

Somewhere along the road, I realized that that *is* my summary. It's not a failure to give students a clear takeaway. Rather, it's just something different that I want them to take away: I'm in this with you, and I also have no idea. More precisely, I fill in why the puzzles are hard with specific content: If you want to say A, here are the questions you need to be thinking about, and if you want to say B, here is what you need to be ready to address. (I suspect this was all my supervising faculty needed from me.) But whatever the specifics of the puzzle I present to them and the challenges for solving it, the theme is always the same: this is really hard. Far from offering a nice summary at the end of a class, I have come to see my job as complicating the narrative for students. Our class discussion should be the *beginning* of their exploration, not the end of it.[1]

At the beginning of every course, I lay out the ground rules of philosophy for my students. I give them three guidelines:

1 In philosophy, our goal is not to *be* right. Our goal is to *figure out* what's right.
2 Because our goal is to figure out what's right rather than to just insist that we're right at the outset, we have to practice humility. We must go into (nearly) every conversation knowing we may be wrong.
3 Because our goal is to figure out what's right and because we might not already have the right answer, we have to consider (most) other views charitably.[2]

I tell students that these will be our starting points for the course, and that the course itself will serve as an argument for these rules. But importantly, I also emphasize how countercultural these rules are.

I like to think of these as the School Speed Zone rules: excellent in theory, but no one actually follows them. Why do we have reduced speed limits in school zones? Because tiny humans with fragile bones and poor impulse control are somewhere near the road. Slow down! That is objectively an *excellent* rule. If we were designing society from the ground up, that rule would enjoy broad bi-partisan support and be an excellent starting point for further compromise. But think about it: when's the last time—without a visible police cruiser parked nearby—that you *actually* dropped below 20 miles per hour in one of those zones? We get flashing lights and everything, but we're so caught up in other stuff we forget why the rule was so important in the first place. To me, the rules of philosophy are just like this. They're excellent—world-changing, in fact. But we're so caught up in other stuff, they take careful attention to follow, and they aren't our default way of approaching disagreements or hard questions.

Consider, for instance, the rule of humility. Anyone can see why this is a good rule: I'm fallible. It would be arrogance of the highest order to believe that in the history of humankind, I alone have it all figured out. Gather round, listen to me, and you shall become wise. No. Obviously not. Students get this immediately. But then I ask this: when's the last time you argued with someone—or even saw a view that differed from yours—and *seriously* entertained the possibility that you may be wrong? It's rare. And that makes sense, because we're socially conditioned not to view discussions that way. We're socially conditioned not to set (1) as our goal, and without (1), (2) and (3) seem optional at best and—if our goal is to win rather than to learn—counterproductive at worst. Imagine, for a moment, that a candidate in a presidential debate says, "That's a good question. I'd need to think about that more," or "You know what? You're right, and I'm going to change my position on that." Considering an alternative position as the potentially correct position? No. Absolutely not.

It may be tempting to write this off as merely part of the absurdity of the arena of politics, but that's too cheap and easy. Consider formal debates someone might participate in during high school, such as a debate team. Their job is (usually) to defend to the bitter end the position they either choose or are assigned.[3] They start with their conclusion, and their task is to defend it relentlessly, come hell or high water. Sure, there will be a period when they encounter objections, but even then, the task is usually to *respond* to the objections. The task is rarely if ever framed as *considering* the objections, *reflecting* on whether and how those objections may impact the position being defended. For that matter, what does it mean that we task one side to listen *for the purpose of* responding? Practically, sure, it's likely that someone can think of some questions or concerns about a view presented. But don't we typically tell people that you ought to listen actively rather than be thinking about what you might say next? Both teams are taking as their starting position that they are right, and the other side is wrong, and they are proceeding accordingly.

Of course, one need not be a member of a competitive debate team to experience this. Classes are frequently split up for debate and given similar rules: this side of the room defends X, and this side defends not-X. Go! Sometimes, this is set up as assigning students to defend a position that is not their own. I confess that my own discomfort with this practice is likely a reflection of the highly politically charged and sensitive topics my own classes cover (e.g., race, gender, family), coupled with the realization that for me, many of these topics are quite abstract while for many of my students, they are constant considerations. What is an interesting policy question to me may be an embodied fear for my students. I'm not inclined to require students to disclose their own views on many things—and indeed stress that I never assume that because they are testing out an idea they endorse that idea—and I'm even less inclined to require that they adopt a position that conflicts with their own.[4] But more importantly, I never want to set class up in a way that reinforces the social norms about arguments, according to which you assume you're right from the beginning and your job is to show why the other person is wrong. Bonus points if you can make them look stupid or evil along the way. So much of how we engage with different views sets us up for failure when it comes to following the most basic rules of discussion in philosophy. How, then, can we help students not only practice following those rules but come to see why those rules are such good starting points? My answer at this point in my teaching career is constant reminders that this is really hard, and that I'm in this with them.

Depending on the size of the class, I have various practices I use to model and help students cultivate humility. In smaller classes, I do a semester-long journal project. For this project, students write 250 words about some moral issue they consider quite easily and obviously answered.[5] I give each student a list of readings to do that make compelling arguments for the other side. Then, the students submit 500 words. I give them my own questions or objections, and they submit 750 words. At this point, students have a meeting with me, and we go over what questions or issues remain. At each stage, I stress to students that it is entirely up to them how they process the questions or objections. Their task is to reflect on the issue, not to defend a particular position. Perhaps the objections are clarifying such that they make their own view stronger. Perhaps the objections rattle their commitment to their initial view. Perhaps the objections strike them as irrelevant for various reasons. It is entirely up to students what to do with those objections. Ultimately, students submit 1000 words and a critical reflection on their experience. Importantly, their critical reflection asks one question: did you ever consider that you might be wrong?

In class discussion following the submission of the final journal and their critical reflection, students are asked to talk about their *experience* with the project. I do not ask them to present their view or where they've landed, but rather to talk about *what it was like* to get that feedback, how they processed it, what they learned about how they respond to challenges throughout the project. Over the years, this journal project has become one of my favorite assignments for exactly this moment. (Well, this moment and the fact that students frequently comment that they would lose sleep thinking about how to respond to some of the questions. I don't enjoy their sleep deprivation, but I do like knowing they are *feeling* how hard this is.) The rules I outlined at the beginning of class seemed so obvious at the time, and students have been asked to practice them throughout the course, and yet they still find that the rules are exceptionally hard to follow. Most students say they never considered that they might be wrong, and that they did in fact always think about how they could respond to the objections. Most students view the objections as obstacles to overcome on their way to defending their initial position. Many report that they have become better at navigating conflict and disagreement, and not interpreting a professor's feedback as a personal criticism of them. But across multiple classes and hundreds of students, I can count on one hand the number of students who said they did consider that they might be wrong.

To be clear, their original position may be right! And I stress as much in class. My goal isn't to change their minds or to convince them they're wrong. But I'm not after the content itself; I'm after the practice. Was your goal to figure out what's right, or was your goal to show that your view was right? Did you consider that you might be wrong? Did you charitably interpret challenges in service to figuring out what's true? Mostly—almost always—the answer is no. And students chuckle at the realization. They endorse the rules. They think the rules are obviously good ones. And yet, they struggle to follow them. They forget to slow down in the school zone. Again, this is really hard. But if we can get to the place where we see how hard it is, we can begin the real work of figuring it all out together, in dialogue with one another.

In large, lower-level classes, I use decision grids and webs. In a decision grid, my goal is to show the challenges a defender of any particular position will face. (See Appendix A.). I am explicit with students: no one in this debate is philosophically off the hook. Everyone has questions they face; everyone has tricky things to consider. My goal is to show that this is hard *for everyone*. There is no one position that avoids scrutiny; no one position that will have me as the professor saying, "You're right. Thanks for settling that debate for us." As a bonus, it helps shape discussion because it outlines clearly for students where their energy should go as they defend a particular point. Importantly, it lets me add to the drumbeat of "this is really hard" a reminder that I am not immune from the challenges. Students may not know where on the decision grid I fall, but they know I fall somewhere, and they know I face challenges. I am upfront about this: I am in this with you. This is hard for me, too. I don't have this all settled. Let's keep trying to figure it out.

Webs are my version of whole-course summaries. (I feel certain this is *not* what my supervising faculty had in mind in graduate school.) For webs, I make a circle that includes the specific topics we covered during the course, and then I show lines connecting the various topics. (See Appendix B.) Consider a course in bioethics. What we say about consent matters for, say, ethical research. But research doesn't occur in a vacuum, so surely we must give some thought to how we allocate resources, which can be tricky if we're looking at something like organs, and wait! Oh! Hey look! Consent is back! The web is admittedly my mic drop moment, and students talk about it even after the class ends. (Indeed, I show them the web and then shamelessly send them off to do course evaluations.) But here's the point I make to them: we tend to ask questions in isolation and in ways that make the answers appear obvious. If we ask only "is it permissible to conduct life-saving research using non-human animals," there will certainly be disagreement, but it's all too easy in isolation to think it's clear that your own answer is correct. If, however, we see that how we answer this question has implications for how we answer questions about other issues, we can start to see how very hard the question really is. Again, this is really hard.

With all three resources—journals, decision grids, and webs—I make the same point to students, and this point becomes the drumbeat of the class: this is hard, but that's a *good* thing. Why is it a good thing? Why not throw your hands up and lose hope? Because the sooner we see how hard the questions are, the easier it is to follow the starting rules. It's our knowingness that gets in the way of following rules we know are good. It's not upsetting to see how hard a question is, or how seemingly intractable a moral puzzle may be. The difficulty can undermine our confidence that we're right, and that itself can remind us of the importance of the rules of humility and charity. After all, if I am convinced some question is genuinely hard to navigate, I'm more likely to be charitable toward those who answer it differently than I would. "I don't know" is a reason to dig in, not a reason to give up. It's the only reasonable starting point for meaningful exploration; it may just take an entire semester to get to it.

Here's what I tell students: I am unabashedly idealistic about what the world might be like if more people practiced humility and charity, and this manifests as an absurdly intense faith in the way philosophy classes are poised to change the world as we know it. So now, the way I summarize individual class meetings and entire courses is to get us all to the *beginning* of the real work. This is really hard. I don't know the answer. Now let's begin.

Appendix A

Table 20.1 Decision grid: Cochlear implant debate © Brynn F. Welch.

Cochlear implants are an individual parent's decision	Cochlear implants are acceptable, but so is deafening a child	The government should not fund the bionic ear	Cochlear implants are acceptable but not required if the child is born to Deaf parents	Deafness is a disability	Cochlear implants are always morally required	Deafness is a cultural identification, but an "exceedingly narrow" one	Cochlear implants are always morally wrong	Deafness is a cultural identification, but the culture provides sufficient opportunity to ensure the child's right to an open future
– What should guide the parent's decision? – Are there decisions parents should not be free to make? If so, what? And why?	– Are there decisions parents should not be free to make? If so, what? And why? – Are there ever natural conditions/states with which we ought not to interfere?	– How do we justify favoring the interests of the Deaf community over the interests of the child/child's parents? – When should we respond to social inequality by changing the individual rather than the society? – Does the government then have additional responsibilities to ensure an accessible society?	– Are there decisions parents should not be free to make? If so, what? And why? – Does this commit the parents (or society) to additional responsibilities for the child's future?	– Define disability. (This might require defining norms, explaining what counts as an undesirable abnormality vs a desirable one, etc.) – How do we justify rejecting the claims of those who suggest otherwise?	– How many opportunities are parents required to provide their children? – How do we justify favoring the child's interests over the interests of the Deaf community?	– How many opportunities are parents required to provide their children? – When should we respond to social inequality by changing the individual?	– How do we justify favoring the interests of the Deaf community over the interests of the child/child's parents? – How do we determine when a parent is free to make decisions for their child?	– Is it then permissible to deafen a child? – Are accommodations morally required?

Appendix B

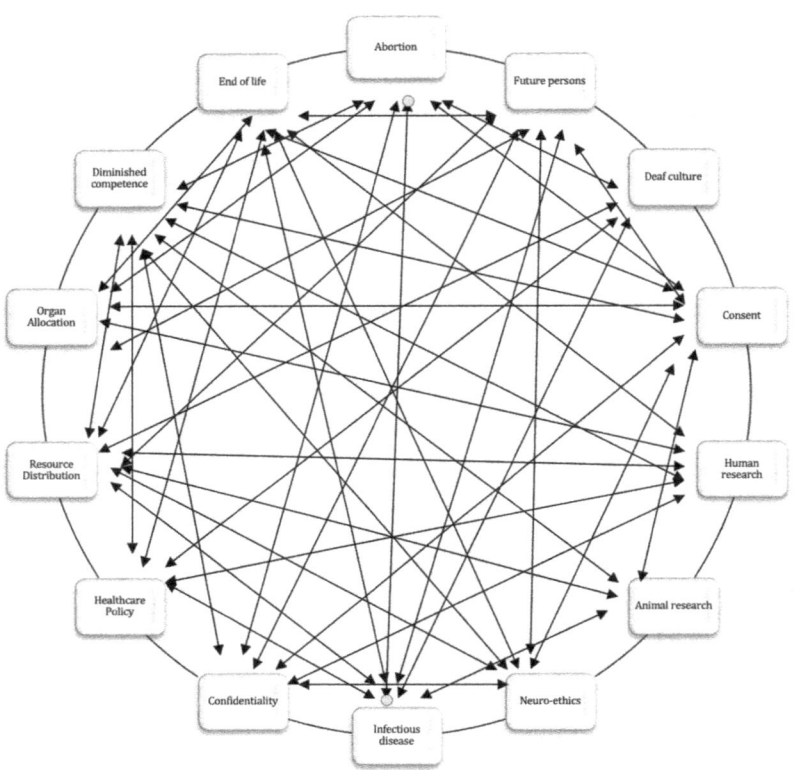

Figure 20.1 A web showing connections between topics named each week in a Bioethics syllabus and the connections between these topics. © Brynn F. Welch.

Notes

1. Thanks to Matt King for framing things this way.
2. In the interest of full disclosure, I spend some time on what counts as an open question. I believe that in a classroom setting, there are some questions that are harmful to entertain as a merely academic exercise. As such, I do not entertain those questions in my class.
3. I should note that having observed the National High School Ethics Bowl competitions, I was inspired by the idea that students learn it isn't a strike against their team if they find themselves modifying or even changing their position, since the goal is careful reflection rather than argumentative victory. We should all be so lucky to be trained this way from an early age.
4. I should note that the value of such practices is not lost on me. Putting students in these situations can certainly help them better understand a variety of complex arguments and how the objections fit into the overall picture, the activities can help generate student engagement and trust between students, and as someone who struggled quite a bit with speaking in class the value of encouraging structured class participation is certainly appealing.
5. The same rules apply as in note (2). In this case the rule is nonnegotiable because there are arguments that I simply will not engage with even for the point of this exercise.

21

A Student's Reflections

Anna E. Ulrey

"I treat the first phase of a research project a bit like being lost out at sea," my independent research advisor remarked in our first meeting regarding my project. Unbeknownst to her, I had spent the last two years as a philosophy major in a similar state. By the beginning of junior year, I completed the pre-medicine requisites and fulfilled the course requirements for my major, but I never felt I landed somewhere substantial in either field. Through developing my independent research project and the empowering mentorship I found with my advisor, I discovered how to *learn* philosophy rather than sit passively in class while a professor taught at me. This prepared me for the following semester when I enrolled in a discussion-based learning course in philosophy. I intend to explore what made these experiences valuable as learning endeavors and why I believe philosophy is best taught and learned through discussion-based learning.

In the second semester of my freshman year, I enrolled in a social-political philosophy course. Though cut short by the pandemic, it was in this course that I acquired my first taste of discussion-based learning. My previous philosophy courses had been primarily lecture-based and lacked much of the student-led discourse that made the course challenging and engaging to me. Though the course still featured lectures, my classmates were a tight-knit group comfortable with proposing new ideas and questioning each other. This facilitated a learning environment salient with exploration of meaningful and relevant issues to the learners that composed it. We discussed real issues experienced by real people in the real world, which can often get lost in learning environments that center around a single contributor and lack open communication from other perspectives.

A few semesters later, I began my own research project utilizing a narrative approach to address weight discrimination in medicine. It was inspired in small part by a class on narrative medicine I took the prior semester and in larger part by the aforementioned social-political philosophy course. The project was to be entirely based on using accessible, narrative-based tools to address very real problems faced by very real people. The project—generously supported by my research advisor—culminated in a successful paper, but that was not the most valuable development to come from the project. Rather, the rich philosophical discussions we conducted in service to the project yielded more intellectual and moral growth than any of my academic endeavors to date. I learned to seek to understand first, to be charitable in discussion, to withhold assertions without questions, and a slew of other skills vital to meaningful academia.

This prepared me for the following semester when I enrolled in my first solely discussion-based learning course in philosophy, in which students led the discourse during class. Our wheels spun a bit at first, but the professor employed a system based on summary sheets that supported the discussion-based format and steadied the pace of the course. Each summary sheet consisted of the primary question, the thesis, and a 500-word summary of the assigned reading. Each student was responsible for one summary sheet throughout the course, alongside 2–3 discussion questions based on the reading. The class meeting began with a brief discussion of the summary sheet before tackling the discussion questions. At times, the professor jumped in with a comment to refocus the conversation or guide it in a new direction, but the course was primarily student led. The summary sheets facilitated opportunity to both practice analysis of academic material and appreciation for unique perspectives and understandings.

The structure of this course allowed for more engaged and meaningful contributions from students than a quick interjection during lecture typically would. In lecture-based courses, a student could raise their hand and ask a question, and the professor might entertain the question for a bit or ask to talk after class before continuing with their lecture. Conversely, in this discussion-based course, one student proposed an objection to the text and we spent much of that class meeting debating this single objection. While in other courses this may be viewed as wasting the meeting on a single point, we instead recognized the rare opportunity to organically develop our skills as philosophers and members of society. We practiced active listening, asking questions first (*not* obvious to many students), charitable understanding, and productive communication. In sum, we learned how to be active agents in philosophy rather than passive observers.

Moreover, discussion-based learning provided an avenue for us to talk openly with each other about topics often excluded from undergraduate curricula but philosophically rich and pertinent to our understandings of ourselves and the world around us—death, living well, and legacy to name a few. We students agreed that the course was unlike others we had taken, and for a while I chalked that up to lucking into a good group of students. Though that may contain a bit of truth, I have since realized that it had much more to do with the influence and power of discussion-based learning.

These are the cornerstone experiences that have changed the way I learn within and apart from the field of philosophy. They reflect how I believe philosophy is best taught and learned—through encouraging personal engagement with and collaborative discourse about the material rather than traditional lecture-style learning.

Part III

Exercises and Assessments

22

A Primer for Assessing Dispositional Growth

David W. Concepción

Think aspirationally. Imagine that you bump into a student who took your introductory course four years ago. During the conversation you ask: What is the most important thing that has stuck with you from your time in my course? What do you hope the answer will be? Please make a list of the top five things you might be proud or pleased to hear. If you had to pick, which item on the list would you most want to hear? No, really, take a moment before you continue reading, and actually write a list. Whatever you wrote are your *real* learning objectives; they are what you really care about even if they don't match the three to five bullet points starting with an active verb on your syllabus.

Which type of learning objective have you identified? Suppose we divide learning objectives into three types: content mastery (Which information do you know?), skill development (What can you do?), and dispositional growth (What are your character strengths?). There is nothing especially revelatory about this way of dividing types of learning, and for other purposes another taxonomy might be better. But this trichotomy allows us to see especially clearly how unusual philosophers are.

In over twenty years of leading faculty development events, I've noticed trends. Natural scientists focus most on content mastery, and professional disciplines stress skill development most. Perhaps it is unsurprising that humanities professors emphasize dispositional growth over skill development and content mastery. It's not that we don't want our students to know what Descartes said in the second meditation, it's just that philosophers—especially when thinking aspirationally—care more that our students become, for example, less dogmatic. No less than others, philosophers see the instrumental value of written communication skills, but philosophers also tend to care a great deal about another outcome of evaluative writing, the value of becoming intellectually humble. Philosophers are not alone in emphasizing dispositional learning objectives, but we do tend to emphasize them more often and more deeply than almost everyone outside of the humanities and more so than a majority of others within the humanities. Because so many philosophers emphasize delicious, deeply human, and enduringly valuable all-purpose character development, it is no wonder that a person who believes that content mastery is the only (appropriate) type of learning objective might ask philosophers questions that seem to devalue our teaching.

I've been told by administrators in charge of assessment that I may not have intellectual humility as a learning objective because it is unobservable and thus immeasurable. This directive rests on a mistake. Assessment coordinators are right to insist that evidence of student learning be direct. What they mean is that claims about student learning must be evidenced by the work of the student, and not, say, the reputation of the graduate program they are in. But it is a mistake to understand this particular direct/indirect distinction as suggesting that judgments regarding student learning are based on direct observations of students' minds or characters.

All judgments regarding student learning are inferential. For a teacher to evaluate what a student knows or knows how to do, or the state of a student's character, the student must produce and submit an artifact (e.g., an exam or essay) or performance (e.g., a presentation). It is the artifact or performance that the teacher evaluates; teachers evaluate externalized proxies. Even in an oral exam or a simple conversation, it is the words and the speaking, not the mind or character, that teachers immediately encounter. All learning is assessed inferentially through proxies.

If all assessments of student learning are inferential, then assessment of dispositional growth is not different in kind from assessment of content mastery. Whether a student has grasped the content of Descartes's second meditation (i.e., content mastery), improved their ability to organize ideas into *modus ponens* format (i.e., skill development), or become more curious (i.e., dispositional growth) are all determined by inference from an externalized proxy.

Of course, which proxy data should be produced so that reliable inferences about student learning can be made differs considerably. Multiple-choice exams are pretty reliable markers for content mastery, but they are not perfectly so since students may guess, cheat, or otherwise select answers in any number of ways that are not grounded in what they know. But multiple-choice exams tend to be quite unreliable grounds for inferences regarding skills. Cognitive awareness of where a needle should be placed to successfully draw blood (i.e., content mastery) is necessary for quality performance as a phlebotomist but an unpracticed would-be phlebotomist with such knowledge has not developed a skill through practice. A phlebotomist-in-training should draw from an anatomical substitute until in the judgment of a relevant expert they are skillful enough to practice on live clinical volunteers. In general, the trick is for teachers to ask students to produce proxies that are likely to accurately represent the not-directly-observable state of the student with regard to the learning objective in question.

Aspirationally thinking philosophy teachers frequently express hope that their students will grow, among others, the following dispositions: curiosity, intellectual humility, comfort with ambiguity, and fair-mindedness. What artifact could a student produce or what behavior might a student perform such that it would be appropriate for a teacher to infer that the student has become more fair-minded? An essay assignment where a student must charitably present rationales for thinking their own reasoning is flawed strikes me as a good proxy for fair-mindedness. A student whose writing comes to have more and increasingly challenging yet charitably presented criticisms of their thinking as the semester goes on gives a philosophy teacher pretty solid evidence that the learning objective "improve fair-mindedness" has been substantially met, just as a multiple-choice exam can give a biochemist good evidence that a student has met the learning objective "understand the Krebs cycle."

Two observations are especially important here. First, both the biochemist using multiple-choice exams and the philosopher using essays involving charitable criticism are instances of direct assessment. Second, both are inferential. The requirement for direct assessment is not a requirement for non-inferential assessment and there are common proxies that allow for easy assessment of dispositional learning objectives.

So, which proxies should philosophers ask students to create or perform? How should we assess for dispositional growth? I hope it's obvious that the answer is "It depends." Which growth is being targeted? Which content is being used? What is the institutional context within which the teaching and learning is taking place? And most importantly, what is best for the particular students in the particular course?

One thing is certain, however. As Aristotle told us long ago, action is required to grow dispositions. If you want people to become more curious, ask them to act curiously over and over again, and, to the extent possible, make the joy of curiosity palpable. It may be that some reading about or listening to a lecture about curiosity is helpful or even necessary to become more curious, but reading and listening is not sufficient. To become more curious, one must perform curious action.

What is it to act curiously? An obvious but only partial answer is that curious people ask and attempt to answer questions. A teacher targeting an increase in curiosity would do well to (i) give assignments where students ask and answer questions, (ii) provide formative feedback to help students ask more interesting questions and provide more meaningful answers, and then (iii) ask students to create more and better questions.[1]

In general, to develop sequences like those described above—(i) assignment, (ii) formative assessment, (iii) assignment, etc.—all the way to an end-of-course summative assessment, imagine what a person with an appropriate end-of-course level of the trait you want to help students develop would do on given a particular assignment. That is, imagine the ideal end product of the best student in your class. Then figure out what to ask students to do, including the order you will ask them to do it and when and which feedback you will give them between attempts, so that at the end of the semester they (almost all) are able to produce successful proxies.

Instructive rubrics help students learn by directing their attention to the central features a successful proxy must have. Fundamentally, rubrics are descriptions of what an assessor needs to see in an artifact or performance (a proxy) to justifiably conclude that the desired learning has occurred. But many teachers are not accustomed to creating, and most administrators are not used to reviewing, rubrics regarding dispositional growth. Fortunately, just as dispositional growth is not different in kind from other learning objectives with regard to measurability, rubrics for assignments that ask for proxies of dispositional growth are not different in kind from rubrics for assignments about content mastery or skill development.

Good rubrics describe specific material manifestations that can be judged present or absent, and they do so in terms that are meaningful for students. Weak rubrics are vague; strong rubrics are specific. If one way curiosity is grown is by asking questions, then part of an assignment might be: "After completing the reading, (i) submit a question that the teacher could put on a quiz and (ii) submit two questions about an idea or ideas in the reading that you would like to discuss with your classmates." (For contrast, a weaker assignment might say something like "After completing the reading submit 100 words that demonstrate curiosity.") The key here is that the assignment and rubric describe the characteristics of a full credit-earning proxy, and not the learning objective. A grading rubric for this small example assignment might be: "Submission contains a potential quiz question" and "Submission contains two potential discussion questions." Of course, rubrics for larger essay assignments contain more elements, but the principle is the same. Good rubrics contain specific elaborations of the characteristics of successful proxies.

Dispositional learning objectives are sufficiently measurable that, to please an assessment coordinator, philosophers could even do pre-intervention and post-intervention assessments and report the results numerically. We could ask students to perform a task on the first day of class and then ask them to perform the same task on the last day of class. We could measure how much questioning occurs in the written answers students provide in both the pre-test and post-test, rating them on a ten-point scale. One person might improve from a three to a seven on the curiosity scale, while another improves from a four to a five. That is, many of the specific types of assessment that might be desired by a particular employer can be adapted to a philosophy course focused on dispositional learning objectives. In addition to being direct, both the humanistic and dispositional learning objectives of philosophy are as observable and measurable as any other.

Can we be certain that students have developed the desired disposition simply because they manage to produce an artifact or performance akin to that which the virtuous person would produce? No. But neither does the biochemist know for sure that the student scoring 100 on an exam has understood the Krebs cycle. All sorts of proxies serve as evidence for the assessments we want to make; multiple-choice exams are not the *sin qua non* of observable and measurable assessments.

Lastly, it is worth emphasizing explicitly that the argument here is for parity. There are many different types of learning objectives and as part of a total education none is better than another (although the fact that I have chosen teaching philosophy as a profession shows which I prefer). The claim here is merely that, with the right proxies, dispositional learning objectives are just as observable and measurable as any other. Only a failure of imagination about what a good proxy is would lead one to conclude otherwise.

Coda

What if the objection is not that dispositional growth is unmeasurable but that it is not "objective-worthy"?[2] Some people assert that philosophy doesn't teach anything worthwhile. This objection seems to imply that a response focused on the intrinsic value of dispositional growth will be met with suspicion and derision. I have three reactions. First, this implication should be rejected. "Because it is intrinsically valuable" is a perfectly fine answer to the question "Why should dispositional growth be pursued?"

Second, for the sake of argument, let's accept the instrumentalist restriction. There are many types of instrumental benefits and burdens. Being intellectually humble is typically instrumental to having a meaningful life, being fair-minded seems instrumental to having great inter-personal relationships, and being comfortable with ambiguity has certainly helped many people I know live with low levels of anxiety. Audre Lorde makes the point better than I can: "As we learn to bear the intimacy of scrutiny, and to flourish within it, as we learn to use the products of that scrutiny for power within our living, those fears which rule our lives and form our silences begin to lose their control over us" (1977).[3] Philosophy has high instrumental value.[4]

The above types of instrumental value are frequently preemptorily excluded from the range of acceptable answers by the critic. Such a critic unsatisfied with the first two responses—intrinsic value and non-career & non-financial instrumental value—is revealed as assuming that a college course is worthwhile if and only if it contributes to career and financial goals. Of course, other things being equal (when possible) it is good for people to become able to meet their physiological and safety needs (Cf. Maslow). It's the inference to the value of college courses that is the problem. I think the following inference is false: If (when possible) it is good for most people to position themselves to meet their physiological and safety needs, then college courses that do not directly attempt to help students better position themselves to meet their physiological and safety needs are unjustified. To defend the rejection of this inference is beyond the scope of this chapter. The point here is that dissembling attempts to shroud value commitments in technical language should fail. The "not objective-worthy" objection is *not* a technical issue internal to a discussion of assessment. This criticism is political. The disagreement is about what a curriculum should contain, and which courses an institution should offer.

Sometimes within the laid bare "proper curriculum" debate a philosopher will be accused of being an indoctrinator. I reserve the term "indoctrinator" for a person who aims to have another person (dogmatically) hold a belief or beliefs the indoctrinator wants them to hold. An indoctrinator desires belief-compliance. As dispositions are not beliefs, a teacher targeting dispositional growth is simply not an indoctrinator on this definition. Nevertheless, since a sensible way to help people grow fair-mindedness is by having them evaluate beliefs unlike their own, it is likely that a philosopher will put unpopular beliefs before their students, and many of these beliefs are exactly those that our imagined critic will think would not be expressed in a proper curriculum. Here the indoctrination "criticism" is revealed to be nothing more than the "critic's" desire to not have people experience certain ideas. Perhaps the critic believes that the experience of the idea will result in a person believing it, and the critic does not want the person to believe it. In such a case it is the critic who is pursuing (negative) indoctrination. Even when disguised in wholesome rhetoric regarding freedom of thought and harm prevention, I believe the authoritarian censorship of this critic should be named and resisted, especially when the value of sifting and winnowing is as high as it is.[5]

Third, it's worth noting that even if we grant what we shouldn't—that a college course should be offered if and only if students will have better career opportunities and/or income potential by completing it—philosophy fairs quite well. The National Association of Colleges and Employers lists eight career readiness competencies—traits and skills—that employers most desire their employees to have.[6] Employers regularly say, "We can teach an employee the technical stuff, we need good people." To get hired and advance in most careers certain dispositions—including curiosity and open-mindedness—are particularly helpful, and philosophy is especially effective at helping people develop them. Even more relentlessly, data suggest that philosophy majors do better than most non-STEM majors with regard to income ten years after graduation.[7] Bluntly, on average, a successful philosophy major pursuing a career in accounting is likely to rise to middle management faster than a successful accounting major despite having an initial deficit with regard to technical accountancy skills because the philosophy major will have more finely developed workplace competencies.

Notes

1. Philosophers especially interested in fostering curiosity should examine Weston, Anthony and Stephen Bloch-Schulman (2020), *Thinking through Questions: A Concise Invitation to Critical, Expansive, and Philosophical Inquiry*, Indianapolis: Hackett.
2. Thanks to Brynn Welch for raising this objection.
3. See also Ruth Ginzburg, "Philosophy Is Not a Luxury," in Claudia Card ed., *Feminist Ethics* (1991) Lawrence, University of Kansas Press, 126–45. (P.S., no relation to RBG).
4. An excellent and more thorough argument that aligns with what is said here is "5 Reasons to Major in Philosophy," https://www.youtube.com/watch?v=sZTrFpl09s8&t=1s.
5. For more on how teaching for dispositional growth is not indoctrination, see David W. Concepción and Juli Thorson Eflin (June 2009), "Enabling Change: Transformative and Transgressive Learning in Feminist Ethics and Epistemology," *Teaching Philosophy* 32:2, 177–89, especially 185–7 and Jeanine Weekes Schroer (June 2007), "Fighting Imperviousness with Vulnerability: Teaching in a Climate of Conservatism," *Teaching Philosophy* 30:2, 185–200.
6. https://www.naceweb.org/career-readiness/competencies/career-readiness-defined/.
7. https://dailynous.com/value-of-philosophy/charts-and-graphs/.

Reference

Lorde, Audre (1977). "Poetry Is Not a Luxury." *Chrysalis: A Magazine of Female Culture* 3: 7–9.

23

Dialogue, Virtue, and Assessment: Teaching for More Than Technical Proficiency

Kristopher G. Phillips

Introduction

Teaching philosophy can be a *transformative* experience for students and faculty alike (Burroughs 2013; Phillips 2019; Croce and Pritchard 2022). Following the distinction made by L.A. Paul (2014), we might think it's obvious that a philosophical education can be *epistemically* transformative, but we do little more than gesture toward the personally transformative aspects—if we consider them at all. Whatever the reasons that we might shy away from the personally transformative aspects of education—whether out of concern for being morally accountable (Curren 2020) or simply because assessment techniques tend to be overly narrow and quantitative in nature (Baehr 2021: 172)—the ways in which we educate our students are often

---

Thanks to Cassie Finley for all of the thoughtful discussions that resulted in this chapter. Additionally, I would like to thank Gretchen Ellefson, David Nelson, and Trinnity Prisco for helpful comments on an earlier draft of this chapter. Finally, I owe a deep debt of gratitude to the students in my Fall 2022 Philosophy of Education class at Southern Utah University for a semester's worth of discussion about what education is, what it ought to be, and perhaps more importantly, what sorts of things definitely *do not* work in a philosophy classroom.

influenced by both how we conceive of the discipline of philosophy itself and the limitations of our assessment methods. Additionally, financial and political pressures exerted on universities to provide a good "return on investment" for students influence the practice, methods, pedagogies, and even ideas within the philosophy classroom. The result is that we often prioritize skills that are directly or obviously applicable to students' future financial success.

While it is likely true that philosophy programs can and do cultivate skills that are broadly applicable in today's society, the mere possession of such skills neither guarantees, nor even makes likely, that students will be motivated to use them properly (Battaly 2016: 165–6; King 2021: 22). Yet, even if students end up employing the sorts of philosophical skills and tools philosophers teach, it is not at all obvious that a focus on broadly applicable skills will do much more than produce what Martha Nussbaum calls "useful profit makers with obtuse imaginations" (Nussbaum 2012: 142).

In this chapter, I offer advice for how to frame our classes, and by extension our undergraduate degree programs, with the aim of moving beyond mere technical proficiency by re-centering the intellectually and personally transformative potential of teaching philosophy through dialogue. I draw on the growing body of literature discussing intellectual virtues and education, then offer ideas for how we can both assess philosophical skills *and* meet the lofty ideal that, as Nathan L. King puts it, "you should go to college because it can help develop your character, particularly your intellectual character" (King 2021: 13).

Presenting Philosophy to Our Students

There is a common misconception that one is really only *doing* philosophy when they are engaged in research; that teaching is a sort of necessary evil or the part of the job we have to perform in order to do the "real work" (Cahn 2022). The mistake lies in thinking that there is an in-principle distinction between engaging peers over philosophical issues and engaging students in philosophical discussions. When speaking to other specialists in our subdiscipline, we may convey information differently than we would when speaking to a broader audience of philosophy faculty. In the latter case, surely nobody would think they have ceased doing philosophy; rather they would recognize the need to make adjustments in order to accommodate their audience. The same goes for our courses—the adjustments may be more drastic, but this is a difference of degree rather than kind.

Yet, it is not always the case that teachers engage their students in the practice of philosophy. Often philosophers end up teaching students *about* philosophy rather than *doing* philosophy with them. Conceiving of teaching as a project aimed only, or at least primarily, at imparting content knowledge and argumentative skill gained through rehearsing objections to philosophical views makes students largely passive participants in their education. That is, such an approach does not teach students how to *do* philosophy, it teaches them *about* philosophy. Fortunately, there is a way to frame our teaching that makes students active participants in their education, encourages them to engage meaningfully in *philosophy* itself, lends itself to philosophy's personally transformative potential, and helps to make sense of why we read, talk about, and take seriously philosophical positions that seem so disconnected from every-day life: philosophy as an ongoing dialogue.

(Some of) The Benefits of Presenting Philosophy as Dialogue

Presenting philosophy to our students as dialogue has a number of benefits.[1] These include:

1 Making students *active participants* in their education.
2 Helping to make sense of why we ask students to engage with long-dead thinkers.
3 Helping to block some of the groundless pontificating that novices sometimes bring to philosophical paper-writing.
4 Helping students make sense of the oddities of philosophical writing (anticipating objections, etc.).
5 Better supporting skill development and the cultivation of intellectual virtue than an explicit focus on learning outcomes.

Regarding (1), I take it as given that having engaged, thoughtful students in class makes the experience better for instructor and students alike. When students are brought on as genuine interlocutors regarding philosophical subjects, they feel an ownership over the material that they would not gain by passively listening to, or watching others (typically *us*) engage in or with philosophy. Engaging students in dialogue about philosophical issues not only affords them ownership over the content but also serves as an opportunity to cultivate the virtues (understood as a disposition to exercise philosophical skills at the right times and in the right way) we want students to gain more organically, and more frequently, than when we assign papers or exams.

When we present philosophy as an ongoing dialogue that has taken place across a couple thousand years, this helps with (2): making sense of why we still take long-dead philosophers seriously. Historical philosophers contributed to the discussion in important and interesting ways and we will find ourselves in a better position to contribute if we understand what has been said before. Even if philosophers of old were wrong about much or all of what they said, we should still take the time to hear them out. After all, these were smart folks who probably had interesting reasons for being wrong. More broadly, *presuming* that someone is wrong or has nothing to offer contributes to philosophy's well-documented perception as hostile to diversity. To be clear, I am not suggesting that canonical figures from the past face the same sort of challenges that members of marginalized communities face in academic philosophy today. Quite the opposite—even within history of philosophy circles, the voices principally amplified belong to affluent white men. The very fact that the historical canon is remarkably homogeneous is a symptom of philosophy's reluctance to take alternative perspectives seriously. Framing philosophy as dialogue allows room to make explicit that certain people are left out of the conversation by challenging the underlying assumptions that have encouraged such problematic omissions.

For many students approaching philosophy for the first time, philosophy classes seem to be an ideal opportunity to share all of the big ideas they have. This often takes the form of (3), discussing massive ideas too quickly and without grounding the discussion in extant philosophical work. Framing philosophy as an ongoing dialogue can help to head this off. Just as it would be poor form to interrupt a group of people already chatting and announce, "Everybody shut-up! I have something interesting to say" and then subsequently refuse to engage with anyone else, it is inappropriate to barge into the *philosophical* dialogue and share whatever is on one's mind (unless you're Alcibiades, perhaps). A dialogical framing helps students see *why* it is important to understand, charitably interpret, and engage with folks who are already in the discussion.

Regarding (4), it is easy to forget that many of the features of philosophical writing we take for granted are baffling to those approaching it for the first time. For instance, in most texts we anticipate and respond to objections. Many students initially find such behavior perplexing—it gives the impression that philosophy is little more than "talking in circles." While explicit dialogue as a philosophical presentation style has all but died off, most philosophical texts still involve some sort of *intratextual* dialogue between the author and various interlocutors (Phillips 2019: 51; see also Concepción 2004: 365–7). By pointing to the different "voices" within a philosophy paper and encouraging students to think about the paper as engaging in a dialogue with other philosophers, we can help students understand how papers hang together and ultimately move past the frustration that stems from the idea that philosophy just seems to go in circles.

Finally, (5) philosophy-as-dialogue helps cultivate virtues better than an explicit focus on learning outcomes does. In a recent study, Kristina M.W. Mitchell and Whitney Ross Manzo found that "the use of learning objectives has no effect on student performance" (Mitchell and Manzo 2018: 469). So why use them to frame our pedagogical practices? I've argued elsewhere that we shouldn't: crafting courses to fulfill predetermined outcomes is actually less successful than just *doing* philosophy with students when it comes to cultivating a philosophical disposition (Phillips 2017, 45–6; Phillips 2019: 47). Engaging in a philosophical dialogue with students allows virtues to develop organically as a result of philosophical practice in a way that rigid, backward-designed courses do not.[2]

For these reasons, we ought to adopt a philosophy-as-dialogue framing for our classes. Furthermore, we ought to frame philosophical dialogue in terms of the cultivation of intellectual virtues. In a recent paper, Cassie Finley sketches what she calls a "virtue dialogue theory" (Finley 2023). The ideally virtuous interlocutor, Finley argues, will not only be one who appeals to the appropriate standards of evidence, primarily communicates what they believe to be true statements (in good faith), and makes cogent arguments, but is also one who listens attentively, exercises intellectual humility, and responds genuinely. Such a practice encourages students and faculty alike to engage carefully and critically with a shared aim of seeking the truth through logical principles, while recognizing the character-based aspects of a philosophical dialogue. By engaging students in virtuous dialogue, we help to cultivate philosophical virtues and encourage students to practice the associated skills through discussions about philosophical issues. Since those skills are central to engaging with philosophers, dialogue of this type will bring the skills about naturally as a consequence of our focus on having a virtuous dialogue and being a virtuous interlocutor.

Assessing Student Development, Virtues, and Transformation

In many ways, lecturing about philosophy is easier than having a philosophical dialogue with students. When we lecture, we have control over the framing and presentation of ideas, can tease out fine-grained distinctions, and can make adjustments based on nonverbal cues from our audience. Yet, such a "control posture" makes students passive participants in the educational process, precludes dialogue, stifles spontaneity, and limits opportunities to get to know our students (Baehr 2021: 73–8; see also Freire 2018). Despite the benefits, ceding control over the classroom is both difficult and unnerving. After all, we are the experts in the room and there are things students *need* to know. This is why being thoughtful and intentional in crafting and grading assignments is particularly important. I will not offer specific assignments here. Rather I will discuss general principles for crafting and assessing them—and thereby assessing student development in terms of their intellectual virtues (in other words: assessing students as *thinkers*).

A dialogical framing for our philosophical pedagogy lends itself to holding students to extremely high standards for clarity, structure, accuracy, working through texts, and articulating these things in their writing. The dialogical virtues we model for our students, highlight in class when students exhibit them, and practice in discussion are no different from how we expect students to engage with the philosophers they read and write about. We need to articulate to our students that just as they should actively listen to and accurately represent the thoughts of their peers, we expect them to do the same with texts. It is here that we can cultivate close reading, charitable interpretation, critical engagement, and other skills we hope students learn. However, merely possessing the skills alone is not enough—students need to know how to use them well and when to use them appropriately. Even more than this, they need to be *motivated* to employ these skills in appropriate ways—hence the virtue dialogue framing. By encouraging students to conceive of their writing as an extension of an ongoing philosophical dialogue, the assignment becomes less a task aimed at honing transferrable skills and more an exercise in having a virtuous dialogue—albeit a more formal expression thereof.

This means, too, that when we give feedback to our students, it's especially important to frame feedback appropriately. Perhaps unsurprisingly, it's my position that we should consider our feedback on written work as an extension of the dialogue. Students have shared their thoughts in a more formalized way with us and we are in a position to help them clarify, expand, correct, or adjust their contribution to the discussion. Once again, the way in which we frame the feedback is critical; there is some reason to believe that thorough, careful, and direct feedback on writing can be overwhelming, discouraging, and have a negative (or no) impact on students (Ackerman and Gross 2010).

Such a worry could be sharpened by the virtue framing—a virtue education is about the student's character, not merely their work. However, it's possible to circumvent both concerns. In philosophy we have a tendency to personalize and psychologize our criticisms. How often in question-and-answer sessions do we accuse the *speaker* of various intellectual vices? Such phrasings are problematic for a couple of reasons. First, in psychologizing on behalf of the speaker/author, we go well beyond the actual evidence; they might have good, but unstated, reasons for *seeming* to make a particular mistake. Second, and this is especially important when thinking about student interactions, it makes the feedback about the person rather than the ideas or presentation. A subtle shift in the language we use in our interactions with students, especially on written work, from, e.g. "you're being uncharitable" to "this presentation is uncharitable," takes the emphasis off of the student and places it instead on the presentation of ideas. In making this shift, we are in a position to remind the student that a virtuous intellectual character is something at which we have to work and, like any highly skilled activity, to do it well requires that one has their mistakes pointed out to them. At the same time, it does not *essentialize* the mistake; it's not that the *student* is uncharitable, this presentation of the idea(s) is uncharitable. The latter is something we can work on, the former at least sounds as if it is not. When we offer feedback about the *work* rather than the *student* and frame such feedback in terms of helping the student cultivate the sort of intellectual character that will enable them to flourish in their engagements with others, students appreciate as much feedback as we're able to give.

We also ought to communicate how the learning process is likely to progress across the degree program. I suggest that student progress parallels the meditator's progress over the course of Descartes's *Meditations*. Just as the meditator backslides, falls into old habits, hits dead-ends, and occasionally has massive insights which propel her forward only to backslide again, progress in learning philosophy is rarely linear. Students will have "aha!" moments, immediately followed by the exhausting recognition of how many new problems just came into view. As students progress in philosophy, learning can and does *require* apparent backslides. Some backslides may occur early on because they are new to philosophy and arrive overconfident in their background beliefs (not unlike the meditator's experience in the *First Meditation*), while others may come about because we push them to adjust the scope of their thinking and writing (as in the *Third Meditation*). A student may experience somewhat linear development in one respect—say, in writing textual or argument analysis papers—to the point that they become reliably proficient in writing essays for their classes. However, once they've gained that proficiency, it's important for their development that we encourage them to move beyond that narrow domain to, for instance, incorporate relevant secondary literature. Since the student was competent in textual analysis, but had very little experience incorporating secondary literature, they will feel as if, and probably actually will, produce lower-quality work in this new area than they would have if they had stuck to working from primary texts.

This apparent backslide is a necessary part of the learning process. In order to become an excellent thinker overall, one must push beyond the mastery of just one aspect of thinking. If the meditator had simply stopped at the *Cogito* and rehearsed that truth repeatedly, I doubt we'd bother with the *Meditations* at all. Taking skills we've cultivated and applying them to novel contexts will result in mistakes but will offer opportunities for further development and growth. By framing our teaching in terms of virtuous dialogue, we can help cultivate virtues while recognizing, and sharing with students, that the quality of their work will necessarily fluctuate as part of their development. Such a framing empowers students to separate the evaluation of their work from the evaluation of their development as a learner. Rather than punishing students for taking risks (by grading them down for "making more mistakes"), we can applaud students for trying to develop stable intellectual dispositions (virtues) across contexts while correcting missteps. This helps students find the motivation to push past the inclination to continue writing "safe" papers and instead take risks and develop their philosophical skills.

Conclusion

By framing our classes in terms of cultivating a virtuous intellectual character through philosophical dialogue, we are better able to achieve a wide variety of goals we have as instructors. The experience within the philosophy classroom can be epistemically and personally transformative for both instructor and student alike and can push students to take ownership of their education in ways that extend well beyond the traditional narratives tying education to workforce readiness or transferrable/marketable skills. In fact, by approaching our teaching and assessment in terms of a virtue-dialogue framing, we avoid the pitfalls that arise from an overreliance on narrowly prescribed assessment methods while helping students develop the skills and the motivation to refine and apply them in novel contexts. Doing so often means ceding some control over the classroom, but that does not necessarily mean sacrificing high academic standards. The virtue dialogue approach reinforces the need for clarity, precision, and critical analysis by situating the value of these traits in something decidedly familiar to students—dialogue.

Notes

1. In their "Statement on the Teaching of Philosophy," the American Philosophical Association explicitly states that "Verbal interaction, in which ideas can be articulated and examined, questions asked, positions debated, and arguments presented and criticized, is essential both to the activity and discipline of philosophy and to philosophical education" (Schacht and Iseminger 1995).
2. I think there are two related problems here: First, what I call the "paradox of practicality." Parallel to the paradox of hedonism, when we focus on "practical" outcomes (skills), we actually do worse in cultivating them than we would by just doing philosophy with students. The paradox is closely related to the second problem: "Goodheart's Law." Named for British Economist Charles Goodheart, the idea is that once a measure becomes

the target, it's no longer a good measure. This is exactly what we see in higher education assessment; the metrics by which we assess "learning" are no longer assessments so much as they are targets in themselves. We have made a practice of trying to get students to "mastery" or whatever, rather than using the tools to see where they are. As a result, faculty are able to gamify assessment and students are able to gamify learning.

References

Absher, Brandon (2021). *The Rise of Neoliberal Philosophy: Human Capital, Profitable Knowledge, and the Love of Wisdom*. Lanham: Lexington Books.

Ackerman, David S., and Barbara L. Gross (2010). "Instructor Feedback: How Much Do Students Really Want?" *Journal of Marketing Education* 32(2): 172–81.

Baehr, Jason (2021). *Deep in Thought: A Practical Guide to Teaching for Intellectual Virtues*. Cambridge, MA: Harvard Education Press.

Battaly, Heather (2016). "Responsibilist Virtues in Reliabilist Classrooms" in Jason Baehr (ed.), *Intellectual Virtues and Education: Essays in Applied Virtue Epistemology*, 163–83. New York: Routledge.

Burroughs, Michael D. (2013). "A Different Education: Philosophy and High School" in Sara Goering, Nicholas J. Shudak, and Thomas E. Wartenberg (eds), *Philosophy in Schools: An Introduction for Philosophers and Teachers*, 179–89. New York: Routledge.

Cahn, Steven (2022). "Professors as Teachers." *Blog of the American Philosophical Association*. January 3. https://blog.apaonline.org/2022/01/03/professors-as-teachers/. Accessed February 21, 2022.

Concepción, David W. (2004). "Reading Philosophy with Background Knowledge and Metacognition." *Teaching Philosophy* 27(4): 351–68.

Croce, Michel, and Duncan Pritchard (2022). "Education as the Social Cultivation of Intellectual Virtue" in Mark Alfano, Colin Klein, and Jeroen de Ridder (eds), *Social Virtue Epistemology*, 583–601. New York: Routledge.

Curren, Randall (2020). "Transformative Valuing." *Educational Theory* 70(5): 581–601.

Descartes, Rene (1985). *Discourse on the Method*. Vol. 1, in *The Philosophical Writings of Descartes*. Eds John Cottingham, Robert Stoothoff, and Dugald Murdoch. Cambridge: Cambridge University Press.

Finley, Cassie (2023). "Virtue Argumentation, Virtue Dialogue, & Aristotle." *Educational Theory* 73(2): 153–73.

Freire, Paolo (2018). *Pedagogy of the Oppressed*. 50th Anniversary Edition. Trans. Myra Bergman Ramos. New York: Bloomsbury Academic.

Hadot, Pierre (1995). *Philosophy as a Way of Life*. Ed. Arnold I. Davidson. Trans. Michael Chase. Malden, MA: Blackwell Publishing.

King, Nathan L. (2021). *The Excellent Mind*. New York: Oxford University Press.

Mitchell, Kristina M. W., and Whitney Ross Manzo (2018). "The Purpose and Perception of Learning Objectives." *Journal of Political Science Education* 14(4): 456–72.

Nussbaum, Martha C. (2012). *Not for Profit: Why Democracy Needs the Humanities*. Princeton: Princeton University Press.

Paul, L. A. (2014). *Transformative Experience*. Oxford: Oxford University Press.

Phillips, Kristopher G. (2017). "Is Philosophy Impractical? Yes and No, but That's Precisely Why We Need It" in Lee Trapanier (ed.), *Why the Humanities Matter Today: In Defense of Liberal Education*, 37–64. Lanham: Lexington.

Phillips, Kristopher G. (2019). "The Kids Are Alright: Philosophical Dialogue and the Utah Lyceum." *Precollege Philosophy and Public Practice* 1 (1): 42–57.

Schacht, Richard, and Gary Iseminger (1995). "Statement on the Teaching of Philosophy." *Proceedings and Addresses of the American Philosophical Association*: 96–100. https://www.apaonline.org/general/custom.asp?page=teaching. Accessed January 27, 2023.

24

Student Transformation through Civic Engagement Projects

Monica "Mo" Janzen and Ramona Ilea

Many philosophy professors strive for transformative learning to take place in their classroom. Similarly, when we imagine meeting students five or even ten years after our classes end, we hope that rather than remembering just specific content, students feel that something significant in their lives shifted as a result of their time in our classroom. In this chapter, we'll focus on a specific civic engagement (CE) project we call the Experiments in Ethics and show how it can transform student lives. We'll suggest ways others can connect CE projects to other student success initiatives and offer some resources to get started.

L. Dee Fink writes that "significant learning [also called transformative learning] requires that there be some kind of lasting change that is important in the learner's life" (2013: 34). Fink argues that significant learning then has six central components (2013: 35):

- foundational knowledge (what most of us call course content)
- application of learned content
- integration or connecting the content to others' ideas
- a human dimension where learners learn about themselves and others
- caring about the content by developing dispositional feelings or values
- learning how to learn

When students have foundational knowledge, they understand important class ideas. Application of content asks students to learn how to use the knowledge that they gained and develop skills like critical thinking and analysis. Integration helps students see that their knowledge can be useful or connect to other types of knowledge they have. The human dimension of learning helps students see themselves in a new way and understand that they can become different persons. When students learn to care about a specific topic, they are energized to continue learning and make it a part of their lives. Finally, learning how to learn helps students see the value in learning and what is necessary to be lifelong learners, gaining skills that can help them be successful in their lives (Fink 2013: 36).

Many philosophy instructors focus on foundational knowledge, application, and integration; they want students to understand philosophical ideas, apply, and analyze them. While it is true that we want our students to do this too, we also want to help students become more than critical thinkers in a classroom. We want students to connect class materials to their own lived experiences, learn how to become capable citizens, and see themselves as individuals who can make changes in their lives and the lives of others. In addition, we want our students to develop specific practical skills that they will use for the rest of their lives, like time management and taking a project from start to finish.

How do we achieve all this? We developed a CE project we call the Experiments in Ethics. CE projects differ from other forms of engaged learning in a few significant ways. CE projects require that students both design and carry out actions in the world. So, unlike some forms of service learning or straight up volunteering, CE projects require students to utilize their own agency or self-authorship (Hawthorne et al. 2016; Ilea and Hawthorne 2011; Iverson and James 2013; Janzen and Ford 2020).

CE projects can encompass the length of a semester (one large project) or they can be smaller, independent but interrelated projects spread throughout the semester. We used to use the first approach—semester-long projects—for many years. But, after thinking more about the way in which students learn, we changed our approach in 2016 and built a new CE project we call the Experiments in Ethics. Our goal was to scaffold student learning and help students build skills throughout the semester more deliberately. Rather than one big project, students work through a series of small-scale, interrelated assignments or "experiments" where students "try out" or "experiment" with ideas we are learning in class.

Because these projects occur throughout the semester, doing them creates a cycle where students learn new content, do an experiment related to the content, reflect, and then get our feedback. In this way, students are gaining foundational knowledge in class, and are asked to apply and integrate this knowledge in their lives. In addition, this cycle provides the scaffolding for students to develop agency and work toward more substantial experiments. For instance, the first experiment requires student to write a letter to someone asking them to make a change, an intermediate experiment asks students to contact a legislator or cultivate a virtue, and the last experiment asks student to design their own change-making activity. It is through this iterative process that students begin to experience the human dimension of learning, dispositional changes that help them feel more hopeful and able to make changes (the caring dimension of learning) and gain important skills (learning how to learn).

The central element of the Experiments in Ethics is the Organize an Activity experiment which occurs near the end of the semester (see Table 24.1). The rest of the experiments should be conceived of like an "a la carte" menu. Different instructors may use different experiments depending on their teaching context (for the type of institution at which they teach and their class sizes), the content they cover, their pedagogical goals, or a desire to cultivate or hone a particular skill essential for their students (see Table 24.2).

We have assessed the Experiments in Ethics and have good evidence that they achieve their aims; students gain important communication, citizenship, practical, and critical thinking skills (Hawthorne et al. 2016; Janzen and Ford 2020). We believe that these skills increase student agency and help change student attitudes about what they can accomplish in their own lives and in their communities (Hawthorne et al. 2016; Janzen and Ford 2020; Janzen, Hole and Ilea 2021) and develop hope for the future (Hole, Janzen and Ilea 2023). Thus, our assessments show that students are achieving transformational learning.

Many campuses have student success initiatives such as promoting undergraduate research and thinking more deeply about inclusive and welcoming practices for all learners. Because the Experiments in Ethics is rooted in transformational learning, it can help on these fronts as well. We use the Experiments in Ethics in an introductory ethics class. Students have shared the results of their Organize an Activity experiments as part of campus showcases that promote creative scholarship and undergraduate research. While the Experiment in Ethics is not like typical philosophical research

Table 24.1 The Organize an Activity experiment © Monica Janzen and Ramona Ilea.

The Organize an Activity experiment is the central element of the CE project.

Experiment	Task	Student examples	Connection to transformational learning
Organize an activity	Identify an ethical issue the student cares about Organize an event or campaign to make a positive change Provide documentation of actions and write a reflection connecting actions to course materials Turn in all evidence and tips for future students Present to the class	Student organizes a walk to benefit an organization working to end eating disorders Student organizes a campaign to ban bottled water on campus Student organizes shoe collection for a local organization benefiting people experiencing homelessness Students organize a group to create goody bags for seniors at a local senior living facility	Students draw on lessons learned earlier in the semester (scaffolding) before initiating an activity. Students gain motivation to engage with others, present arguments, and think of counterarguments. Students exercise their own agency as they design an action and develop the skills to implement it. Students see themselves as agents of change as they complete an action that makes a difference.

on a topic, it can help students make deep connections and integrate their knowledge in new and original ways to the student. So, just like a beginning biology student can share a poster about an experiment where they took class materials and applied them in a new and thoughtful way, beginning philosophy students can do the same.

Additionally, the Experiments in Ethics are built on inclusive and equitable practices. We scaffold experiments so all learners are supported and met where they are. For instance, when students write their change making letter (one of the first experiments), we spend time explaining how the writing in this class works. In addition to scaffolding the writing, we are also scaffolding the other types of learning—we invite students to start

Table 24.2 Scaffolding optional experiments. Reproduced with permission.

The experiments described here are options for instructors to include as ways to provide scaffolding for the Organize an Activity experiment.[1]

Experiment	Task	Student examples	Connection to transformational learning
Email and call political representatives	Email and call one's political representatives about issues the student cares about	Student calls their senator about a bill impacting LGBTQ people Student emails their representatives asking them to support a budget bill	Caring and developing dispositional values and attitudes
Change making letter	Identify an ethical issue that personally affects the student Identify a specific person who can do something about that issue Write a letter making an argument for the change that needs to be made	Student emails the head of the campus cafeteria asking for more vegan options Student writes to elders at her place of worship asking for dancing policy changes Student writes to her parent's doctor asking to stop prescribing painkillers for the parent	Students connect philosophical arguments to their lives and examine actions that may lead to changes
Changing a habit or developing a virtue	Identify a virtue or habit to cultivate or change For 7 days, work to make this change Provide documentation of actions and write a reflection connecting actions to course materials	Student eats vegan meals for a week Student limits their use of phones Student tries to learn Hawaiian (their grandparents' language) using Duolingo every day	This assignment creates space for self-reflection and helps students examine a deliberate effort to make a change in their own lives

Experiment	Task	Student examples	Connection to transformational learning
Volunteer activity	Identify an organization that tackles an ethical issue Volunteer at least 3 hours Provide documentation of actions and write a reflection connecting actions taken to course materials	Student packs food at the local food bank Student helps gather signatures for a petition initiated by a nonprofit organization Student helps plant trees with local group	Students differentiate volunteering for an organization (charitable action) and organizing an activity (justice focused action) and students make connections between what is happening in their communities and course materials
Summative reflection	Reflect on the Experiments in Ethics objectives Write a reflection, drawing on any relevant class materials	Students write that the Experiment in Ethics teaches them ways to make life better for themselves and others Students comment that they have a new perspective at the end of the course Students believe they are better equipped to make, organize, and carry out civic actions	Students make connections across course content and unite the experiments as a singular assignment, reflect on self as agent, and reflect on responsibility in civic life

thinking about changes others can make by writing a letter or signing a petition. A next step might be thinking about changes in their own lives, like changing a habit or developing a virtue. In this way, students move from connecting and integrating to a more human dimension and caring about learning. Students can choose which issues are important to them and have significant freedom to decide which actions they want to tackle.

Can you do this on your campus? Yes, you can! We have been doing CE projects for many years. We have been presenting about it and even created a website to share materials and help others follow suit (www.EngagedPhilosophy.com). While many think what we do is cool, few adopt a similar set of experiments in their classes. Some worry that it asks too much of students or will bring unwanted problems. We can assure you that in our many years of teaching using CE projects, we continue to be impressed, inspired, and motivated by our students. Implementing the Experiments in Ethics can be a lot of work, but it is possible. Please reach out to us if we can help! We encourage philosophy professors to think for the first time (or again) about civic engagement (CE) projects.

Note

1. Parts of this table were revised and reproduced from Janzen and Ford, 2020.

References

Fink, L. Dee (2013). *Creating Significant Learning Experiences: An Integrated Approach to Designing College Courses*. San Francisco: Jossey-Bass.

Hawthorne, Susan, Monica Janzen, Ramona Ilea, and Chad Weiner (2016). "Cultivating Citizenship: Student Initiated Civic Engagement Projects in Philosophy Classes" in Julinna Oxley and Ramona Ilea (eds), *Experiential Learning in Philosophy*, 101–16. New York: Routledge.

Hole, Benjamin, Monica Janzen, and Ramona Ilea (2023). "Radically Hopeful Civic Engagement." *Teaching Philosophy* 46(22): 291–311. https://doi.org/10.5840/teachphil2022512173.

Ilea, Ramona, and Susan Hawthorne (2011). "Beyond Service Learning: Civic Engagement in Ethics Classes." *Teaching Philosophy* 34(3): 219–40. https://doi.org/10.5840/teachphil201134331.

Iverson, Susan V., and Jennifer H. James (2013). "Self-Authoring a Civic Identity: A Qualitative Study of Change-Oriented Service-Learning." *Journal of Student Affairs Research and Practice* 50(1): 88–105. https://doi.org/10.1515/jsarp-2013-0006.

Janzen, Monica, Benjamin Hole, and Ramona Ilea (2021), "Civically Engaged Philosophy as A Way of Life." *American Association of Philosophy Teacher's Studies in Pedagogy* 6: 141–55. https://doi.org/10.5840/aaptstudies20232354.

Janzen, Monica, and Catherine Ford (2020). "Scaffolding Civic Engagement Projects: A Study into the Effectiveness of Supported Small Scale, Independent, Student-Designed Projects." *Transformative Dialogues: Teaching and Learning Journal* 13(3): 9–29. https://journals.kpu.ca/index.php/td/article/view/461.

25

Discussion, Self-Assessment, and the Discussion Moves Framework

Christopher Blake-Turner

---

1 Introduction

For many of us, improving discussion skills is a key learning outcome for most philosophy courses.[1] But discussion skills are tricky both to promote and to assess. Often, we give learners a sense that discussion is important, and give them some opportunity to practice, without much guidance or evaluation. Sometimes, if we try hard, we might offer participation grades. But this is fraught, not least because of the ways such assessment metrics are likely to be influenced by our own biases, as well as to exacerbate preexisting injustices. In this chapter, I try to suggest how we might do better. I start by giving a case for why we might want to do better, and end by sketching how I've attempted to do better in my own classes.

2 Why Participation Grading Sucks and What We Need to Do Better

The default pedagogy for discussion typically goes something like this. Discussions are carried out during the course of a class. An instructor tries to evaluate learners' contributions to discussions and on that basis awards participation grades. The problem is that this pedagogy sucks. Don't feel bad if you use it. I've used it. I think most instructors have, in part because we don't know what else to do. I hope this chapter will offer a concrete alternative. But first, let me explain why participation grading sucks. Doing so will help us get clearer on what we need to do better.

Participation grading fails to address the two main issues when it comes to helping learners gain or refine discussion skills. The first is one of guidance, the second one of assessment.

The *Guidance Problem* is that it's not always clear how to help learners improve their discussion skills, beyond having them engage in discussion. It's worth stressing at this early point that engaging in discussion regularly enough is an important necessary condition for improving discussion skills. All skill development requires practice. If you really want learners to get better at discussion skills, you need to give them opportunities to practice the skills (Rocca 2010). But we surely need to do more than provide opportunities for discussion. The Guidance Problem is about how to go beyond just giving learners the chance to practice: how do we offer learners guidance that will help them improve their discussion skills? This is a problem because it's not obvious what kind of guidance will be useful. We need to find a way to steer between two unhelpful extremes. On the one hand, we need to do better than vague injunctions that are not easily implemented: "Try to ask better questions," "Try to go deeper rather than staying at the surface." On the other hand, the more we tend toward specific guidance, the more we run the risk of getting embroiled in the discussion ourselves, depriving learners of the ability to hone their own discussion skills (Ladenson 2001: 68–9; see also Gregory 2007). Generalizing from my own case, it's all too easy to try and make a clinical intervention in a discussion only to find oneself taking the discussion over completely.

Participation grading typically does little to address the Guidance Problem. Of course, you could supplement a pedagogy anchored around participation grading by offering guidance of various kinds. But participation grading does so badly at addressing the second problem that any worthwhile discussion pedagogy must solve that I think it's worth changing tack altogether.

The *Assessment Problem* is how to determine whether learners are in fact achieving the hoped-for levels of discussion capability. People typically use participation grades to try and assess learners' discussions contributions directly. But this is problematic in many respects. Here are three.[2]

First, participation grading is demanding for the instructor. Trying to keep track of conversational contributions, let alone accurately assessing them, takes a lot of attention and effort. Even in small classes, it's hard to do this well. In larger classes, it's all but impossible. Learners can break into smaller groups, but then the instructor has no way of tracking what's going on in all the groups at once.[3] Second, tracking participation is likely to be affected by implicit biases that disadvantage marginalized learners. Even with the best will in the world, and even with ample time and attention, instructors are subject to the same biases as others (Dee and Gershenson 2017). This might lead them to overemphasize the contributions of those from privileged groups, and underemphasize the contributions of those from less privileged groups. For instance, confirmation bias might lead an instructor to focus on the best contributions made by discussants from relatively privileged groups, while focusing on the less good contributions of underprivileged discussants. Third, participation is affected by preexisting injustices in other ways. Certain learners are more likely to contribute in class, especially to discussions that are being assessed by an instructor. These learners skew whiter, maler, ciser, richer.[4] Learners who have been furnished neither with the cultural capital nor the confidence they need to succeed in such situations may find it harder to do what we're asking of them.

So, participation grading is fraught in various ways. In trying to develop a better pedagogy of discussion, we must face two problems: one of guidance, and one of assessment. I'm going to say something about addressing each problem separately, before offering a way of making headway on both at once.

3 The Discussion Moves Framework

To make progress on the Guidance Problem, I've started employing what I call the *Discussion Moves Framework* (DMF). The idea is to give learners some discussion "moves," specific types of speech acts that they can deploy in philosophical discussion. An example of a discussion move is *offer an objection*. Offering objections to claims is an important part of much philosophical discussion, but learners often feel awkward about disagreeing with one another and they rarely realize that they can (and should) try to offer objections to claims they agree with, including their own.[5] Giving learners this specifically as a move to try out can help with that. Another example of a discussion move is *recapping the dialectic*. This is something that those with significant philosophical training are good at and can deploy in ways that help to contextualize contributions, and to keep track of the overall shape of a discussion and what's at stake. But it's the kind of thing that isn't obvious if one has never thought about doing it before. So part of the advantage of the DMF is to make the implicit explicit, a key principle of inclusive pedagogy (Jacquart et al. 2019: 121–3). Some learners may well have learned by osmosis or otherwise that certain conversational moves are useful in philosophical contexts. But others have not. Making these moves transparently available helps close that gap. Moreover, it does so in a way that offers specific, implementable guidance without risking the instructor's taking over the discussion.

3.1 Which Moves?

The two moves mentioned above—offering an objection and recapping the dialectic—are taken from Olivia Bailey's (2021) fantastic resource "But How Do I Participate?"[6] Bailey lists twenty moves (plus a bonus move of *listening carefully*) that range from restating a claim, to offering a case, to asking about the big picture. These are the kinds of moves that good philosophical discussants are able to deploy aptly, but that are not obviously good contributions in the eyes of novices.

Bailey's list of moves is not meant to be exhaustive. It's a good starting point in that it both (i) offers learners some concrete moves to try out and (ii) gets them thinking of contributions to discussions as moves within a larger practice, rather than as just isolated verbal episodes.[7] A fruitful way to get beyond Bailey's list is to ask learners themselves what moves are missing. One that often comes up when I've done this is something like *making a claim*. It's helpful to add it, perhaps as move zero, just to get into the spirit of making the implicit explicit.

A limitation of Bailey's list is that it focuses almost exclusively on what we might call *cognitive* rather than *social* discussion moves.[8] Cognitive discussion moves change the logical structure of the discussion space. They put new claims on the table, or offer new reasons for accepting existing claims, or offer objections, and so on. Such moves are crucial for productive philosophical discussion. If a discussion is to be a productive enterprise in the service of doing philosophy, rather than just a bit of banter or a nice chat, then reasons must be proffered, scrutinized, accepted or rejected, and so on. But discussions are not just exchanges of reasons between Cartesian egos. They unfold at particular times and places, and are carried out by flesh-and-blood persons, who bring to them their own contingent, socially shaped identities and values. This means that a good philosophical discussion should be good not just *qua* philosophical but also *qua* discussion, construed as a human activity. As cognitive moves shape the rational landscape of the discussion, social moves shape its human landscape. *Thanking someone for their contribution*, or *apologizing for a contribution that misfired*—neither of these moves in themselves changes the standing within the space of reasons, or gets us closer to the truth. But moves like these help the discussion go well at a human level and not merely a rational one.[9] Especially when the discussion involves controversial or otherwise difficult issues, it's important to deploy moves to make sure that participants' needs are being taken care of, and not just the needs of the putatively inevitable march of dialectic toward truth.

Let me be clear about this. I want learners to be able to have discussions where they feel uncomfortable or challenged. But I believe that they are better able to have such discussions if they are explicitly thinking about their interlocutors as humans with various needs and limitations, and not just machines for spitting out reasons and objections. In my experience, a discussion is much more likely to lead to and through uncomfortable territory in a productive way if learners deploy social moves (whether they frame them that way or not). Moreover, I think it's helpful to remind learners that discussions are social human practices, and not just abstract argumentative structures in logical space.

I've offered some moves, starting with Bailey's list, and suggested that relying on moves can go some way toward meeting the Guidance Challenge. But how should one introduce such moves to a class? I'll give one way of doing so, but first I'll revisit the Assessment Problem.

4 Self-Assessment

No one pays as much attention to what a discussant does in a discussion as the discussant themselves. My suggestion to meet the Assessment Problem is to leverage this tendency toward discursive solipsism by having learners assess their own contributions to discussion. This solves part of the Assessment Problem by assigning a tractable division of labor: each participant has their contributions tracked by one single person only; since that person is themselves, they are especially well placed to keep track. The obvious downside of self-assessed discussion is that novice discussants are not in a good position to accurately evaluate their contributions to discussion. This is a general problem for trying to learn new things on your own: you're not altogether sure you're doing a good job.

This limitation is real, but I think worth living with. The way I've learned to live with it is to explicitly move to assessing discussion skills indirectly. I have learners reflect on how discussions go, sometimes including rating their performance. But their grade is pass/fail based on the reflection. So they can rate themselves low and receive full credit. Instead of direct assessment by the instructor, learners assess themselves, and what's graded is their reflection and engagement, not the quality of their discussion. Shifting the focus of assessment from directly evaluating discussion quality to assessing reflection and engagement has several benefits: the instructor's implicit biases are removed; learners that don't do as well in traditional discussion settings aren't disadvantaged as much; learners get to think about their own discussion contributions carefully; learners' grades aren't dependent on inexpert judgments of discussion contribution. In my experience, the tradeoff has been well worth it.

5 Self-Assessment and the Discussion Moves Framework

Moving to self-assessment and employing the DMF are separable. You could have learners assess themselves without using discussion moves. And you could employ the DMF while having instructors try to assess learner discussion. But combining self-assessment and the DMF is especially effective. Here's how I've done it recently in a fifty-person, intro-level class (without TAs).[10]

Throughout the semester there are four "formal discussions." I do lots of discussion in class, but the formal discussions are marked out as special in that I set a time limit for them and tell learners that *this* is the discussion they will then be asked to write a reflective self-assessment about. I break learners into small groups, and typically start with an icebreaker and ask learners to introduce themselves to each other. The formal discussion then starts. At the beginning of the semester I provide questions for the formal discussions, based on the course content for that week, for them to chew on. By the end of the semester I provide no guidance for the formal discussions whatsoever. (I warn them that this is coming.) I typically set a timer for the formal discussions for 15–25 minutes, depending on the length of the class period.

After each formal discussion, learners complete a Discussion Self-Assessment (DSA). So, four times over the course of the semester, learners have to pay close attention to a discussion *qua* discussion. They have to pay close enough attention to the formal discussion to be able to use discussion moves in ways that make sense, and to then assess how effective their contributions were. Because it's often helpful to have an idea for how this might work, concretely, here's the specific process I implement. The first DSA is not framed in terms of discussion moves. I just ask them: (i) what they did well and badly; (ii) to highlight a contribution that a group mate made, and say why it was helpful; and (iii) to commit to doing something to improve their discussion contributions the next time. Between DSA 1 and DSA 2, I have learners read Bailey's piece. For the second formal discussion, I ask them to deploy a move of Bailey's. DSA 2 then asks similar questions, but this time framed in terms of discussion moves. For instance, instead of asking what they can do better next time, I ask them to commit to two of Bailey's moves to try out in the next formal discussion. I also ask learners to rate their contribution to the discussion out of ten. DSA 3 is very similar. At some point, either before or after DSA 3 depending on the class, I introduce the distinction between cognitive and social moves, and ask the class to come up with some examples of each kind of move that aren't on Bailey's list. DSA 4 is the last discussion-related assignment of the semester so, as well as asking about how the last formal discussion went—both in terms of cognitive and social moves—I also ask learners: how, if at all, their approach or ability with respect to discussion differs from their former self at the beginning of the semester; and what, if anything, will they take away from the discussions and DSAs going forward into their life beyond the class.

I grade these assignments pass/fail. Learners pass the assignment for making a good faith effort (charitably construed) to reflect on the discussions. I make this explicit, stressing to learners that their grades do not depend on how they say the discussions went. If a discussion went badly, they should say that (and say why they think that was, and what they might be able to do better about it next time). Together, the DSAs comprise 10 percent of the course grade; I don't assess discussion in any other way, though there are lots of unassessed opportunities for discussion in small and large groups throughout the semester.

There are of course many ways a set of assignments like this could be varied and tweaked. My aim here is to sketch a concrete implementation of self-assessment and the DMF, without overwhelming you with too much detail that probably isn't relevant to your own teaching context. I invite you to take what's useful, and be inspired (or provoked) to do better by what isn't.

6 A Final Worry

You might be skeptical at this point. *This is all well and good*, the skepticism runs, *but there's no way of knowing whether learners in fact get better at discussing as a result of this pedagogy!* To some extent, I recommend biting this bullet. But I think that most of the time we're biting this bullet whether we admit it to ourselves or not. In many teaching contexts, I don't think there's an unequivocally good (accurate, unbiased, and so on) way of assessing discussion directly. Attempts to do so via various measures might be reassuring. They might even be worth implementing for the benefit of administrators. But I don't think we should fool ourselves into thinking that they're giving us a good sense of how learners' discussion skills are improving (or not). Moreover, the pedagogy does give *some* data points for learners' discussion skills: their reflective self-assessments. These are no doubt fraught in various ways, but it's not clear they're less probative of how learners are doing than traditional participation grading.

7 Concluding Voices

One of the reasons I often include improving discussion skills as a course learning outcome is that I want students to be able to speak their minds clearly and to have their voices heard. So I'll end by letting students who've engaged with this pedagogy speak for themselves. Here are three learner responses to how their approach to discussion changed over the course of a semester.

> *The class discussions have helped teach me what it means to have a respectful and open conversation. Topics covered in the class are often heavy topics ... Every classmate has a different view or side on every issue. I have learned how to accept and understand opposing sides to an argument, regardless of my own opinion. By putting my own bias aside, I have been able to better understand*

why people align with different sides of an issue. Whether it be with friends, family, work, or other groups, I know that I will be a much more effective communicator.

In the early stages of the semester I'd like to say I was pretty shy, well more nervous to talk about things. This day and age we are so sensitive I was afraid and stepped on eggshells with basic questions. I also did not quite understand how to ask a philosophical question without it being extremely simple. Now I feel a lot more confident speaking in class and connecting with others close in age without anyone getting upset (not visibly at least) and am more enticed to ask questions as well as rebuttal.

Thinking back to the beginning of the semester I remember myself not being as outgoing or assertive. I remember that I was afraid to voice my opinion. However, now these past few weeks, I have been more open about my views and morals because I am getting comfortable with my own opinions now. I am also able to use more social moves in a way that I could not before such as making eye contact which was a more difficult skill for me at first since I was so unsure of my views at the beginning of the semester.

Notes

1. I'm very grateful to Joanna Lawson and Brynn Welch for reading and offering extremely helpful comments on a draft of this chapter. Thanks also to participants at my Teaching Hub presentation on this material at the 2022 Central APA in Chicago, in particular: Dave Concepción, John Koolage, Claire Lockard, Fritz McDonald, and Jake Wright.
2. I'm influenced in part here by Norlock (2016), whose focus is on how participation grades disadvantage learners with social anxiety. I also encourage you to learn from Bell (2021), whose paper only recently came on my radar. Bell makes some of the same points I'm about to, but supports them in greater detail and also develops other concerns with participation grading.
3. Even for those instructors who have teaching assistants, it's unlikely one will have enough assistants to make the group sizes small enough to be manageable.
4. This was the b-side to Daft Punk's more famous hit.
5. For the reasons given by Dotson (2011), I resist characterizing *all* philosophical discussion as involving objections.
6. I wish I could remember who first put me on to Bailey's piece. I suspect it was Rebecca Scott, who has long been using discussion moves in the service of improving learners' discussion skills.

7. I say "verbal" as the focus is on oral discussion. But much of what I say applies to written discussions, for instance via online forums.
8. I owe this distinction and the terminology to Dave Concepción.
9. I don't mean to endorse the idea that the rational and human-emotional dimensions are completely separated. But it's worth making the distinction as philosophy instructors often focus on what I am calling the cognitive elements of discussion.
10. I've done similar things to good effect in upper-level courses.

References

Bailey, Olivia (2021). "But How Do I Participate?" https://obailey.weebly.com/uploads/1/0/5/6/105611057/bailey-but-how-do-i-participate-2021-edition.pdf.

Bell, Elizabeth (2021). "Participation Grades: An Argument for Self-Assessments, the Potential to Reproduce Inequalities, and Preventive Suggestions." *Teaching Philosophy* 44(4): 449–85. https://doi.org/10.5840/teachphil2021518146.

Dee, Thomas, and Seth Gershenson (2017). "Unconscious Bias in the Classroom: Evidence and Opportunities, 2017." *Stanford Center for Education Policy Analysis*. https://eric.ed.gov/?id=ED579284.

Dotson, Kristie (2011). "Concrete Flowers: Contemplating the Profession of Philosophy." *Hypatia* 26(2): 403–9. https://www.jstor.org/stable/23016554.

Gregory, Maughn Rollins (2007). "A Framework for Facilitating Classroom Dialogue." *Teaching Philosophy* 30(1): 59–84. https://doi.org/10.5840/teachphil200730141.

Jacquart, Melissa, Rebecca Scott, Kevin Hermberg, and Stephen Bloch-Schulman (2019). "Diversity Is Not Enough: The Importance of Inclusive Pedagogy." *Teaching Philosophy* 42(2): 107–39. https://doi.org/10.5840/teachphil2019417102.

Ladenson, Robert F. (2001). "The Educational Significance of the Ethics Bowl." *Teaching Ethics* 1(1): 63–78. https://doi.org/10.5840/tej20011113.

Norlock, Kathryn J. (2016). "Grading (Anxious and Silent) Participation: Assessing Student Attendance and Engagement with Short Papers on a 'Question for Consideration.'" *Teaching Philosophy* 39(4): 483–505. https://doi.org/10.5840/teachphil201612259.

Rocca, Kelly A. (2010). "Student Participation in the College Classroom: An Extended Multidisciplinary Literature Review." *Communication Education* 59(2): 185–213. https://doi.org/10.1080/03634520903505936.

26

Argument Diagramming as a Teaching Tool for Philosophy

Maralee Harrell

Introduction

In my experience, philosophy teachers teaching a wide variety of subjects often rely on their students having a particular skill set they can deploy to be successful—the ability to analyze, understand, and evaluate an argument. Unfortunately, it is often the case that students are not taught these skills explicitly, and this causes students to struggle in the courses that assume these skills.

When I first started teaching, I was surprised to learn that students were mostly unable to read philosophy texts, especially primary sources. They seemed to be able to get the general idea of a text, but they often did not recognize that the text presented an argument. Instead, they would read the text either as a story or as a textbook. This type of reading was plain when, for example, students were asked to summarize a philosophical text. Summaries usually consisted in restating the claims, in the order in which they appeared.

One hypothesis is that many undergraduate students lack a schema for *reading* philosophical arguments. Most have schemas for reading stories or textbooks, developed from years of literature and science courses. These schemas tell them what to look for when reading; if it's a story, then they should find the main characters, conflict, climax, conflict resolution, dénouement, etc., while if it's a textbook, they should interpret the claims as established facts that may be collected as they read.

What they needed then, was an alternative schema, and what I had to do was give them a corresponding graphic organizer and teach them how to use it. This graphic organizer would be a sort of representation they can create as they find the relevant parts of the text. An argument diagram (AD) is just this sort of representation. In such a diagram, text boxes are used to represent claims, and arrows and lines are used to represent connections. Thus, if we consider an argument to be a series of statements in which one is the conclusion, and the others are premises supporting this conclusion, an AD is a visual representation of these statements and the inferential connections between them.

For many years I taught argument diagramming in all my classes just to teach students how to read, understand, and evaluate arguments. Eventually, I began exploring more ways to use this tool for more pedagogical purposes. I now use argument diagramming in my classes not only to teach students to read philosophy, but also a variety of additional skills.

In this chapter, I briefly describe how I use argument diagramming to teach students to (a) read and analyze philosophical texts, (b) collaborate with others to read and analyze philosophical texts, (c) write papers that explain the analysis of a text or give an argument for a particular claim, (d) engage in productive peer review, and (e) engage in meaningful revision. First, though, let me explain what an AD is.

Argument Diagrams

An AD[1] is a visual representation of the content and structure of an argument using a very basic graphical structure comprised of nodes and edges.[2] For example, consider the following argument:

> I think everyone would agree that life is worth protecting and that the environment sustains all of us. It stands to reason, then, that we need to protect the environment. One particular threat to the environment is the emission of greenhouse gasses. This is because greenhouse gasses trap the energy of the sun, causing the warming of the planet, and the warming of the planet could have catastrophic effects on the environment. So, we just can't avoid the conclusion that we need to reduce greenhouse gas emissions.

For the AD, I represent the claims as the nodes (text in boxes) and represent the inferential connections between claims as the edges (arrows indicating the direction of inference), and all the excess verbiage[3] is removed (see Figure 26.1).

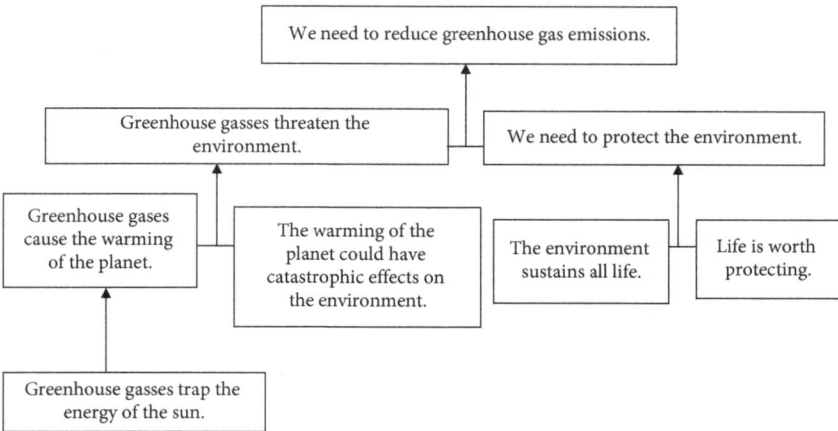

Figure 26.1 An argument diagram representing an argument for reducing greenhouse gas emissions. © Maralee Harrell.

Previous research suggests that teaching students argument diagramming can significantly enhance their critical thinking (Harrell 2011; Twardy 2004; van Gelder 2003; van Gelder et al. 2004), writing (Harrell and Wetzel 2015), and collaboration skills (Chouta et al. 2017; McClaren et al. 2011).

Reading

When I assign reading in my class, I want the students to do more than just have their eyes pass over all the words. I want them to engage in close reading, to determine the argument, and to evaluate it critically.

The idea here is to get the students to use an AD as a kind of graphic organizer. As they read, they should be noting the parts of the text that should go into the boxes or that indicate how to connect them with arrows. I encourage my students to circle indicator words and underline main claims. They can take different paths in the construction of the AD. On one path, they can start with a blank generic AD, and then fill it in, adding and deleting boxes and arrows as they go along. On another path, they can put all the main claims in boxes first, and then figure out how the boxes should all be connected.

To teach students how to do this analysis, I make several resources available to them. First, I assign an online tutorial I have created that teaches the basics of claims, inferences, arguments, and creating ADs. Second, I give them examples of ADs I have constructed, along with detailed explanations of how I determined which claims should go in the boxes and how the claims should be connected by arrows (Harrell 2016). Finally, I give them access to online tools specifically designed to build ADs.[4] The advantage of an online tool over pencil and paper is the ease with which they can add and delete boxes and arrows, move boxes and their attached arrows around the space, and generally just experiment with different versions of the AD until they decide on the right one. Generally, I assign students weekly summaries and AD homework in which they must diagram the argument in a particular text and offer a written summary. In the feedback for these assignments, I give them a copy of my solution, emphasizing that ADs are a kind of interpretation of the argument, and there is not necessarily only one right way to do it. This way, students get regular feedback, and their diagramming skills improve.

Collaboration

During my education, I spent several years taking and then teaching math and science courses. Working on homework assignments with other people in the class was always a good way for me to learn and was always something I encouraged my students to do. Further along in my career, I struggled to find ways for my philosophy students to take advantage of these activities in which math and science students regularly engage. If I assign AD homework, however, the students can work together to read texts and determine how best to represent the argument.

Let's say that Anna and Ben are working on their AD homework together on an assignment that asks them to summarize Aquinas's five ways of proving the existence of God. They each read the text and then engage in a discussion about how to create an AD that accurately reflects each argument. In doing so, they will engage in metacognition in which I always want my students to engage. Since they are working together, they must articulate their reasons to each other for identifying certain claims as the text they should put in the boxes, and deciding how the boxes are inferentially connected. To do this they will have to engage in very close active reading and think aloud about the text. After they collaborate on the ADs, each student can write and submit their own summaries of the arguments based on the diagrams they jointly created.

Writing

As a student, when I had an assignment to write a paper, I was often encouraged or required to create an outline first to help guide my writing. Doing this outlining never really helped me, probably because I don't remember any of the instruction I received on how to do it productively. I find now that many of my students are in the same situation. For such students, I encourage them to construct an AD of the argument they want to present. Thus, I ask them to focus on the core substance of the paper, without needing to decide ahead of time the order of their paragraphs, etc. This encourages them to consider what reasons they have for their thesis and how many premises they need to express these reasons.

Additionally, I can help them in the beginning with creating the diagram. This means they can start their paper without having to stare at a blank page trying to figure out what to write first. During a help session, I ask for their thesis and their basic reasons to believe it. The first step does not include what they consider "real writing"; rather, they can start with just a few words in the AD boxes. We can then discuss how to make the diagram represent better the argument they had in mind.[5] Then, after they have an AD they are comfortable with, the first writing they have to do is just translate what's in the boxes into complete sentences. In addition, they can think ahead of time what is the best way to explain the argument in the AD. This pulls on previous knowledge they have about how ADs correspond to written work, which they learned by diagramming others' arguments.

Peer Review

Many authors have noted that having students review each other's papers may seem efficient, but it's not since, to do it right, students need to be trained on how to do it. But with AD, they've already learned how to use the tool that they will use for peer review.

Let's say Anna and Ben are engaged in peer review, and Anna is reviewing Ben's paper. Whatever the prompt for the paper is, it must contain an argument. During peer review, Anna reads Ben's paper and creates an AD that reflects her understanding of Ben's argument. As she does this, she notes places in the paper in which the writing makes it difficult for her to decide what goes in the AD boxes or how the boxes should be connected. Then

Anna presents Ben with her notes and AD. In the best case, Anna's AD does adequately represent the argument Ben was trying to convey. If not, Anna and Ben can have a conversation about why Anna's AD does not match what Ben had in mind, and about the places in the writing that made it difficult for Anna to figure out the argument.

Revision

Revision is often difficult for students, especially after an ordinary peer review session. Students tend to focus primarily on grammatical or spelling errors, rather than the structure of the argument or the clarity of the exposition. Thus, when it's time for revision, students are confused about what should be changed; and when they ask for help, they generally have vague questions like "How do I fix it?"

Let's say that after Anna and Ben's peer review session, Ben comes to my office hours for help with his revision. After his peer review session with Anna, he has a set of more or less concrete questions to ask, starting with "How do I explain my argument so a classmate would understand it?" We can then spend *productive* time discussing ways in which he can revise his paper, focusing on making his claims clear, and describing the inferential connections better. And, instead of being focused on telling me what he knows, Ben can focus on the content of the paper from the point of view of the audience.

Conclusion

Ultimately, I think one of the best things about using argument diagramming in all these aspects of my courses is that the students only have to learn to use one cognitive tool throughout the course—the entire course structure (not content) is based on the correspondence between texts and ADs. Thus, the students don't have to learn one kind of procedure to read, another kind of procedure to write, yet another to peer review, etc.

Notes

1. Definitional clarification: many scholars use the terms "argument diagram" and "argument map" interchangeably. I do not. As I will use the terms, an argument *diagram* is a visual representation of the content and inferential

structure of a single argument (Reed et al. 2007); an argument *map* is a visualization of a debate that includes many arguments (Horn et al. 1998). Here I am interested in the pedagogical practice of teaching students how to construct argument diagrams.
2. There are, of course, many different models for diagramming arguments, and each has its own ontology, syntax, and semantics. For example, in the Toulmin model, there are boxes for different kinds of statements (claim, warrant, etc.) and arrows can point to either boxes or other arrows. In my classes, which consist mostly of first- and second-year college students, I use a modified Beardsley-Freeman model as it is very easy to learn the basics. For an overview of the development of argument diagramming, as well as a description of many models, see Reed et al. (2007).
3. For my purposes, "excess verbiage" is defined loosely, and is intended as a guide to help students (re-) write complete, independent statements in the boxes of the diagrams. For example, students do not include the premise/conclusion indicator phrases in the boxes; these phrases are instead "represented" as arrows in the diagram. Additionally, I advise my students to eliminate discounts, repetition, assurances, and hedges. As their argument analysis skills become more sophisticated, these guidelines are relaxed, and students can consider the differences between, for example, claims made with hedges and claims made without hedges.
4. Three such tools are iLogos, which I helped create (https://www.eberly.cmu.edu/ilogos/), MindMup from Simon Cullen (https://www.mindmup.com/), and LASAD from Bruce McLaren (https://www.informatik.hu-berlin.de/de/forschung/gebiete/cses/software/lasad/lasad).
5. In fact, not infrequently at this stage, students will change their minds about the argument they were going to write, as seeing the AD may show them in what ways their original idea was insufficient. It is good for them to realize this at an early stage rather than when the paper is nearly finished.

References

Chounta, Irene-Angelica, Bruce M. McLaren, and Maralee Harrell (2017). "Building Arguments Together or Alone? Using Learning Analytics to Study the Collaborative Construction of Argument Diagrams." In *Making a Difference: Prioritizing Equity and Access in CSCL*, 12th International Conference on Computer Supported Collaborative Learning (CSCL) 2017, Volume 2, Brian K. Smith, Marcela Borge, Emma Mercier, and Kyu Yon Lim (eds), 589–92. Philadelphia, PA: International Society of the Learning Sciences.

Harrell, Maralee (2011). "Argument Diagramming and Critical Thinking in Introductory Philosophy." *Higher Education Research & Development* 30(3): 371–85.

Harrell, Maralee (2016). *What Is the Argument? An Introduction to the Practice of Philosophy*. Cambridge, MA: MIT Press.

Harrell, Maralee, and Danielle Wetzel (2015). "Using Argument Diagramming to Teach Critical Thinking in a First-Year Writing Course" in Martin Davies, Ronald Barnett and B. Ennis (eds), *Palgrave Handbook of Critical Thinking in Higher Education*, 213–32. New York: Palgrave Macmillan.

Horn, Robert E., Jeffrey K. Yoshimi, Mark Deering, and Russell McBride (1998). *Mapping Great Debates: Can Computers Think?* Bainbridge Island, WA: Macro VU Press, 165–84.

McLaren, Bruce, Oliver Scheuer, Maralee Harrell, and Armin Weinberger (2011). "Will Structuring the Collaboration of Students Improve Their Argumentation?" In *Lecture Notes in Computer Science: Artificial Intelligence in Education*, 15th International Conference, Gautam Biswas, Susan Bull, Judy Kay, and Antonija Mitrovic (eds). Berlin: Springer-Verlag, 6738: 544–6.

Reed, Chris, Douglas Walton, and Fabrizio Macagno (2007). "Argument Diagramming in Logic, Law, and Artificial Intelligence." *The Knowledge Engineering Review* 22(1): 1–22.

Twardy, Charles R. (2004). "Argument Maps Improve Critical Thinking." *Teaching Philosophy* 27: 95–116.

van Gelder, Tim (2001). "How to Improve Critical Thinking Using Educational Technology." In *Meeting at the Crossroads: Proceedings of the 18th Annual Conference of the Australian Society for Computers in Learning in Tertiary Education*, Gregor Kennedy, Mike Keppell, Carmel McNaught, and Tom Petrovic (eds). Melbourne: Biomedical Multimedia Uni, The University of Melbourne. 539–48.

van Gelder, Tim (2003). "Enhancing Deliberation through Computer Supported Visualization" in Paul A. Kirschner, Simon J. Buckingham Shum and Chad S. Carr (eds), *Visualizing Argumentation: Software Tools for Collaborative and Educational Sense-Making*, 97–115. New York: Springer.

van Gelder, Tim, Melanie Bissett, and Geoff Cumming (2004). "Cultivating Expertise in Informal Reasoning." *Canadian Journal of Experimental Psychology* 58(2): 142–52.

27

A Jigsaw Lesson for Symbolic Logic

Russell Marcus

Jigsaw lessons were initially developed in the 1970s by Elliot Aronson in response to poor performance and low self-esteem of Black children in the wake of school desegregation. They are perfect for active learning in philosophy classrooms, fostering collaboration and interdependence. The core idea of this cooperative structure is to emphasize the importance of each student's contributions to a classroom community. In a jigsaw structure, students work collaboratively on a complex task with several (ordinarily three to five) distinct aspects. Each student focuses on one aspect. These distinct aspects combine like puzzle pieces into the larger task and students learn about all of them. Jigsaws can be used for a single lesson or for long-term projects. Jigsaw lessons are especially effective in philosophy classrooms because they promote the active and social learning and conversation that are characteristic of our discipline, historically and globally.[1] This chapter presents an overview of the jigsaw structure and instructions for a sample jigsaw lesson for translation using identity in first-order logic.

Each student in a jigsaw structure is a member of two distinct groups: a base group and a work group (Figure 27.1). (Base groups are sometimes called home groups, jigsaw groups, or cooperative groups; work groups are sometimes called expert groups or counterpart groups.) Students ordinarily begin in base groups, in which they choose, or are assigned, one aspect of the larger project. Next, we reshuffle the class, with all students moving to distinct work groups where they attempt to master their assigned aspect of the larger task. In work groups, students collaborate with members of

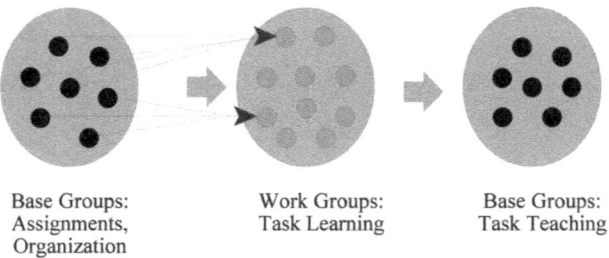

Base Groups:	Work Groups:	Base Groups:
Assignments,	Task Learning	Task Teaching
Organization		

Figure 27.1 The three steps of the jigsaw lesson. Each member of each base group attends a work group with a different topic, and then returns to their original base group. © Russell Marcus.

different base groups to learn their aspect of the larger project well enough to teach it. Finally, all students return to their base groups and each one in turn teaches the other base group members what they have learned, combining the pieces of the puzzle. At the end of the lesson, each student in each base group has had the opportunity and responsibility both to teach their aspect of the larger task to the other base-group members and to learn each part of the complete project from the others in their group. Because of the distributions of tasks, there are no free riders in a jigsaw: everyone contributes.

Instructors can develop jigsaw lessons from any activity that can be divided into distinct parts. For example, an ethics instructor could construct a jigsaw out of a case study, forming, say, four work groups that each focus on how different moral theories assess the case: utilitarianism, deontology, virtue ethics, and feminist ethics. An instructor teaching a unit on free will in an introductory philosophy survey could design a jigsaw around three different responses to a Frankfurt case: the libertarian, the hard determinist, and the compatibilist. Below, I describe in detail a jigsaw with five work groups in a logic class (Figure 27.1).

For greater efficiency in single class meetings, the first base-group step may be omitted and students can start in work groups and then form base groups out of members from different work groups. For longer jigsaw activities, group projects that last over weeks or even whole semesters, students may convene their base groups or their work groups repeatedly. The same base groups can even be used for distinct activities, with different work groups. In a philosophy of education course, I dedicate two weeks at the end of the term to a jigsaw project in which students in base groups design an ideal school. First, we convene five work groups to review material for the five antecedent units of the course: knowledge, human nature, learning, teaching, and community. Later, a different set of four work groups focuses on aspects of the schools designed by the base groups: curriculum, pedagogy, physical space, and connection to community. Students get to collaborate with lots of others in the class, sharing collaborative research and developing greater expertise on areas of particular interest.

Students are typically and naturally actively engaged during jigsaw lessons. Instructors can judge whether their students need motivation in addition to the specific learning goals of the lesson, for example, a grade on the complex task. Students mainly need to trust that the moving parts, which can seem complex at first, will resolve appropriately. Instructors must communicate confidence in both the effectiveness of the activity and how to manage it.

During class, the instructor may roam through different groups, providing support, but the instructor's work is mainly behind the scenes, in preparation. To foster interdependence, it is useful to use jigsaws to introduce new concepts so that the members of the base groups really need to be taught by each of the experts coming out of the work groups. Thus, work groups need materials to help them to develop that expertise, one for each aspect of the larger project, preferably roughly equal in difficulty. These materials should be crafted so that students can learn them quickly enough to be able to teach them to their base groups. The topics should be substantial enough to justify the use of class time, yet not too difficult for the students to master without extensive help from the instructor.

While the instructor of a jigsaw lesson is focused on facilitating the organization of the lesson and on the content of the assigned tasks, students in jigsaw lessons, as in any cooperative learning situation, are often also anxious about interpersonal social issues. We may hope that our classes are immune to hierarchies and cliques and that our students collaborate eagerly and productively, focusing entirely on philosophical content. That may not be the case. Cooperative lessons often bring out social complexities, as students are required to interact directly and explicitly.

Still, jigsaw lessons, because of their structured interdependence, can mitigate some social problems present in other cooperative structures. Aronson developed the jigsaw specifically to improve social interactions in recently desegregated schools, attempting to replace a competitive atmosphere with a cooperative one. The interdependent structure and its social factors were the primary content of the jigsaw at its inception. Especially long-term uses of jigsaws can improve relationships among students.

Random group assignments, done transparently in class, can also minimize the deleterious effects of social hierarchies. Allowing students to choose their own base groups can reinforce existing social structures. Random assignments presume and display no preference among students, leveling the playing field.[2] The simplest method for transparent random base-group assignments is to have the students count-off by the number of groups that will be formed. To make forming base groups a bit more fun, I sometimes have students use homemade jigsaw puzzles of pictures of philosophers printed on card stock and laminated. This technique is tricky, since you never know precisely how many you need, given potential class absences, so preparing various options can be useful.

The remainder of this chapter describes a specific jigsaw lesson in a formal logic class.

A Jigsaw Lesson in Formal Logic

Group assignments can be daunting, especially when you don't know who will show up to class on a given day. I'll sketch the lesson for an ideal class size, twenty-five students, and then make some suggestions for adjusting to less elegant numbers.

The main goal for this lesson is to have students learn how to translate English sentences into first-order logic with identity, focusing on five specific tasks:

1 'At least' sentences;
2 'At most' sentences;
3 'Except' sentences;
4 'Only' sentences; and
5 Superlatives.

In our ideal example, base groups and work groups all have five students. First, I divide the class into five base groups. In this first meeting of the base groups, students perform two small administrative tasks: distributing the five tasks and familiarizing themselves with each other. Once they have gone to their work groups and mastered their specific task, they will return to these groups and teach their tasks to the other members of their base groups.

To form work groups, all of the students who chose to work on 'at least' sentences, one from each base group, form one work group. All of the students who chose to work on 'at most' sentences form a second work group, and so on for the other three tasks.

Once the work groups are formed and students are re-settled, I distribute worksheets, prepared in advance, enough for all students. The worksheets each have five sample English sentences and corresponding model regimentations in first-order logic, along with additional English sentences with no translations to logic. Students in the work groups learn from the samples and translate the additional sentences. I emphasize that each student should learn their small task quickly and well enough to teach it to the other members of the base group to which they will return. Work groups ordinarily take ten-to-fifteen minutes to complete their tasks. A sample worksheet for 'only' is included.

Once the work groups have finished, students return to their original base groups. Members of the base group have now all become experts on distinct tasks. In turn, they teach the other members of the group, distributing the relevant sheets, taking about five minutes each. After about twenty-five minutes, each member of the group has had a chance to learn each of the five tasks. Ta-da.

Rarely do classes have such neat numbers, five groups of five students in both base and work groups. Still, it is not too difficult to adjust to odder numbers. The sizes of base groups in jigsaw lessons are ideally determined by the number of tasks and it's important to have at least that many students in each base group, so that no tasks are omitted. If there are more people than tasks in a base group, two students can choose the same task (and work group) and can share responsibility for teaching their task when they return to base groups.

Any number of base groups can work. In large classes, you can have multiple work groups for each task. Imagine a class with sixty students and five tasks. You could have twelve five-person base groups. Five twelve-person work groups, though, would be unwieldy. Groups function best with three to seven students. In larger groups, individual students are too easily lost or ignored. Moreover, the number of individual social interactions that students must navigate increases exponentially with the size of the group. In a group with n members, there are nC_2 one-to-one interactions, a number which gets quite large even for small n (e.g., in a group of six students, there are fifteen one-to-one interactions).[3] Instead, you can have multiple parallel work groups for each task. Rather than one twelve-person work group, consider two sixes or even three fours.

Final Thoughts

Jigsaw lessons can be intense. Students are typically highly engaged and there are lots of moving pieces. During class time, the instructor's job is mainly to direct traffic with confidence and then support the groups as they work. In classes in which time is short, specific time limits for each task must be strictly enforced. I ordinarily complete the logic lesson in fifty-minute classes: five minutes for an introduction in which I outline the jigsaw method and briefly introduce the '='; five minutes for the first base groups; fifteen minutes for the work groups; and twenty-five minutes for the second base groups. That last stage takes the most time because each student has to teach their newly mastered skill.

Lastly, remember that students can be unnerved by surprise changes in class structures and expectations. Because jigsaws require so much moving around and interacting, it is useful to alert students in advance. Or, better still, accustom your students to various creative cooperative structures early and often.

Appendix: Sample Worksheet for Work Group "Only"

I. Translation key

b: Berkeley; d: Descartes; h: Hume; k: Kant; l: Locke; n: Nietzsche; s: Spinoza;
Ex: x is an empiricist; Px: x is a philosopher; Rx: x is a rationalist
Lxy: x likes y; Mxy: x is read more widely than y;
Pxy: x plays billiards with y; Rxy: x respects y

II. Use these five examples with the translation key above to teach yourself and your work group how to work with "only" sentences.

1. Nietzsche respects Spinoza
   Rns
2. Nietzsche respects only Spinoza
   Rns • $(\forall x)(Rnx \supset x=s)$

   3 Only Nietzsche doesn't like Nietzsche.

       ~Lnn • (∀x)(~Lxn ⊃ x=n)

   4 Only Locke plays billiards with some rationalist who is read more widely than Descartes.
      (∃x)(Rx • Mxd • Plx) • (∀x)[(Rx • Mxd) ⊃ (∀y)(Pyx ⊃ y=l)]

   5 Only Kant is read more widely than Descartes and Hume.
      Mkd • Mkh • (∀x)[(Mxd • Mxh) ⊃ x=k]

III. While still in your work groups, determine how to translate these two sentences. After moving back to your base groups, you can use these, along with the five in II, to teach the rest of your group.

   6 Nietzsche is the only philosopher read more widely than Descartes.

   7 Kant is the only empiricist who is also a rationalist.

IV. If you have time in class, or after class if you do not, make sure that you can translate this sentence successfully.

   8 Only Locke and Berkeley are empiricist philosophers respected by some rationalist philosopher.

Solutions to 6–8 are shared with students after class.

   6 Pn • Mnd • (∀x)[(Px • Mxd) ⊃ x=n]

   7 Ek • Rk • (∀x)[(Ex • Rx) ⊃ x=k]

   8 El • Pl • (∃x)(Rx • Px • Rxl) • Eb • Pb • (∃x)(Rx • Px • Rxb) • (∀x){[Ex • Px • (∃y)(Ry • Py • Ryx)] ⊃ (x=l ∨ x=b)}

Notes

1. For evidence of the effectiveness of active learning strategies, see Johnson, Johnson, and Smith 1998 and Freeman et al. 2014. For the importance of interdependence, see Johnson, Johnson, and Smith 2014. See Choe and Drennan 2001: 330; and Morgan et al. 2008 for striking data on undergraduate and graduate students' enjoyment of jigsaw lessons. Morgan et al. 2008 describe some concerns, especially for stronger students, though Aronson et al. 1978 report that high-achieving elementary-school students in jigsaw classrooms suffer no reduction in performance, p 118,

and that enjoyment of school is improved, p 120. Most research on jigsaw lessons focuses on elementary through high school classes. Slavin 1995: 33–5 provides some data on achievement in jigsaw classrooms for younger students. There is less evidence of its use at the undergraduate or graduate level, outside of education or psychology departments, as in Perkins and Saris 2001. See Honeychurch 2012 for a report of successful uses in philosophy. For jigsaws in anthropology, biology, chemistry, geology, history, literature, and sociology classes, see: Choe and Drennan 2001; Resor 2008; and, especially, Mills and Cottell 1998. See also Johnson, Johnson, and Stanne 2000 for data on the success of various cooperative learning techniques, including the jigsaw.
2. For more on cooperative learning group assignments, see Marcus 2010.
3. See Cooper 1990 for discussion of group sizes.

References

Aronson, Elliot (2000–2022). *Jigsaw Classroom* website. http://www.jigsaw.org/.

Aronson, Elliot, Nancy Blaney, Cookie Stephin, Jev Sikes, and Matthew Snapp (1978). *The Jigsaw Classroom*. Beverly Hills: Sage Publications.

Choe, S. W. Tina, and Philippa M. Drennan (2001). "Analyzing Scientific Literature Using a Jigsaw Group Activity." *Journal of College Science Teaching* 30(5): 328.

Cooper, Jim (1990). "Cooperative Learning and College Teaching: Tips from the Trenches." *Teaching Professor* 4(5): 1–2.

Freeman, Scott, et al. (2014). "Active Learning Increases Student Performance in Science, Engineering, and Mathematics." *Proceedings of the National Academy of Sciences* 111(23): 8410–15. www.pnas.org/cgi/doi/10.1073/pnas.1319030111.

Honeychurch, Sarah (2012). "Taking Forward the Jigsaw Classroom: The Development and Implementation of a Method of Collaborative Learning for First Year Philosophy Tutorials." *Discourse: Learning and Teaching in Philosophical and Religious Studies* 11(2): 40–52.

Johnson, David W., Roger T. Johnson, and Karl A. Smith (1998). "Cooperative Learning Returns to College: What Evidence Is There That It Works?" *Change* 30(4): 26–35.

Johnson, David W., Roger T. Johnson, and Karl A. Smith (2014). "Cooperative Learning: Improving University Instruction by Basing Practice on Validated Theory." *Journal on Excellence in College Teaching* 25(3–4): 85–118.

Johnson, David W., Roger T. Johnson, and Mary Beth Stanne (2000). "Cooperative Learning Methods: A Meta-Analysis." https://resources.ats2020.eu/resource-details/LITR/CooperativeLearningMethods.

Marcus, Russell (2010). "Observations on Cooperative-Learning Group Assignments." *The APA Newsletter on Teaching Philosophy* 9(2): 2–5.

Mills, Barbara J., and Philip G. Cottell Jr. (1998). *Cooperative Learning for Higher Education Faculty*. Phoenix: The Oryx Press.

Morgan, Bobbette M., Alma D. Rodríguez, and Graciela P. Rosenberg (2008). "Cooperative Learning, Jigsaw Strategies, and Reflections of Graduate and Undergraduate Education Students." *College Teaching Methods & Styles Journal* 4(2): 1–5.

Perkins, David V., and Renee Saris (2001). "A 'Jigsaw Classroom' Technique for Undergraduate Statistics Courses." *Teaching of Psychology* 28: 111–13.

Resor, Cynthia (2008). "Encouraging Students to Read the Texts: The Jigsaw Method." *Teaching History: A Journal of Methods* 33(1): 20–27. findarticles.com/p/articles/mi_hb302/is_1_33/ai_n29427184.

Slavin, Robert E. (1995). *Cooperative Learning: Theory, Research, and Practice*. Boston: Allyn and Bacon.

28

Teaching with Puzzles

David O'Brien

People love a good puzzle, and philosophy teems with puzzles.[1] So puzzles have a natural place in the philosophy classroom. Most of us already use them, in one way or another, in our teaching. But we can underestimate—certainly I used to underestimate—just how much we can usefully do with puzzles in the classroom. I'll briefly describe how I teach with puzzles, explain why I think it's worth doing, and suggest some possibilities for using the method in more advanced settings.

1 How I Do It

The way I teach with puzzles has three phases—setup, solving, and reflecting.[2] In the setup phase, I present the puzzle, piece by piece, to students. The goal is to engage students' sense of puzzlement at the puzzle. In the solving phase, students work together at solving the puzzle. The goal is for students to begin to produce hypotheses about how to solve it. In the reflection phase, students work with each other and with me to start to test their hypotheses. The goal is for students to think comparatively about various solution hypotheses and thereby begin to understand the underlying issues that generate the puzzle.

To illustrate what that looks like in practice, here's a case study. The puzzle is loosely adapted from Derek Parfit's discussion of the repugnant conclusion (1984).

I begin the setup phase by introducing the kind of puzzle we're going to think about: I'm going say three things, each of which I think is quite plausible, but not all of which can be true. The puzzle arises from an unusual set of choices: I'm faced with a set of buttons, each of which would dramatically affect how the distant future will be, and I have to choose which to press. If I press "A," I'll produce in the distant future a large population with great lives. If I press "B," I'll produce a different population, twice as large, with slightly less great lives. And so on—until, if I press "ZZ," I'll produce a still different population, gargantuan in size, all with just barely tolerable lives.

Then it's on to the description of the puzzle itself. I present it like this. The first puzzle piece is my judgments about each of the adjacent pairs of buttons. A large population with great lives is very good, but it seems even better, overall, to have twice as many lives that are nearly as great. And the same reasoning applies to the comparison between any individual pair of adjacent outcomes. So my first judgment is that:

(1) ZZ > YY, and YY > XX, and …, and B > A

But—the second puzzle piece—it looks like a very plausible principle that, if one thing's overall better than the second and the second's overall better than the third, then the first is overall better than the third. So my second judgment is that:

(2) If ZZ > YY, and YY > XX, and …, and B > A, then ZZ > A.

But—the final puzzle piece—when I directly compare the prospect of pressing "ZZ" with the prospect of pressing "A," I simply find it impossible to believe that I'd making be things better by producing a gargantuan number of barely tolerable lives rather than a different, but still large, number of great lives. So my third judgment is that:

(3) It's not true that ZZ > A.

The final element of the setup phase is my underlining that, although each of those three sentences, when I considered it individually, seemed very plausible to me, they just won't fit together. If I start with any two of them, then I can't consistently add the third. So something must have gone wrong in my thinking somewhere—but what exactly? That's the puzzle, as I present it to students.

There are several things worth noting about the setup phase. First, I deliberately introduce the puzzle as a request for students to *help* me. That's an important motivator. People like being in a position to help others. (So it helps to select a puzzle that, like this one, I really do find puzzling.) Second, it's helpful to introduce the puzzle in such a way that, for each puzzle piece, there's at least one way of rejecting it that corresponds to an interesting and substantive philosophical position. (So it helps to select a puzzle, like this one, in which that's true.) Third, introducing the puzzle is often a good time to canvass students' preliminary questions; that can lead naturally into the solving phase. (In the case of this puzzle, for example, students sometimes want to know whether the population that comes to exist would know what else might have happened. Eliciting such questions can help students to begin to orient themselves toward a solution hypothesis.)

In the solving phase, students then get to work developing and testing solution hypotheses. I usually have them do this in smaller groups of 3–4 people. The only further instructions I give are these. Try to spend some time thinking about as many ways out of the puzzle as you can—even ideas that might not seem initially promising or sensible. And: if you have a thought that seems important, try to work carefully to figure out exactly which piece of the puzzle your thought would show to be mistaken. (In this case, for example, it's initially quite natural for some students to hypothesize that ZZ isn't as bad as it first appears, and so it's clear enough that rejecting [3] is a live option. Likewise, it's initially quite natural for some students to think that there's some intermediate point in the sequence where the quality/quantity tradeoffs are no longer improvements, and so it's clear enough that rejecting [1] is a live option. By contrast, getting students to see what it would be to reject [2]—i.e., what it would be to deny that "better than" is transitive—is more challenging.)

There are a couple of things worth noting about the solving phase. First, the hardest thing for many students is to "translate" their initial thoughts about the puzzle into a definite problem for some individual puzzle piece (or even to identify which puzzle piece their thought poses a problem for). I often circulate among groups to try to help them figure out how to do this. Second, and relatedly, sometimes students are inclined to want to reject the very terms of the puzzle. That must, of course, remain a possibility: if a puzzle contains some hidden incoherence, it wouldn't be surprising if it generates inconsistency. Most often, however, apparent resistance to the puzzle itself turns out to be a disguised basis for rejecting one or more of the puzzle pieces. (In this case, for example, some students are inclined to initially say that you "can't compare" the options or that one of the puzzle pieces is only "kind of" true. But under judicious questioning, these initial thoughts often resolve themselves into substantive views that correspond to rejecting a particular puzzle piece—e.g., into the view that it would be equally good to press any of the buttons.)

In the reflecting phase, students come together with me to present and compare their solution hypotheses. This is in one way the most important phase. It's the time at which students get resources from each other (and from me) that point them toward further thinking and writing. It's often the moment when, for some students, a vaguely articulated solution hypothesis finally crystallizes. It's a time at which I help them draw connections between different solution strategies. It's often the time when I can work to sustain interest in the puzzle. (Hearing other people's differing approaches to a puzzle is a great way of motivating you to say what you *still* like, or now like *less*, about your own approach.) It helps me nudge students toward thinking harder about exactly which puzzle piece is the one that their idea targets, or to help them diagnose why it seemed difficult to "fit" a solution hypothesis to a particular puzzle piece. (Sometimes, for example, a student will have had an idea that could be developed in more than one direction.) And it helps me start to draw out with students the basis for rejecting different puzzle pieces—i.e., to draw out the different substantive views that underlie students' initial hypotheses.

There are a couple of things worth noting about the reflecting phase. First, it's typically the phase in which I work hardest. A class of 20–30 students typically has at least 6–7 very different reactions to the puzzle. It's hard work to keep track of the different proposals, to help students develop nascent proposals, and to exercise judgment to know when it's time to leave a nascent proposal at a point where it's clearly developed enough for now and needs further thought to be given to it in later work. Second, it's often unpredictable where students will bestow their attention. So I usually have pre-prepared sketches of a variety of solution hypotheses ready to introduce if needed. Third, because students typically have *lots* to say at this point, I usually have to exercise a bit of judgment about when to cut things off and segue to integrating the puzzle session into the class's broader goals.

I've focused here, as a case study, on the puzzle about the repugnant conclusion. That case study helps, I hope, to see in some detail what a class session focused on puzzle-solving might look like. But it's worth re-emphasizing the sheer *variety* of puzzles around which one might design a class session. Some puzzles focus on abstract issues in mid-level theorizing within a particular subfield of philosophy; the puzzle about the repugnant conclusion is an example. Other puzzles focus on larger-level issues that frame an entire subfield of philosophy; the apparent tension between free will and determinism is an example. Still other puzzles focus on local issues more directly connected with everyday life; an example might be the apparent tension between the (seeming) appropriateness of diminishing anger or grief at past injustice and the (seeming) persistence of the reasons for anger or grief at past injustice.³ These different kinds of puzzles will generate, and call for, very different kinds of student engagement. So, even if the case study above doesn't align with your particular pedagogical goals or context, it may be worth considering whether a different kind of puzzle might do so.

2 Why I Do It

Students who are working in the way described above are doing a variety of valuable things. From a purely logical point of view, of course, what they're doing differs only trivially from the more usual classroom method of reconstructing a valid argument, considering sub-arguments that support its premises, and then considering objections. From a psychological point of view, however, what they're doing is very different.

Interpersonally, they're learning to reason with each other about a common problem. The puzzle frames a philosophical problem as *everyone's* problem; after all, no one can accept the inconsistent set. The only common enemy, so to speak, is the puzzle itself (or perhaps Parfit!) So students are primed to begin philosophical work under the guise of a cooperative endeavor.⁴

Substantively, the puzzle primes students to clarify their thinking and to explore logical space. If you know you have to reject at least one puzzle piece, then you're motivated to find out *which* one is the culprit; so there's motivation to develop vague thoughts to the point at which you can identify what proposition they're an objection to (as opposed to resting content with vague dissatisfaction about an argument whose conclusion you reject). And because, in the solving phase, you're trying to figure out which proposition is the one that you might be rejecting, you're primed to genuinely explore different attitudes you might take toward the puzzle.⁵ Relatedly, the puzzle method also primes students to commit to ideas in an *experimental* spirit (rather than committing too quickly to accepting, or rejecting, different substantive views). And, finally, because other views about the puzzle are encountered, not as objections to what you say, but as competing solution hypotheses, the puzzle method primes students to take opposing substantive views—in effect, objections to their own favored view—seriously as genuine competitors rather than as irritants or afterthoughts.

Pedagogically, the puzzle method often alters the character of what's happening in the classroom—both between me and other students, and among students themselves. The puzzle method primes students to think of themselves as *co*-investigating a problem with me and with each other. Rather than priming students for the (psychologically more difficult) challenge of contradicting an author, or a peer, or me, it primes students to want to tell others how they went about a problem-solving task, and how their approach compares, for better or worse, with how others went about it. The puzzle method also helps with bigger-picture pedagogical aims. It can lead naturally to better motivation for written assignments. (You've developed a thesis; you've already begun defending it; and substantive objections to your proposal, in the form of alternative strategies to solving the puzzle that you've heard other people explore and defend, are vividly present for you.)[6] And it can lead naturally to better motivation for reading assignments. ("You've tried to solve it. Now look at how this author tried to do it." It's easier to read actively, and to be on the lookout for problems with other solution strategies, when you've already tried your own hand at solving something.)[7]

That's the *promise* of teaching with puzzles. As with any pedagogical tool there are also challenges. It can be a challenge to find puzzles that are *both* sufficiently freestanding that they can be introduced efficiently (so as to leave classroom time for the pedagogically crucial solving and reflection phrases) *and* that aren't isolated from other course topics or disconnected from students' concerns. It can also be a challenge to manage some students' discouragement. Puzzles are fun, but they're also frustrating. When one starts to sense just how complex a good philosophical puzzle is, the puzzle can seem (not just engagingly challenging but) counter-engagingly daunting.

3 Doing More with It

I hope that gives a sense of how and why I think teaching with puzzles can be useful in the philosophy classroom. More importantly, I hope it helps to suggest to you ways of refining or improving the basic idea I've described. I'll conclude by briefly suggesting two ways in which I think the method might usefully be deployed in more advanced settings.

The first kind of advanced application is to use puzzles to help students grasp the important distinction between reasons that count *for* a thesis and reasons that count *against* some alternative to that thesis. This distinction emerges quite naturally from presenting philosophical issues in puzzle form. It is clear enough, for example, that the apparent transitivity of "better than" is a consideration that counts *against* rejecting [2] in the puzzle about the repugnant conclusion, but is not a consideration that counts in *favor* of, say, rejecting [3] (since rejecting [1] would be just as consistent with it as would rejecting [3]). That's one way in which teaching with puzzles can help students to sharpen and make more careful their thinking about philosophical problems and the considerations that bear on them.

The second kind of advanced application is to encourage students to think about *generalizations* of a puzzle and to consider how solution strategies might succeed, might need to be revised, or might fail, in more general instances of the puzzle. For example, there are arguably analogs of the puzzle about the repugnant conclusion within a single life (Quinn 1990; Temkin 2012). Can some strategies for solving the interpersonal case be generalized to such intrapersonal cases? If so, does this count in their favor? If not, why not? Considering such generalizations is a way for students in more advanced settings to refine and test solution strategies more carefully. Relatedly, students can be led over the course of a suitably designed semester to begin to see patterns emerging in different puzzles—i.e., to see them as puzzles of the same type. And, correspondingly, this can lead them to begin to recognize general strategies for solving puzzles of a given type.[8] For example, arguably a characteristic kind of tension arises in cases in which: (a) unless the facts about some domain were objective, our judgments about it couldn't be vindicated, but (b) the kinds of objects or properties that would be needed to vindicate these facts being objective seem objectionably mysterious or hard to square with other commitments we have. Broadly constructivist views (which, again arguably, seem to come close enough to recovering the relevant kind of objectivity about the domain but without positing objectionably mysterious objects or properties) then emerge as one kind of general-purpose solution strategy to this puzzle type. Considering such sets of puzzles is thus a way for students in more advanced classes to be led to a more integrated, and more synoptic, understanding of the philosophical landscape.

Notes

1. See Cohen (2013).
2. See Polya (2004/1945).
3. See Marušić (2020) for discussion.
4. See Darby and Lang (2019) on the emotional dimension of learning.
5. See Cohen (2013) on framing effects in argument presentation.
6. See Ambrose et al. (2011) on introducing longer writing assignments in "scaffolded" fashion.
7. See Concepción (2005) on motivating active reading.
8. See Ryle (1954).

References

Ambrose, Susan, Michael Bridges, Michele DiPietro, Marsha Lovett, and Marie Norman (2010). *How Learning Works: Seven Research-Based Principles for Smart Teaching*. San Francisco, CA: Wiley.

Cohen, Gerald Allan (2013). "How to Do Political Philosophy" in Michael Otsuka (ed.), *On the Currency of Egalitarian Justice, and Other Essays in Political Philosophy*, 225–35. Princeton: Princeton University Press.

Concepción, David W. (2005). "How to Assure Student Preparation and Structure Student-Student Interaction." *Discourse: Learning and Teaching in Philosophical and Religious Studies* 5(1): 107–19.

Darby, Flower, and James Lang (2019). *Small Teaching Online: Applying Learning Science in Online Classes*. San Francisco, CA: Wiley.

Marušić, Berislav (2020). "Accommodation to Injustice" in Russ Shafer-Landau (ed.), *Oxford Studies in Metaethics Volume 15*, 263–83. Oxford: Oxford University Press.

Parfit, Derek (1984). *Reasons and Persons*. Oxford: Oxford University Press.

Polya, George (2004 [1945]). *How to Solve It: A New Aspect of Mathematical Method*. Princeton, NJ: Princeton University Press.

Quinn, Warren (1990). "The Puzzle of the Self-Torturer." *Philosophical Studies* 59(1): 79–90.

Ryle, Gilbert (1954). *Dilemmas*. Cambridge: Cambridge University Press.

Temkin, Larry (2012). *Rethinking the Good: Moral Ideals and the Nature of Practical Reasoning*. Oxford: Oxford University Press.

29

Students Make Pudding

Stephen Bloch-Schulman

1 What Seems to Be the Problem

Philosophers recognize the challenge of naïve relativism and how it undermines the kind of learning they want students to experience in class. If any answer, any opinion, is equally valid, there is no real purpose to the careful work we want students to do. I suspect philosophers who do any normative work are also, as am I, worried about naïve relativism as a normative stance; I am excited to talk through complicated views of relativism with students and take those views very seriously. What I am talking about, and worried about, is the use of naïve relativism in the classroom as a conversation-stopper and a derailing of the important work we and students do to improve as critical thinkers. (And one might learn a lot about their students by attending to when, in particular, such moves are clung to most. I often see it emerge in relation to a particular set of topics, especially when matters of racial injustice are brought into the classroom in terms white students find hard to avoid; for an excellent resource on this, see Matt Whitt's excellent "Other People's Problems: Student Distancing, Epistemic Responsibility, and Injustice.")

That is, I see a certain naïve relativism as a stumbling block to any real philosophic engagement and thus to philosophic learning, and it is that kind of naïve relativism that I am discussing here and that I have seen in class.

There are many common approaches that philosophers use to address naïve relativism. When I was a student and, today, I still see two as the most common within the discipline:

1 Philosophers use (or suggest that others use) particular argumentative strategies to convince students of the costs of naïve relativism. There are many ways to do this and a common argument I see is for the faculty member to walk through some noxious outcomes of naïve relativism—for example, showing that the naïve relativist cannot criticize Nazis. "Unless you want to think Nazis might be morally acceptable," they conclude (or imply), "you need to reject naïve relativism."

2 They speak about the values that a student who offers a naïve relativist view is trying to uphold: they might highlight the students' desire to enact humility and value the recognition of differences that are easily bull-dozed over when we make normative claims about how people should live, especially when we admit our own limited context and knowledge and how norms change over time and between cultures. But then they show some reason that naïve relativism fails to meet these goals: that it isn't actually humble because it means that no one can criticize them and they have no need for self-reflection which might lead to learning; and that valuing differences is best done through specific norms that are not relative (e.g., that one should not discriminate against someone on the basis of their racial identity).

Certainly, a careful argument can be persuasive and sometimes is.

Earlier in my teaching career, when I worked with students who would push a naïve relativist position, I would make these kinds of arguments too. Sometimes they would work and I would be glad to be done with that particular problem. But often they did not. And they did not, I suspect, because of what this approach—directly arguing against naïve relativism—may fail to consider, namely, that naïve relativism in students may well be a rejection of the importance and value of argumentation and persuasion. Whether students do it for this particular reason or not, in my experience, it is when students are pushed to consider views they would rather not, or consider for longer and in more nuanced ways than is comfortable for them, that naïve relativism is most likely to rear its clichéd head. I have come to see the work naïve relativism does for students in a class, more than anything else, as an attempt to forestall thinking, to act as a "conversation-stopper." (I take this term from Richard Rorty, who uses it for somewhat analogous concerns.)

If that is the case, then an argument against naïve relativism is largely beside the point or may be counterproductive: it might be beside the point because it is not clear that students care about naïve relativism as a belief, and it may be counterproductive because arguing about naïve relativism takes the focus away from the issues that may be most important (e.g., in thinking seriously about injustice). Arguing against naïve relativism takes students at their word: as if they are committed to naïve relativism in the first place.

2 The Real Problem as I See It

I don't know any student who, when push comes to shove, actually lives as a naïve relativist. In this case, neither the pushing nor the shoving need be particularly forceful. A single gentle poke will do: I don't know that I have met a student who would, regardless of what they espouse in class, actually be fine with randomly assigned grades because I claim that "that is what I believe is right."

The problem is not, as far as I can tell, that there are students who need to be persuaded against naïve relativism, exactly. It is rather that, in trying to stop further conversation (and further thinking), students offer a view in class that isn't the way they live. In normal circumstances, when a professor asks a question and wants students to talk about their beliefs in class, I think what the students are offering is what their "classroom self" wants to admit/ wants to show themself to believe. It feels like asking someone to show up to a formal dinner event: everyone is on their "best" behavior, only in this case, "best" here should be understood as "best I can offer in relation to the power-structures that are the classroom/professor-asking-a-question" setting. They bring their classroom self to class and when asked about a belief, that is who answers. It is the contemplative, disengaged, supposedly disembodied self who answers, with nothing particular and concrete at stake (other than looking a certain way in class). It is often a self that suspends disbelief in the discussions in a philosophy class; we can say what we wish in this space, it is merely the game we play here. Not that that doesn't mean it can't get heated and people cannot act like it matters deeply. They can. In the way we do when we play games. But it is the structure of the classroom, with its given set of goals, that determines the typical ways students take up their agency, as one might say if one were obsessed with *Games: Agency As Art* by C. Thi Nguyen. (Not that I know anyone who fits *that* description at all.) Somehow, they come to class as a seventh-level circle of the moon Druid, and we act like that person in class is them (or all of them).[1]

I am not really interested in their contemplations or their espoused classroom beliefs. I *am* interested in their performance as "student who is showing they are interested in X or Y" and how this performance can be used to avoid thinking and facing difficult truths. That is, I am interested, as Hannah Arendt liked to say, in "thinking what we are doing" (Arendt 1958: 5), and in this case, asking students to think what they are doing (rather than what they are espousing); and I am particularly interested in asking them to think what they are doing when the rules of the classroom game are not overdetermining their claims and behavior. Even as they might say they are naïve relativists (in their own language), I don't see them *doing* along the lines of naïve relativism. One might call my focus Bloch-Schulmanian/Schwitzgebelian pedagogies, if one weren't worried about how hard that would be to pronounce. Eric Schwitzgebel argues against the intellectualist view of beliefs, wherein beliefs are to be understood as what one says one believes when one sincerely looks within themselves (Schwitzgebel 2021). Schwitzgebel offers, as an example, a graduate student who proclaims and believes he believes that all human beings are morally equal and should be treated with respect. He writes papers that define and further this stance and he thinks he thinks it. But he treats people differently based on their position in the social hierarchy of his community, treating, for example, the person who clears his table at the restaurant quite differently than the fancy philosopher he is getting to dine with. Schwitzgebel asks, in this case, if we should take "belief" to be that which this graduate student proclaims (even when he does so sincerely) or if we do not have to take into account that if he *really* believed what he said, he would act differently and therefore, based on his actions, we know that he does not (or does not univocally) believe in his stated principles of equality for all. (For those who know his work, I hope the resonance with Charles Mills's worries about classical philosophers not really believing their own espoused principles, and the need for Black students to pretend, is visible here.)

It is with Schwitzgebel's skepticism that I take with a grain (or a shaker) of salt the beliefs my students proclaim in class as if they know and are expressing their real beliefs. What they espouse may be part of their beliefs, definitely, and I certainly see them as beliefs they want to believe and want to think they believe. But that is far from saying that it accurately names something about what their beliefs are. And I want to be clear: I am just as skeptical about the espoused beliefs of others who are not students in the class and about myself: I don't think I know my own beliefs, either.

And, with Schwitzgebel and Arendt, I want to know how the students *do* (and thus something like "what they really believe" or, maybe like "what they believe when they are not contemplating what they believe in a classroom game"). I want to know what beliefs they perform, not what they say they believe, and I want students to be shining a critical light *there*. I want students to critically consider their beliefs, and in that way, I suspect I am quite typical for philosophers. Where I suspect my approach is unusual is that I don't care (much) what students say they believe, especially in class, because I don't think they know what they believe. I don't think any of us do. I think their beliefs need to be brought out, shown indirectly, reverse engineered through a critical examination of the actions they take and what those actions say the student must believe (whether they know it or not).

Put another way: students can claim in class and in their written work to be naïve relativists all they want; I am skeptical.

Then how might I ask them to reveal the beliefs that they live by when they are not espousing? How do I get them in their day-to-day clothes eating in their day-to-day way (instead of dressed up fancy, on their "best" behavior); what they eat and how they act with their friends, say, at the school cafeteria? (I am not asking how they act or dress on a Saturday night. That, I am quite sure, is either way above or way below my pay-grade.)

So, instead of arguing against a view I don't think they actually hold (or, at least, don't hold univocally), I try to get them to *do* something and then reflect on what they have done so they (and I) can see that their actions show something essential (maybe not all, but a lot) about what they really believe.

3 The Pudding and Its Proof

When naïve relativism is holding students back from fuller engagement in the activities of the class, when they use it to stop conversation and thought, I use a process where students see the problems with naïve relativism through their own actions and commitments. (It also, as a delicious benefit, works well for teaching growth-mindsets and what progress in philosophy looks and feels like.)

Specifically,

> 1   I give students an assignment that is the right amount of challenging: the task needs to be sufficiently nuanced and complicated that I am

confident that the work of every student could be improved (even as some will do better than others on this initial assignment). But it cannot be too challenging. I am trying to find an assignment that I am convinced will be quite hard at the time I give it, but that with some help, with some extra skills, the student will be able to have done recognizably better than when they first started. For me, this is often a close reading of a text with a question to answer about the text.

2 When they submit the assignment to me, I don't hand it back or grade it yet. I keep it in pocket until step 5 of *the proof*.

3 I help students get better at doing the specific tasks needed for the original assignment by leading specific hands-on, multi-iterative training and guidance. That is, they learn a skill and practice it and then get feedback on it and try it again until it is clear they have improved that skill. This training could include class discussion, work on fallacies, work in logic, reading relevant texts. Whatever the training is, I only move on to the next step when I am convinced that their skills in the relevant task have been notably improved. This might take two or three class periods, though it is sometimes shorter and sometimes longer.

4 When I am convinced that students have the skills to perform the original assignment better than they did initially, I ask them to do the same original assignment again (still having not gotten feedback from me on their first attempt).

But here is the kicker:

5 In class, without having read or graded the initial homework assignment, I hand back each student's original work. I explain that I have not looked at the work and have no idea to what extent it is or is not good work. I ask them to take some time to compare their earlier and later attempts to do the assignment. I sometimes encourage them to do so in conversation with others at their table. It is at that point, with both their own earlier and later work in hand, with better skills, and with some time to consider, that I offer them a choice: A) they can select which of the two I will grade (and it will count for both assignments) or B) they can submit both and I will choose one randomly (and the one chosen randomly will count for both assignments). They must also include a written description of why they chose the option they did.

I have never had a student submit both for me to randomly choose which one to grade. They always choose one and describe why it is better. Through this process, they have thus shown themselves that there are standards and that when their grade is on the line, they *do* recognize that there is reason to prefer one answer to the other (almost always, they see that their earlier work is not as strong as their later work), and thus that they are not equal.

When this works the right way, and in my experience, it consistently does, I return to the explicit discussion of naïve relativism to point out how their own actions reveal their own skepticism of the position. That is, students, through this process, are enacting the kinds of commitments that reveal to themselves the problems with naïve relativism and the benefits of the skills I have taught them, and the value of their own work. When I point these out to them, I rarely have to say much more. They see it. I have not done an empirical study on the effectiveness of this method but have used it often and find that when students confront their own work, with their grade on the line, that it makes the questions and problems of naïve relativism real for them. They see, through the process, how they *do* think one answer is better than the other and if that is true, then that naïve relativism will do them no benefit. Students have, in the end, cooked the pudding wherein they find their own proof.

Note

1. This was a description offered by Rebecca Scott to a text message where I claimed that I had a "D&D emergency." If you want to know about D&D and how to use it in class, you should talk to her.

References

Arendt, Hannah (1958). *The Human Condition*. Chicago: The University of Chicago Press.

Mills, Charles (1998). "Non-Cartesian Sums: Philosophy and the African-American Experience" in *Blackness Visible: Essays on Philosophy and Race*, 1–20. Ithica, London: Cornell University Press.

Nguyen, C. Thi (2020). *Games: Agency as Art*. New York: Oxford University Press.

Rorty, Richard (1994). "Religion as Conversation-stopper." *Common Knowledge* 3(1): 1–6.

Schwitzgebel, Eric (2021). "The Pragmatic Metaphysics of Belief" in Dirk Kindermann, Andrea Onofri, and Cristina Borgoni (eds), *The Fragmented Mind*, 350–75. New York: Oxford University Press.

Whitt, Matt S. (2016). "Other People's Problems: Student Distancing, Epistemic Responsibility, and Injustice." *Studies in Philosophy and Education* 35: 427–44.

30

Prisoner's Dilemma and Prisoner's Delight: A Simple Activity That Helps Students See the Complexity of Others

Joshua DiPaolo

How can we help students avoid simplistic narratives about the difference of Others?

It's Spring 2018. I'm teaching Philosophy of Race to thirty-five students at a university in the middle of Kansas, thirty-five students at a university in the middle of Kansas. Thirty of them are white. This is my second year teaching here. Incidentally, I am also married to a native Kansan who graduated from this very university fourteen years earlier. I know these students and their backgrounds well. I know what they were taught about race growing up, and I know what narratives they encountered.[1] Moreover, I care very much about these students and their learning. So far in the semester, for many of them the course has been one disturbing revelation after another. One student who came into the class deeply skeptical of the contemporary significance of race now frequently expresses her resentment toward the omissions of her previous education: "Why was I never taught any of this?" Her experience in the class, she said, felt like she was one of the prisoners escaping Plato's cave. She was feeling the pain of coming out of darkness into daylight. Many of her classmates echoed this sentiment throughout the semester.

Working through Elizabeth Anderson's book *The Imperative of Integration*, we are about to discuss a problematic racial narrative I know they've heard a million times growing up. Many of them probably accept it themselves. Following Anderson, we will encounter this narrative when we consider a common answer to these questions: Who is responsible for reducing disadvantage in Black communities? Only members of those communities? Or do people outside those communities bear responsibility? Anderson addresses this argument: disadvantage in Black communities results from dysfunctional behaviors inherent to the members of those communities, so people outside those communities owe no assistance to people in them. That's a fancy way of saying something my students had heard before. White folks aren't responsible for helping Black folks in Black ghettos; their choices—crime, young single-motherhood, fiscal irresponsibility, lack of commitment to education—cause their suffering. This is just *who* they are: they're criminals, they lack traditional family values, they don't care about school.

A tempting narrative lies behind this argument. It is tempting to believe that people who behave radically different from us must *be* radically different from us. *We* would never do *that*. *They* must lack *our* values. Tempting. But false. Radically different behavior does not necessarily reflect radically different values. Two people with the exact same values may behave differently when facing different circumstances. To you and me, this is obvious. It's not to my students. Not in this context. But if I could get them to grasp this insight, it could have far-reaching consequences for their thinking. It could produce a gestalt shift; a new way of seeing the old. I knew I had to get this right. I couldn't bury a lesson like this in a lecture on the fundamental attribution error or in a head-on abstract discussion of the argument.[2] I wanted students to *experience* this lesson. I wanted it to *stay* with them. What could I do?

I had a hunch there was an activity I could create to get students to fall for a version of this tempting narrative, directed at their classmates. They knew each other well enough. They knew they were not radically different from each other. If I could get them to make this mistake, to wrongly assume they were in the same circumstances and thereby fail to see the influence of circumstance on each other's decision-making, I knew the lesson would stick. I'm a big fan of using games in teaching. I suspected a game would work. Games allow us to try on different agencies.[3] That was what I needed: I needed students to be the agents in this experience, to judge each other as agents, and to realize those judgments were based on an incomplete view of the bigger picture. Then they would be prepared to examine the tempting narrative as it applies to race. Here is what I came up with. It's simple. But it was powerful.[4]

I split the class into two "societies." I "segregated" these societies into two sides of the room, sitting students far enough apart so they couldn't hear the other group's discussion. I gave each student the rules of a simple game. Ultimately, each student had two options: Cooperate or Defect. They were allowed to discuss with members of their group what they should do. During the discussion, I randomly assigned each person a partner from their own society without telling them who their partner was—I would reveal this only after they had made their choice. Being paired with a partner attached stakes to the consequences of their decisions. They weren't just picking one of two inconsequential options; they were Cooperating with or Defecting against one of their classmates. But here's the thing. What students did not know, and did not realize for a long time, was that *the two societies were playing different games*. Society 1 was given a classic Prisoner's Dilemma. No matter what the other person does, the rational option is Defect. Society 2 was given a version of the less familiar Prisoner's Delight. The incentive structure is the opposite: no matter what the other person does, the rational option is Cooperate. This was by design. I wanted to concoct a situation where on the whole the students in different societies behaved radically differently from each other. Once students "locked in" their decisions, I told them who their partner was and, starting with Society 1, I asked each student to share with the class whether they would Cooperate or Defect.

The crucial thing to keep in mind here is how Society 1's behavior appears from the perspective of Society 2, and vice versa—*not knowing they're playing different games*. One by one, students in Society 1 (Prisoner's Dilemma) chose Defect. From the perspective of Society 2 (Prisoner's Delight), *this is crazy!* You must be absolutely cutthroat, not to mention irrational, to Defect. Defecting made no sense!

I should say: I was nervous coming into class that day to run this exercise. It was risky. It could totally flop. But I'll tell you what: as I heard students in Society 2 react to Society 1's decisions, I knew I had them. They were shocked. "What's wrong with these people?!" their gasps and laughter seemed to shout! Then we went to Society 2. No one had caught on yet. As each member in Society 2 agreed to Cooperate, the people in Society 1 reacted in corresponding fashion. To Cooperate is to be a real sucker! Cooperating makes no sense. Nevertheless, the results were clear: most in Society 1 Defected while everyone in Society 2 Cooperated.

Then I asked Society 1 to explain their decisions to Society 2. Why would you Defect? To make it more fun, I raised the stakes by jokingly asking why they would betray the classmate with whom they'd been paired: "Come on, Evan! Why would you do that to Sarah?!" It took everyone some time to uncover my devious plan. But before it dawned on them, some argued vigorously in favor of their own decision and against the decisions they saw in the other society. "It was so obvious that Defecting was the right decision!" "How could anyone choose not to Cooperate?!" And so on. Eventually, some started to catch on to the fact that they were playing different games. Then I revealed the truth to the entire class. But not too soon, not before the damage was already done.

Game theory experts might identify holes in this activity if it were meant as an analogy to some specific real-world situation. But it wasn't. It was about giving students a particular experience. Students were guilty of making the tempting but fallacious inference I wanted them to make: that different behavior implies different values. It didn't occur to them that they were playing different games; it didn't occur to them that the difference in their behavior was explainable in terms of having the *same* values in *distinct* situations, with distinct costs and benefits assigned to the ostensibly "same" action. Once students realized this, the narrative's flaw was inescapably clear. The people in Society 1 were no different from those in Society 2—after all, they were randomly assigned! What was different was the incentive structure.

Now they were ready to confront the argument addressed by Anderson. They were ready to think critically about what "dysfunctional behavior" in poor Black communities actually means. Perhaps staying in school in a ghetto doesn't pay the way it does outside the ghetto; perhaps being friendly to strangers doesn't pay the same way; perhaps avoiding crime doesn't either. Perhaps differences in behavior don't necessarily indicate a difference in values; maybe they indicate a difference in situation with different costs and benefits associated with the available options.

The rest of the semester students frequently mentioned how much they enjoyed this experience. And they were quick to bring its lesson into the discussion when it was relevant. Students also mentioned that they wished we had more experiences like this in class. I wish that too! Unfortunately, I'm not that creative.

Let me conclude with a caveat and a generalization. First, this activity requires deception. Even mildly deceiving students may not be everyone's cup of tea. I respect that. But even if you don't mind a little teacher-to-student deception, there are limits worth considering. You don't want to create an environment of distrust, especially when teaching charged topics like race. For this to go off without a hitch, the timing and relationships must be right. I work hard in my classes to develop a learning environment where students are comfortable with each other and with me. When I ran this activity, it was about four weeks into the semester. Students generally felt like they could trust me. As far as I could tell, the deception had no negative impact.

Second, although this activity arose in the context of teaching Anderson, that has nothing to do with its success. It was all about the tempting narrative. That narrative pops up all over the place. A key takeaway in James Rachels's classic essay "The Challenge of Cultural Relativism" is that apparent differences in values need not reflect fundamental moral disagreements. How could a family abandon their children in freezing cold temperatures on the tundra? They must be monsters! Oh ... they're facing extremely different circumstances from the rest of us. A more contemporary example concerns women acting as YouTube propagandists for misogynistic groups (Llanera 2023).[5] Why would women act as shills for misogyny? Don't they have any self-respect? Oh ... maybe in their misogynistic, oppressive communities the main way to acquire universally sought after goods—respect, belonging, meaning—is to advance the misogynistic cause.

That last example may raise alarm bells. It shouldn't. *Not* falling for the tempting narrative doesn't settle issues of morality and blame. Rather, shoving that simplistic narrative aside opens up space to address the real, the hard, and the complex questions of political evaluation and moral responsibility. Only after students are prepared to acknowledge the complexity of others are they equipped to make genuine headway on these pressing questions.

Acknowledgments

Thanks to Gina Schouten and Brynn Welch for feedback on this chapter. Thanks to Brynn for inviting me to contribute to this brilliant volume. Special thanks to Sarah Riforgiate for all her encouragement and guidance in the Peer Review of Teaching Fellowship program I was participating in when I was teaching my philosophy of race class at Kansas State University. The work I did in that fellowship helped me vividly remember that 2018 semester and improved my teaching. Thanks Sarah! Above all, thanks to my students in that class not only for being guinea pigs for this exercise, but also for being excellent students who taught me so much.

Appendix

These are the instructions I gave to students, one group received the Delight instructions, the other received the Dilemma instructions, the other received the bottom half. I explicitly describe the payouts in the instructions to minimize the chance that confusion would ultimately determine their decision. Finally, I am including these exact instructions in this piece to show how robust the effect was. Notice the two stories have nothing to do with each other! One is about rowing a boat, the other about being a criminal. When I originally came up with this activity, it was rushed—a stroke of inspiration late the night before class. So I just used the standard Prisoner's Dilemma story and the first story of Prisoner's Delight I'd found (from Bryan Skyrms's (2009) Tanner Lectures *Evolution and the Social Contract*). Despite the different stories, the activity worked; students argued for a while before even mentioning the details of their story. Nevertheless, I recommend making the stories match to reduce the likelihood of the cat prematurely getting out of the bag.

Prisoner's Dilemma/Prisoner's Delight

Delight

You and your partner are sitting on the shore of a lake in your rowboat. You each have a set of oars. You have been out fishing all day and have a hot dinner awaiting you across the lake. Each of you can choose whether or not to row.

If you COOPERATE by rowing, then you'll receive 3 units of happiness (when your partner rows you'll get there fast) or you'll receive 1 unit of happiness (when your partner doesn't row you'll get there, but slowly).

If you DEFECT by not rowing, then you'll receive 2 units of happiness (when your partner rows because you'll get there but not as fast as if you both rowed) or you'll receive 0 units of happiness (when your partner doesn't row because you won't make it across the lake).

In other words:
    If you *both* COOPERATE, you'll receive 3 units of happiness.
    If you COOPERATE and your partner DEFECTS, you'll receive 1 units of happiness.

If you DEFECT and your partner COOPERATES, you'll receive 2 unit of happiness.

If you *both* DEFECT, you'll receive 0 units of happiness.

Suppose you only care about getting as much happiness as possible.

What do you choose: COOPERATE or DEFECT?

Dilemma

You and your partner are members of a criminal gang. You've just been arrested and imprisoned. Each of you is in solitary confinement with no means of communicating with the other. The prosecutors lack sufficient evidence to convict the pair of you on the principal charge. They hope to get both sentenced to a year in prison on a lesser charge. Simultaneously, the prosecutors offer each of you a bargain. You can betray the other and defect by testifying that the other committed the crime. Or you can cooperate with your partner by remaining silent. The offer is:

If you DEFECT by betraying your partner, you'll serve 2 years in prison (if your partner betrays you) or you'll serve 0 years in prison (if your partner remains silent).

If you COOPERATE by remaining silent, you'll serve 3 years in prison (if your partner betrays you) or you'll serve 1 year in prison (if your partner remains silent).

In other words:
  If you *both* DEFECT, you'll each serve 2 years in prison.
  If you DEFECT, but your partner COOPERATES, you will go free (0 years in prison)
  If you COOPERATE, but your partner DEFECTS, you will serve 3 years in prison.
  If you *both* COOPERATE, you'll each only serve 1 year in prison.

Suppose you only care about minimizing time in prison.

What do you choose: COOPERATE or DEFECT?

Notes

1. In case you're less familiar with these students: most of them grew up in politically conservative communities where their high school history teachers informed them that the Civil Rights Movement solved race and racism. It hasn't been a real problem in years. Obama's election was proof!
2. For a classic discussion of the fundamental attribution error, the tendency to attribute behavior exclusively to an agent's dispositions and ignore powerful situational determinants, see Nisbett and Ross (1980).
3. Nguyen (2020) makes this point, which I intuited inchoately at the time, explicitly and beautifully.
4. See the Appendix for the actual handout I used.
5. See also Friedman (2008).

References

Anderson, Elizabeth (2010). *The Imperative of Integration*. Princeton: Princeton University Press.

Friedman, Marilynn (2008). "Female Terrorists: Martyrdom and Gender Equality" in Ibraham A. Karawan, Wayne McCormack, Stephen E. Reynolds (eds), *Values and Violence: Intangible Aspects of Terrorism*, 43–61. London: Springer.

Llanera, Tracy (2023). "The Misogyny Paradox and the Alt-Right." *Hypatia* 38(1): 157–76. First View: doi.org/10.1017/hyp.2023.4. 1–20.

Nguyen, C. Thi (2020). *Games: Agency as Art*. Oxford: Oxford University Press.

Nisbett, Richard, and Lee Ross (1980). *Human Inference: Strategies and Shortcomings of Social Judgment*. Englewood Cliffs: Prentice-Hall.

Rachels, James (2019). *The Elements of Moral Philosophy*. New York: McGraw Hill Education.

Skyrms, Brian (2009). "Evolution and the Social Contract" in Grethe B. Peterson (ed), *The Tanner Lectures on Human Values Vol. 28*, 47–63. Salt Lake City: University of Utah Press.

31

Will the Gendered Division of Labor Be an Issue in Your Generation? An Exercise

Harry Brighouse

One of the first times I taught about the gendered division of labor in my *Contemporary Moral Issues* course, a student articulately challenged the relevance of the issue to her and her peers. I had assigned the key chapter of Susan Okin's classic, *Justice, Gender and the Family*, which argues that the gender system violates fair equality of opportunity, because girls are socialized to be carers (and boys aren't), therefore end up disproportionately in caring (and therefore lower paid) labor, and, because they take the lion's share of the burden of caring labor in the home, end up lower paid than their spouses; and yet they face a high probability of a divorce after which they will not be able to share in their spouse's greater earning power. (I disagree with Okin about Rawls—I do not in fact think that the gender system violates *Rawlsian* fair equality of opportunity given the way that Rawls conceives of subject of justice—though I agree with her that if the mechanisms she identifies are at work there *is* a social injustice.) For her empirical case, Okin relies heavily on Lenore Weitzman's study of divorce.

My student said this research was not relevant to her generation. Putting aside the now well-known methodological worries about Weitzman's study, I was rather unnerved to figure out on the spot that the women she studied were in the generation of my students' grandparents or, in some cases, great grandparents. I wouldn't want to draw conclusions about my own life course from studies of my grandparent's generation either, especially if my parents and teachers had insisted that my own circumstances were entirely different, and even less if I were aware (as some of the women are) that so soon after admitting women as equal participants many universities now have to practice affirmative action for men in admissions to get close to equal sex-ratios.[1] I pointed all this out to the students, and then, again on the spot, tried to figure out a way of showing that the issues, if not the figures, probably are relevant to the current generation nevertheless. I was pretty happy that in five minutes I had them convinced that at least it *might* be relevant.

Since then I have formalized and anonymized the exercise. At the start of each semester I send out a survey with about twenty-five items, asking them what their views are about some of the issues that we'll be studying over the course of the semester, and slipping the gendered division of labor questions into the mix. Here are the gendered division of labor questions:

1 Are you male, or female, or non-binary?
2 During your teen years did you get paid to babysit a non-relative more than ten times?
3 Do you anticipate having children? If not, sit out the exercise.

> Here are three kinds of parenting arrangements:
>
> A) Father-led parenting: the father spends substantially more time than the mother looking after the children and thinking about their well-being over the course of their childhoods.
> B) Mother-led parenting: the mother spends substantially more time than the father looking after the children and thinking about their well-being over the course of their childhoods.
> C) Egalitarian parenting: the mother and father spend roughly the same amount of time looking after the children and thinking about their well-being.

4 Think just about yourself for the moment. Which of A, B, and C best characterizes your expectations for your prospective family life.[2]
5 Now think about your FIVE best friends. Which of A, B, and C best characterizes your expectations for most of their family lives? (e.g., if you expect 3 or more of them to be Father-led, answer A).

I've now been doing this annually for well over a decade. My class, obviously, is not representative of students as a whole, let alone of their cohort. It's not even representative of students at UW-Madison. Usually more than

50 percent of the students are Business majors, and nearly every time more than 50 percent are seniors. But that doesn't matter. This isn't a scientific survey; it is just aimed at showing the students that the gendered division of labor is something that *might* be a real issue (and possibly an issue of justice) for them and their cohort.

The answers to the babysitting question are as you would predict. Well over half the women, and well under a quarter of the men, answer in the affirmative. This shows them that the women are probably better prepared for—they have more practice at—caring for children than are the men.

For (4) and (5), the numbers have changed a little over time. Between 2005 (when I started asking this) and 2013 the following was a representative result:

4.   Men: A 0%; B 85%; C 15%
     Women A 10%; B 25%; C 65%

So the expectations of the men were completely misaligned with those of women. Even this result should give the women pause for thought. Since 2013 the results for the men and women have gradually come into closer alignment, mainly because increasingly more men answer that they expect egalitarian parenting for themselves.[3]

But the answers to (4) for both sexes are still, as they always have been, out of alignment with the answers to (5). Both men and women say that they expect their *friends* to have children who are raised mainly by the mother. Here's a representative set of answers from that early period:

5.   Men: A 0%; B 85%; C 15%
     Women A 0%; B 75%; C 25%

Since 2013 the answers for both sexes have changed a little: now some men and more women say they expect the father to be the main parent for their own children, and a few of both say they expect the father to be the main parent for their friends' children. But, still, their expectations for *themselves* and *their friends* are highly divergent.

When I present the data the students are always startled, then amused, and most concede that their answers for their friends are more realistic than their answers for themselves.

It's still an open question, of course, whether any injustice is operating and, if so, what if anything, should be done about it. The women studied in the research on which Okin relied were not encouraged in school to be high academic achievers in the areas which might yield high-paying careers, and anyway were subject to a high degree of labor market discrimination once they finished school. In the current generation, women have much more educational success and attainment than men, including in areas that lead to high-paying careers. The best academic studies we have suggest that the wage gap between men and women is almost (but not quite) entirely down to choices men and women make about attachment to the labor market after they have children. Jobs are structured so that it is very difficult for couples to share child rearing equally; but nothing in the economy forces heterosexual couples to choose that fathers, rather than mothers, pursue careers while mothers, rather than fathers, step out of or step down from full-time employment. Those unforced choices and/or the cultural norms that influence them may well be subject to criticism at the bar of justice, but it's not at all obvious why, and that tends to be where discussion focuses.

Notes

1. See for example, Susan Dominus, "There Was Definitely a Thumb on the Scale to Get Boys," *New York Times*, September 8, 2023. Retrieved at https://www.nytimes.com/2023/09/08/magazine/men-college-enrollment.html.
2. I don't provide instructions about how to answer if one expects the other parent to be the same sex as oneself, because I don't want to lead the respondent. I assume that a woman who expects to raise children with another woman will answer B. The exercise does not assume a two-parent arrangement: Someone who expects to raise the child alone should answer A or B. Strictly speaking the wording ("the mother" and "the father") does assume that the children will not have more than two parents, though someone who expects to raise a child with more than one other person can probably figure out how to give a good answer.
3. Since 2013 answers to two other questions—"Would you describe yourself as a feminist?" and "Would your friends describe you as a feminist?"—have changed dramatically. Before 2013 few women and fewer men answered "yes" to either of those questions. Now large majorities of both sexes answer "yes" to both. And, amusingly, several of each sex answer "yes" to one of those questions and "no" to the other. My entirely unscientific conjecture is that the key event explaining the change after 2013 is a speech by Ms. Emma Watson at the UN. An alternative possibility, of course, is that the boys have become more inclined to give the answers that they think are the politically correct answers, and it's entirely possible that inclination has increased over time. The sudden change around 2014 is, nevertheless, striking.

32

Feminist Critiques of the Original Position

Susan Kennedy

As an educator, I strive to create an active learning environment that promotes student engagement and interest in the subject matter. To achieve this, I incorporate various activities such as case studies, simulations, and debates into my teaching approach. However, I encountered a challenge when trying to devise in-class learning activities that complemented the underrepresented philosophers on my syllabus. Despite the increasing availability of resources to help instructors diversify their syllabi, I found that there are fewer resources that offer lesson plans and classroom activities to support instructors in fully embracing this goal in their teaching methods.

Given my concern that simply including underrepresented philosophers on the syllabus may not be enough to convey the significance of their contributions to students, I developed a learning activity to establish better alignment between the syllabus and the classroom. Although this particular activity was designed for an introductory course in political philosophy, the aim of amending preexisting classroom activities or creating new ones to support one's teaching of underrepresented philosophers is relevant to other course topics as well.

To foster student engagement with canonical texts in political philosophy, I utilized class activities such as the Prisoner's Dilemma exercise when teaching Hobbes's State of Nature and Harry Brighouse's "Game on Rawls's Second Principle" when teaching the Original Position (Brighouse 2004). Taking inspiration from the latter, I designed an activity to address feminist critiques of social contract theory and Rawls's Original Position (2001). In this activity, students find themselves confronting the assumptions, commonly represented in canonical texts, that human beings are rational, independent, and self-interested adults.

After breaking into small groups, students are asked to negotiate with each other on a set of issues concerning voluntary relationships, basic liberties, and distributive justice. Unbeknownst to the students, half of the groups will receive different instructions for the activity than the others. One half of the class will be asked to imagine themselves negotiating based on the assumptions associated with the canonical figures they have read up until this point. In particular, students will be prompted to recall Hobbes's *Leviathan* (1986) and Locke's *Second Treatise of Government* (1980) which frame the liberal individual at the center of the social contract as one who is atomistic, self-interested, and rational. In contrast, the other half of the class will be negotiating based on feminist considerations that draw attention to mothering persons and parents as well as children and other dependents. Following the small group discussions, a scribe will put their group's answers on the board for the whole class to discuss. To the students' surprise, some groups may have conflicting answers owing to the different background conditions they were asked to imagine. This creates a fruitful environment for the class to discover, explore, and debate the contributions of feminist philosophers. In what follows, I provide the instructions for groups A and B and a brief discussion of the rationale behind the questions and their connections to feminist scholarship.

Group A—Instructions

Breaking news! In light of recent technological advancements, a new human civilization will be built on Mars. While you will remain on Earth, you (and the other members of your group) have been selected to design the foundational principles for this new society on behalf of its new inhabitants. Your task is to assume that the new inhabitants are rational adults who prioritize their self-interest in acquiring a larger share of social goods. You know nothing about their talents, abilities, gender, religious views, etc. Your decisions should reflect a belief in the autonomy and rational decision-making of each individual. You should carefully consider how you will justify your choices to the new inhabitants.

Discuss the following questions within your group for forty-five minutes with the aim of reaching consensus:

1 There will be an upcoming election to nominate a leader for the new society on Mars. Should all members of this society be allowed to vote in the upcoming election?
2 Suppose one of the citizens is refusing to eat and adamantly insists that she wishes to starve to death. Should the state intervene and force her to eat?
3 Should all members of society be allowed to enter and exit personal relationships at will?
4 Should the state be allowed to impose a comprehensive religious doctrine on all members of society?
5 During military service, an individual will be prevented from fully participating in society for nine months. Should this individual be compensated by the state for their role in national defense?
6 Scientists have identified a genetic trait in humans that reveals how compatible their native talents and abilities are with the rest of society. A low compatibility score means that the individual will have diminished life chances. Should individuals who have a low compatibility score with respect to the new Mars society be redistributed and placed in a different society (where their compatibility score is higher) instead?
7 There is a shortage of human organs available for transplant, which means some individuals waiting for a transplant will die. There is a minimally risky procedure to harvest non-vital organs from a living donor, although the donor will undergo a painful recovery from the surgery for three weeks. Supposing that individuals are prohibited from receiving compensation for organ donation, how would you estimate the likelihood that individuals would choose to donate an organ on a scale of 1–10, with 1 being unlikely and 10 being very likely?

Group B—Instructions

Breaking news! In light of recent technological advancements, a new human civilization will be built on Mars. While you will remain on Earth, you (and the other members of your group) have been selected to design the foundational principles for this new society on behalf of its new inhabitants. The new inhabitants will consist of diverse individuals, including adults and families with children, parents, grandparents, spouses, and more. In shaping the societal structure, your decisions should prioritize the well-being of all members of the community, recognizing the importance of caring relations and the way individuals are interconnected and dependent on one another. You should carefully consider how you will justify your choices to the new inhabitants.

Discuss the following questions within your group for forty-five minutes with the aim of reaching consensus:

1. There will be an upcoming election to nominate a leader for the new Mars society. Should all inhabitants be allowed to vote in the upcoming election?
2. Suppose a child is refusing to eat and adamantly insists that she wishes to starve to death. Should parents be allowed to intervene in cases like this and force the child to eat?
3. Should all members of society be allowed to enter and exit their family relationships at will?
4. Should parents be allowed to impose their comprehensive religious doctrines on their children?
5. During pregnancy, women will be prevented from fully participating in society for nine months. Should mothers be compensated by the state for their role in reproduction?
6. Scientists have identified a genetic trait in newborns that reveals their compatibility with adult caregivers. A low compatibility score will result in the child having diminished life chances. Should children be redistributed at birth and placed with those adults who will parent them best?
7. There is a shortage of human organs available for transplant, which means some individuals waiting for a transplant will die. There is a minimally risky procedure to harvest non-vital organs from a living donor, although the donor will undergo a painful recovery from the surgery for three weeks. Supposing that individuals are prohibited from receiving compensation for organ donation, how would you estimate the likelihood that individuals would choose to donate an organ on a scale of 1–10, with 1 being unlikely and 10 being very likely?

Rationale behind the questions:

1. Drawing inspiration from Virginia Held's paper "Non-Contractualist Society: A Feminist View," this question highlights how adults and children may not be entitled to equal rights (e.g., the right to vote), even if they are entitled to equal respect (Held 1987).

2 Similarly inspired by Virginia Held's work, this question highlights how our obligations to one another cannot be fulfilled by non-interference in the case of child rearing (1987, 1993).
3 Drawing inspiration from Anne Alstott's book *No Exit: What Parents Owe Their Children and What Society Owes Parents,* this question challenges the idea that voluntary, contractual relations are an appropriate model for parent–child relationships (2005).
4 This question raises a challenge for the basic liberties that should be afforded to individuals in a state vs. family context, particularly freedom of religion. It often leads to a lively discussion about the extent to which parents may legitimately shape their children's values.
5 For Group A, this question is about inequality in the distribution of benefits and burdens of cooperation, where national security is generally thought to be a socially recognized good. For Group B, this question is posed as a matter of whether pregnant persons should be compensated for their role in reproducing society. This leads to an interesting discussion of whether reproduction is a socially recognized good and whether motherhood is "its own reward" despite the inequalities that result. The version of this question posed to Group B draws inspiration from S.A. Lloyd's paper "Toward a Liberal Theory of Sexual Equality" (1998).
6 For Group A, this question brings to light questions of justice between societies rather than focusing solely on justice within a society. For Group B, this question draws inspiration from the "redistribution challenge" which is a proposal to redistribute children at birth to those adults who can do the best job raising them for the sake of justice. This prompts a discussion of whether individuals are fundamentally separate and detached as opposed to connected as the mother–child relationship seems to demonstrate. The version of this question posed to Group B draws inspiration from the work of Virginia Held (1987), Barbara Katz Rothman (1995), and Anca Gheaus (2012).
7 This question reveals the extent to which altruism can be expected to promote social goods, and prompts discussion of whether various relations in society should be characterized by care rather than mutual disinterest.

While the two groups are likely to provide conflicting answers due to the different background conditions they were asked to imagine, there is also a possibility that the groups may reach certain conclusions that do not align with their respective prompts. For instance, Group B might estimate that individuals would be "very likely" to donate an organ despite not receiving any compensation. This outcome once occurred because the students in Group B had imagined a family member or close friend being in need of an organ, leading the group to reach a consensus that they would readily elect to donate an organ in these circumstances. By prompting students to explain their reasoning, this activity creates an opportunity for the class to reflect on how the different prompts influenced their thought processes. It lays the groundwork for exploring the importance of understanding the perspectives of authors studied in the class, enabling better interpretation and engagement with their work.

Although this activity was originally designed for an introductory course in political philosophy, its goal applies more broadly to any situation where teaching underrepresented philosophers is part of the curriculum. Specifically, the aim of this learning activity was to foster students' engagement with some of the key insights and critiques offered by feminist scholars, rather than simply introducing these ideas as peripheral considerations of canonical texts. This activity encourages students to adopt a critical lens toward canonical texts and continue contemplating alternative perspectives throughout their engagement with them. Moreover, it predisposes students to approach the work of underrepresented philosophers in a different way, as students have become more invested in tackling the issues that have arisen in previous class discussions. The benefit of learning activities like this one is that they show how the work of underrepresented philosophers need not feel like an afterthought, even if this work is only covered in the course subsequent to canonical texts.

References

Alstott, Anne L. (2005). *No Exit: What Parents Owe Their Children and What Society Owes Parents*. New York: Oxford University Press.

Brighouse, Harry (2004). "Game on Rawls's Second Principle." *Crooked Timber*, March 18. https://crookedtimber.org/2004/03/18/game-on-rawlss-second-principle/. Accessed March 1, 2023.

Gheaus, Anca (2012). "The Right to Parent One's Biological Baby." *Journal of Political Philosophy* 20(4): 432–55.

Held, Virginia (1987). "Non-Contractual Society: A Feminist View." *Canadian Journal of Philosophy Supplementary* 13: 111–37.

Held, Virginia (1993). *Feminist Morality: Transforming Culture, Society, and Politics.* Chicago, IL: University of Chicago Press.

Hobbes, Thomas, and C. B. Macpherson (1986). *Leviathan.* Harmondsworth: Penguin.

Lloyd, Sharon A. (1998). "Toward a Liberal Theory of Sexual Equality." *Journal of Contemporary Legal Issues* 9: 203–24.

Locke, John (1980). *Second Treatise of Government.* Indianapolis, IN: Hackett Publishing.

Rawls, John (2001). *Justice as Fairness: A Restatement.* Cambridge, MA: Harvard University Press.

Rothman, Barbara Katz (1995). "Daddy Plants a Seed: Personhood under Patriarchy." *Hastings Law Journal* 47: 1241–8.

33

The Clear and Concise AF Assignment: A Quick and Effective Way to Teach Basic Writing Skills

Dustin Locke

1 Introduction

The ability to write philosophical essays is a complex skill. It is difficult to say what exactly its component skills are, but some of them are just certain basic writing skills. When I refer to these writing skills as "basic," I mean that they are the kind of skills that can and should be learned prior to trying to write philosophical essays. Unfortunately, many of our students come to us without these basic writing skills.

What to do? For many years, I did what most philosophy instructors do: when I wrote feedback on student essays, I commented not just on what students said but on how they said it. In other words, I saw it as part of my job to help students with their basic writing skills, and I dedicated some amount of time to that task, but I did so *in conjunction with* helping students master what we might call the "content" of a philosophy course—that is,

---

Thank you to Alex Rajczi and Brynn Welch for their comments on earlier drafts of this essay, and thank you to Linda Nelson for writing her excellent book *Specifications Grading: Restoring Rigor, Motivating Students, and Saving Faculty Time.*

certain philosophical theories, the ability to spot logical fallacies, the habit of looking for counterexamples, and so on.

Two years ago, I tried a different approach.[1] Before asking students to write proper philosophical essays, I administered an assignment that required them to demonstrate certain basic writing skills. To my delight, the experiment was a great success: the essays my students wrote after completing my new assignment were the best I had seen in nearly two decades of teaching, and it wasn't even close.

I called my new assignment "The Clear and Concise AF Assignment," since it asked students to produce a very short piece of writing that was clear, concise, academic, and focused. While I did have to spend some time grading the new assignment, this time was offset by a reduction in the time I later spent grading essays. In other words, my students were producing remarkably better essays, and they were doing so without any net increase in the amount of time I spent helping them become better writers—a pedagogical win if there ever was one.

This chapter explains how The Clear and Concise AF Assignment works (Section 2), answers some frequently asked questions (Section 3), briefly explains why the assignment is so effective (Section 4), and addresses a common concern (Section 5).

2 How the Clear and Concise AF Assignment Works

The Clear and Concise AF Assignment is administered during the first few weeks of a course. It is suitable for both introductory and non-introductory courses.[2] The instructions are below. I cover these instructions in class, allowing plenty of time for students to ask questions.

Instructions

The goal of this assignment is to ensure that all students have the basic writing skills that will enable them to succeed in this course. By the end of this assignment, students will have the ability to produce writing that is clear, concise, academic, and focused ("clear and concise af").

This assignment embodies the "mastery learning" approach to education. In mastery learning, students are asked to sufficiently master certain basic skills (such as certain basic writing skills) before they are asked to work on more advanced tasks (such as writing philosophical essays). Unlike more traditional approaches, mastery learning is supported by hundreds of empirical studies on what works in education.[i]

This assignment is graded full credit/no credit and counts as 10 percent of your course grade: if you complete it, then 10 percent of your course grade will be an "A;" if you don't, then 10 percent of your course grade will be a zero. That might sound scary, but don't worry! You get three attempts to complete it. Also, I've been using a similar assignment in my introductory philosophy courses for over a decade, and every single student who has tried has passed.[ii]

Here's how The Clear and Concise AF Assignment works. You will have three attempts (maximum) to write a 250- to 300-word essay that is clear, concise, academic, and focused. If you succeed on the first attempt, congratulations, you've completed the assignment. If not, no worries; you have two more attempts! As soon as you succeed, you're finished, and you've earned an "A." If you feel that three attempts is not enough, you may also submit practice attempts between the official attempts, but the assignment can be completed only on one of the three official attempts. [Note to readers: students almost never submit practice attempts, since they make sufficient progress without them.]

Each of your 250- to 300-word papers **must be on a different reading** assigned for this course. You may write whatever you want to write about the reading, provided that your essay is clear, concise, academic, and focused, as defined below.

Clear writing is easy for the reader to understand. Do not assume your reader knows what you're talking about—not even which text you are referring to. For concreteness, you may assume your reader is some randomly selected high school student who has never taken a course in philosophy or anything else relevant to the topic of the text you are discussing.

Concise writing uses no more words than necessary.[iii] It takes work to write concisely: you must go through your paper sentence-by-sentence rephrasing and deleting. Part of this work is emotional work: as several famous writers have said, you must kill—that is, delete—your darlings.[iv]

Academic writing follows all of the specific instructions for the assignment—including being submitted on time, to the proper location, etc.—and uses appropriate formatting and citations. You may follow any standard academic style guide, such as the APA style guide. I do, however, have **two special requirements** here:
1 So that I know that you know how to properly cite, you must have (a) at least one properly-cited quote and (b) at least one properly-cited paraphrase.
2 You must always cite specific page numbers. If the text does not have page numbers—e.g., because it's a webpage—find another way to direct your reader to the specific location in the text you are referring to (e.g., "paragraph 7").

Focused writing does not ramble or simply list ideas—it includes only the ideas that are necessary for explaining one specific thing or making one specific argument. Focused writing takes lots of deleting, rewriting, and reorganizing. For that reason, don't waste too much time trying to figure out what you'll focus on before you start writing—that rarely works. Rather, for your first draft, allow yourself complete freedom to write whatever comes into your head. The process of writing this first draft will help you find one thing to focus on and to figure out what is relevant and what isn't. Once you've done that, light your first draft on fire and start again.

Each of your (up to) three attempts to complete The Clear and Concise AF Assignment is due on a specific date (see course schedule). After each submission, you will revise your paper in light of my feedback, which will help you understand how your paper could have been better. When you submit your next attempt, however, you will write a completely new paper on a different reading. This is how you will demonstrate that you have acquired not (just) the ability to effectively revise a paper in light of my feedback, but the ability to write papers that are clear, concise, academic, and focused.

i. Contrary to what some teachers believe, when you require students to master a skill, and give them multiple tries to do so, students consistently rise to the challenge. If, however, you allow students to earn 'C's and 'B's, some students come to believe that that is all they are capable of. Even more tragically, some *teachers* come to believe that that is all some students are capable of. If you think you are a "B"-student, you are about to learn otherwise: you are an "A"-student who has simply never been given the proper opportunity to succeed. For research on mastery learning see Taveggia 1976, J. A. Kulik 1976, J. A. Kulik, Jaksa, & Kulik 1978, Guskey & Gates 1985, and C.-L. C. Kulik, Kulik, & Bangert-Drowns 1990.

ii. In the extremely unlikely event that you do not complete this assignment, you will have the opportunity to drop the class without record.

iii. Often, you can make your writing clearer by simply making it more concise. At other times, there is a trade-off between clarity and concision. For example, some concept may need some careful explaining, and so making things more concise may actually make them less clear. In these instances, you need to find the appropriate balance between clarity and concision. Sorry about that. Life is hard.

iv. This quote is often attributed to William Faulkner, but I have been unable to confirm its original source.

End Instructions

3 Frequently Asked Questions

In this section, I answer some questions that I frequently receive from other instructors.

1 How do revisions work?

Revisions count toward the "quiz and homeworks" portion of a student's grade, which is separate from this assignment. Students are required to revise every attempt they submit, even if the attempt earns a "complete" (unless there is literally zero feedback from me). As long as the student has made a good-faith effort to revise their attempt, they receive full credit. Since I do not make comments on revisions, it takes only a few minutes to "grade" revisions for an entire class.

2 Do you give students writing prompts?

Instructors may, if they wish, give students specific writing prompts. But since the purpose of the assignment is to focus on form rather than content, I tell students they are allowed to write on any topic, as long as it is explicitly connected within their paper to one of the readings assigned in the course. I give students some examples of what they might do—e.g., explain an argument from one of the readings, relate one of the ideas from one of the readings to something in their personal life, challenge one of the ideas from the readings, etc.—but I emphasize that it is really up to them what to write about.

3 How do you have time to do so much grading?

Very little grading is required to administer this assignment. In a typical class, roughly 50 percent of the students complete the assignment on the first attempt, another 40 percent on the second attempt, and the remaining 10 percent on the final attempt. This means that in a class of N students, I grade something like $N + .5N + .1N = 1.6N$ attempts, or about 1.5N double-spaced pages in total.

4 Mastery Learning and the Power of Specifications Grading

In this section, I'll say a few words about why The Clear and Concise AF Assignment is so effective. My aim here is not to convince you to use the assignment. Whether the assignment is right for you will depend on a number of factors, including most importantly your pedagogical context and goals.

As noted in the instructions, The Clear and Concise AF Assignment embodies what educational researchers call "mastery learning," the central idea of which is that (1) students should focus on acquiring relatively basic skills before, rather than while, trying to acquire more advanced skills and (2) there should be some mechanism for clearly communicating to students which basic skills they are expected to acquire and whether they have acquired them. Of course, skill acquisition is a matter of degree, and students should not be required to "completely" master the skills in question, whatever that might mean. Rather, students should master those skills to a degree such that they can productively work on acquiring the more advanced skills. Mastery learning has been the subject of hundreds of empirical studies, and its effectiveness is beyond reasonable doubt (Guskey and Gates 1985; J.A. Kulik 1976; J.A. Kulik, Jaksa and Kulik 1978; C.-L.C. Kulik, Kulik and Bangert-Drowns 1990; Taveggia 1976).

One particularly clear way to communicate to students which basic skills they are expected to learn and whether they have learned them is to use "specifications grading" (Nilson 2015). In specifications grading, assignments are graded on a full credit/no credit basis, where earning full credit requires producing work that meets all of the assignment's specifications. Crucially, students are given multiple attempts to produce such work. When assignments are graded on a scale (such as F to A or 0 to 100), and a student receives less than the top grade on that scale, there is considerable room for miscommunication over what exactly the student has accomplished. This may be appropriate for certain types of assignments. But when the specific goal of an assignment is to prepare students with certain basic skills that are best acquired before taking on more advanced tasks, the more clearly we can communicate to students whether they have acquired the skills in question the better. Specifications grading is an excellent way to achieve such clarity.

5 Failure Is (Technically) an Option

You may be wondering how I handle cases where a student fails to complete the assignment within the three allotted attempts. The short answer is that in such a case the student receives a zero. The long answer is that *no student who has made a genuine effort has ever failed to complete the assignment.* There are two reasons why.

First, if a student has failed to complete the assignment after two attempts, I email them to come talk to me before their final attempt. During our meeting, I emphasize to them that they only have one attempt remaining and we discuss ways they can maximize their chances of success. I also allow students to submit "practice attempts," and I encourage students in this situation do so.

Second, and perhaps more importantly, I am the one who determines what counts as "completing" the assignment, and I set the standards for completion such that it is incredibly unlikely that a student who makes a genuine effort will not complete the assignment. If you were to administer the assignment and find that some students who you believe are making a genuine effort are nonetheless failing to complete the assignment within three attempts, I would advise you to lower your standards for completion. The goal of this assignment is not to "weed out" bad writers; the goal is to bring all students up to a certain minimum level of writing ability, where the nature of that minimum should depend on one's educational context. If you teach at an institution where it is simply not feasible to set any minimum whatsoever, then The Clear and Concise AF Assignment may not be for you.

Notes

1. I was inspired to do so by the success of a related assignment. See my *forthcoming*.
2. I use it exclusively for non-introductory courses, since I use a different, but related assignment in my introductory courses (see my *forthcoming*).

References

Guskey, Thomas R., and Sally L. Gates (1985). "Synthesis of Research on Group-Based Mastery Learning Programs." *Paper Presented at the Annual Meeting of the American Educational Research Association*, 1–66.

Kulik, Chen-Lin C., et al. (1990). "Effectiveness of Mastery Learning Programs: A Meta-Analysis." *Review of Educational Research* 60(2): 265–99. https://doi.org/10.2307/1170612.

Kulik, James A. (1976). "PSI: A Formative Evaluation." *Personalized Instruction in Higher Education: Proceedings of the Second National Conference*. Center for Personalized Instruction.

Kulik, James A. (1978). "Research on Component Features of Keller's Personalized System of Instruction." *Journal of Personalized Instruction* 3(1): 2–14.

Locke, Dustin (January 2023). "The Levels System: An Application of Mastery Learning." *Teaching Philosophy* 46(1): 1–39. https://doi.org/10.5840/teachphil2022418166.

Nilson, Linda B. (2015). *Specifications Grading: Restoring Rigor, Motivating Students, and Saving Faculty Time*. Stylus Publishing, eBook Collection (EBSCOhost). http://search.ebscohost.com/login.aspx?direct=true&AuthType=sso&db=nlebk&AN=1172122&site=ehost-live&scope=site&custid=s8438901.

Taveggia, Thomas C. (November 1976). "Personalized Instruction: A Summary of Comparative Research, 1967–1974." *American Journal of Physics* 44(11): 1028–33. *aapt.scitation.org (Atypon)*, https://doi.org/10.1119/1.10579.

34

Emile and Sophie on Tinder: Using Social Media as an Assessment for Philosophy

Claire Katz

Philosophy 208—Philosophy of Education

What is education? This question can be asked about both the reality and the ideal view of education: (1) what is education as we know it, that is, how does education function in our society and (2) what ought education be? To investigate these questions, we must think of education as it is practiced in both K-12 schools and the university. The vision of the university and its success depends on the vision and success of pre-college education. This class will take as its point of departure the theme that education is a way in which we "reproduce the world."

Context for the Assignment

For more than thirty years I have been teaching a Philosophy of Education course. I have taught it at every level from introductory to senior, and undergraduate and postgraduate. I usually organize this material as a relationship between treatises on education and treatises on social and political philosophy. In general, nearly all philosophers in the history of western philosophy who wrote a political treatise also wrote an accompanying educational treatise.[1] They understood that to imagine a politically ideal world is also to imagine an educational process that cultivates citizens into that world, even if it is believed, as in the case of Rousseau, one must cultivate the human being before cultivating the citizen. So one aim of the course is for the students in the class to consider at the end of the semester what kind of educational process would best promote the democratic worlds that we believe we support.

This introductory-level Philosophy of Education course attracts a diversity of students with respect to major, class year, ethnic background, gender, and hometown/state. The texts include Plato's *Republic* (in its entirety) and then selected readings from Aristotle, Locke, Rousseau, Wollstonecraft, Mill, Foucault, Althusser, Arendt, hooks, Dewey, and Freire. At the end of the semester, we discuss Jonathan Kozol's *Savage Inequalities*, which the students are asked to read in its entirety. The readings are challenging. I use three different forms of assessment since different students excel in different ways. Students are asked to write essay exams, several papers based on classroom observations, and then they do a final project. The final project, which I simply call a social media project, allows them to be creative, while demonstrating their comprehensive knowledge of the material through an unconventional form of assessment. I inaugurated this assignment in Fall 2016, and it has generated some of the best works I have ever received from undergraduate students.

Let me provide some additional information about the course before moving to the social media assignment:

> **Classroom Observations:** I require my students to conduct three classroom observations and write a short paper for each. Of the three observations, one must involve a visit to a K-12 classroom, while another must involve a college class (though not one in which they are currently enrolled). The third is their choice. Regardless of which class they observe, the first paper, which is due shortly after the semester begins, is typically superficial. The students do not yet know what to look for. By the time they write their third paper, however, they notice that a gifted teacher not only asks questions, but also asks certain *kinds* of questions, those that engage their students intellectually. They notice not only if students are engaged, but also if the engagement is still only student-teacher. They notice how gender differences may have an impact on how a teacher interacts with her class. And so on. In their third paper, more impressively, they seamlessly weave into their writing the philosophical theories they have learned over the course of the semester.

Essay Exams: I include two in-class essay exams. The exam generally has two parts—identifications and two essays, which include a shorter essay and a longer more general essay. I typically provide a series of guide/study questions from which I pull the exam questions. The exams are straightforward and intended to gauge reading comprehension, the ability to make an argument, and frequently to compare/contrast two or more thinkers.

Final Project: The final project for the semester requires the students to use a social media outlet to demonstrate what they have learned in the course. If they choose Facebook, for example, they may begin with an original post that is a passage from Plato's *Republic*. They could generate a thread incorporating the philosophers' views from our readings. Their projects reflect a particular theme in education that is important to them, for example, equality of opportunity. Presenting their projects to the class during the final exam period, my students reveal a part of themselves, for example, their sense of humor, which I could not have captured on an exam or in a paper. All the materials and the assignments lead up to the final assignment, a social media project. They must do a presentation as part of the project.

Social Media Project: Philosophy of Education (PHIL 208)

For all my courses, I want my students to learn to read carefully, think creatively, and write well. I also want them to demonstrate at the end of the course that they have a cohesive understanding of the material. However, in this class I did not want to give a traditional final exam. Instead, I created an assignment that played to my college students' strengths and gave them the freedom to demonstrate what they know using a non-traditional format: a social media project. (See Appendix*.)

For this assignment, the students are asked to teach the class about a theme or a figure in philosophy of education. The catch? They must use a form of social media to accomplish this task. They may do a podcast or a mock-up of, for example, a Facebook page or use images through Instagram. The requirements are as follows: they must incorporate five to seven figures, out of about fifteen (depends on the semester) that we covered in class (with special attention to any thinkers who were not included on the third exam); they must do a presentation and answer questions from the students and from me; and they must demonstrate a sustained dialogue among the figures (not a set of random unconnected citations). That is, they must demonstrate *integrated and comprehensive* knowledge of the topic. This assignment is worth 20 percent or 25 percent of the overall grade, depending on how I construct the syllabus that semester.

The students can work individually or in a group. The groups are formed in different ways. In some instances, students who know each other or met during the class form a group. In other instances, students ask me to facilitate the group formation. For the latter, I will typically use the kind of social media platform they want to use to organize the groups; for example, those who want to do a podcast in one group, etc. If they work in a group, I ask them to keep a "labor log," to mitigate issues that may arise later where one person did not do any of the work in the group.

Presentations

All projects, whether done individual or in a group, must be presented to the class. I arrange for the presentations to be done during the time slot when we would have had a final exam. Scheduling in this way provides two hours, which is enough time to get all the presentations done. I ask the students to allow for five to seven minutes for the presentation. This is an introductory-level class, so while I want the students to have the experience presenting, I don't want them to be terrified. The format for the presentation varies by project. If the project is a podcast, the individual/group might elect just to play the podcast, or part of it, and then discuss what they did. A Facebook page might require more explanation as they share the discussion threads. One pair of students did a series of interviews about different philosophers and talked through each episode. Beyond providing enough explanation of what they did and how it satisfied the requirements for the project, the students do not have to satisfy other requirements for the presentations. I could imagine in future iterations requiring students to ask questions of their peers, but I do not as of yet do that.

I first introduced this assignment in Fall 2016 and with some tweaking of the assignment each semester, these projects/presentations remain among the best pieces of work from students I have received for this course. They are funny, clever, and smart. They demonstrate, in a way that I might not capture on a paper or an exam, that the students have a comprehensive understanding of the course material. And they allow the students to connect the material to a contemporary issue. For example, some students will begin the Facebook or Twitter post by using a current article as the prompt and then bring in both historical and contemporary thinkers to respond to the article. They add their own comments to the thread. They frequently bring in other philosophers to "hijack" the thread as one would see in a Facebook post. In Fall 2019, a group of students did a set of podcasts covering a variety of themes in the philosophy of education. They were so tremendous that I have encouraged them do a set of podcasts comprising interviews of the faculty in the philosophy department about their current research. Another group began their project with Tinder descriptions for Sophie and Emile, the two young people in Jean-Jacques Rousseau's treatise on education. It was nothing short of brilliant and I still chuckle when I think about their presentation. I grade the assignment primarily on satisfying the requirements: a minimum number of philosophers incorporated into their project that demonstrates that they understand the connections among the different thinkers and that indicates a comprehensive understanding of the material from the semester. Course evaluations are done prior to the completion of this assignment but students will frequently write me to express how much they learned from this project—from the additional research to the integration of the material into a coherent presentation. They also enjoyed the freedom to be creative— and funny. When I ask them what I should change or what I should keep in the class, they uniformly respond that I should keep the following: reading Plato's *Republic* in its entirety; doing the classroom observations and the corresponding paper assignment; and the social media project.

Appendix

PHIL 208: Philosophy of Education
Social Media Assignment

*I distribute this and then have a lengthy discussion about it. I also provide class time over the course of the semester for students to work on the project. Finding time to work with other group members outside of class can be challenging.

You have a variety of options to pursue for this project: blog post with comments, simulated Facebook page or original post with comments, Twitter exchange, YouTube video, Instagram, etc. You are welcome to consult with me if you have concerns or questions about how to pursue this assignment. You may work in a small group or by yourself. If you work in a group, you should have a means to ensure that everyone does his/her fair share of the work.

You will present what you did on XX date (date and time our final exam is scheduled).

The presentation need not be done by everyone in the group, if you are working in a group. You should count on about five to seven minutes, depending on how many presentations are being done. I'll be able to give you a firmer time limit once I am sure of the number of groups.

Because we are doing this project instead of a final exam and since there is not a third exam to test the final third of the material, you must include at least one figure/thinker from the last part of the semester.

You should aim to have five to seven different thinkers represented, but you need to make sure that you include any thinkers that were not included on the last exam.

You can be funny, serious, etc. but please be respectful. Keep the language PG or G ... ☺

If you have something that you want me to copy and distribute, send it to me and I'll make copies for the class. If you need it distributed ahead of time, for example, you did a blog post, send it to me and I'll forward to the class.

The idea is to be creative and have fun. The bulk of the grade will come from three things:

- The number of figures you are able to incorporate; for example, if you only do one or two, your grade will decrease.
- How well you can show an understanding of the material from the course that you can put these thinkers into dialogue with each other.
- How much you are able to incorporate other ideas—current events, articles, current trends in education, etc.

You need not have one overarching philosophical argument—as most social media threads demonstrate; there are often smaller side discussions that take place.

If you need me to help you arrange a group, let me know.

Note

1. Here are some examples: Plato's *Republic*, Aristotle's *Nicomachean Ethics*, Erasmus's *The Education of a Christian Prince*, Kant's *On Education* and the catechism at the end of the *Metaphysics of Morals*, Locke's *Some Thoughts Concerning Education*, Rousseau's *Emile*, Hegel's *The Phenomenology of Spirit* (is frequently read as an extension of *Emile*), *and* Mill's *The Subjection of Women*. Most political treatises have embedded in them or adjacent to them an idea for how the individual will be educated into the society.

35

On Writing Fun, Joyful, Open-Ended Exams

C. Thi Nguyen

The last interaction we have with our students is often the final exam. For many of our general education students, this will be the coda to their only brush with philosophy, or even all of the humanities. The final exam is the grand finale. What taste do we want to leave them with? Do we want to transmit the sense that philosophy is a dreary thing, forced on them from the outside? That doing philosophy is trying to meet some imposed external standard, where what looms in their head most strongly is the sense of possible failure? Or do we want to leave them with the sense that philosophy is a live thing, that it can play with new topics—that it matters, and that it can, in fact, be fun?

I have, over the years, come to deeply change my approach to writing exams. I used to write these very stern exams, whose primary goal was to strictly evaluate the students' mastery of the material. My goals, back then, were to deprive the students of choice, to force them to explain each and every bit of key argument from the class. What mattered most was to write an exam that they couldn't weasel out of, that they couldn't conceal some gap in their knowledge.

But my goals slowly changed, and so did my exams. Now I try to write exam questions that are funny, startling, and open-ended. I want to end the

---

Parts of this essay originally appeared on the blog *The Philosopher's Cocoon* on December 11, 2018; other parts originally appeared on the blog *Daily Nous* on August 9, 2022.

class on a lovely note. I want their final structured activity in my class to exemplify the virtues and joys of thoughtful investigation. I give them weird questions—present them with funny situations, novel problems, and new and thought-provoking arguments. I give them a wide range of questions to choose from, so they can pick exactly the topics that get them the most excited. And I give them questions that are open-ended—that I don't know the answer to. And I tell them so explicitly. And the exams are still good as assessment tools. But I'm willing to trade away a bit of perfect assessment, in return for an improved transmission of the philosophical mindset.

Many of us have come to think that good pedagogy is not just about the transmission of information. It is also about trying to encourage a mindset, to foster intellectual virtue. And part of the way to foster that virtue is to model it in the classroom. Instead of just laying out what we think is the right theory, we make a show of open-mindedness and thoughtfulness. We push for dialogue, we speak our worries out loud, and we flip sides in the middle of class. We visibly enact the process of reflection. And for many of us, we try to make the process enjoyable—thrilling, fascinating, and full of wonderful epiphanies. (My students find it particularly striking when they find a hole in an argument I've given, and I react with joy and excitement.) And many of us do it, not just because we feel pressured to entertain our students, but because we are trying to transmit the possibility of finding joy in thinking. But many of us, I find, abandon all that when it comes to exam design. In our exams, we become pure beasts of assessment.

One of my graduate school advisors used to caution against thinking that the only purpose of grading was to render a judgment of student abilities. They said:

> Imagine that you're grading. You give both Dennis and Kate a B on their first papers. But after you've sent out the grades, you realize you'd made a mistake. On further inspection, Dennis' paper is actually worse than Kate's; he actually deserved a B–. Now their second papers come in, and both Kate and Dennis improve a bit on their second paper. Now what grade do you give them? If you value fairness, you should give Kate's paper a B+, and Dennis' second paper a B—the grade it deserves and that's in line with the grades for the rest of the class. But then you won't be performing another vital function of grading. You won't be signaling to Dennis that he has improved; you won't be visibly rewarding his increased effort and skill. Fairness here asks you to give him a B, but many of our other educational goals say you should give him a B+. So what should you do?

I expected them to say: give Dennis the B, because you've got to be fair. But what they actually said was: "Well, it depends a lot on the specifics of the situation. But, in many circumstances, the right thing to do is give Dennis the B+, because the educational signaling function of grading is often more important than strict fairness."

This blew my mind. Because I had never actually separated out those two functions before. There was just this one edifice in my mind: grading. And the presumption was that grading always had to be maximally fair, that that was what the whole thing was for. But grades, they were saying, aren't just for assessment. They can also be used as a teaching tool—a way of communicating to the students, of signaling to them that they're doing better or worse. And I think that line of thinking also applies to how we design exams. Assessment is only one function of an exam. Exams are a structured activity for the student, where we direct them to think in a certain way and about certain problems. They are yet another tool we have to suggest certain intellectual attitudes. And the final exam occupies a very special place. It is the final taste many of our students will have of philosophy. It is the source of that last lingering taste. If we can use tests to get students to *like* philosophical reflection, to *enjoy* critical thinking, to leave feeling that philosophical reflections *matters*, then we should—even if it sometimes comes at the price of a perfectly fair assessment.

So here's the nitty gritty, I teach a lot of introductory ethics and introduction to philosophy. Many of my students are first-generation college students. Many of them are taking the class only to fulfill a requirement. On the very first day of class, I describe the purpose of the class, and tell them exactly what the exams will be like. I warn them, before they're committed to the class, that the exams will be unusual.

The purpose of the class, I tell them, is primarily skills acquisition. They're going to learn to argue, analyze, dissect arguments, and reflect on their own beliefs. Learning particular philosophers and theories is secondary. To that end, I tell them, all my exams have a very particular structure. One-third of each exam is simple questions that check that they did the reading and came to class. These are multiple choice or short answer. The other two-thirds of the exam is going to be a wide array of, frankly, weird and goofy exam questions that will throw new situations and new theories at them, and ask them to apply theories from the class to new ideas and dilemmas. (I also tell them I'll give them plenty of opportunity to practice thinking of their own solutions to things over the entire class.)

For the actual exams, I always offer them a wide range of questions from which they get to choose the ones they're most interested in. And I make most of the questions *open-ended*. It means that I write questions that I don't know the answer to, where I can see all sorts of arguments and approaches, and I don't have even the faintest clue of what the right answer would be. Often the questions ask them to invent new policy or a new theory. I tell them that I have intentionally written questions that I have no idea what the answer is. The point is not to test for agreement with me, but to let them show off their abilities to think for themselves. (I have to tell them this explicitly and repeatedly. Most of my students have an incredibly hard time wrapping their heads around the idea of an open-ended exam question. If they aren't regularly reminded, they can get freaked out during the exam when there's no obvious "right answer.")

There's a hidden sting here, of course. Take a question like, "*What would Aristotle and Susan Wolf think of Instagram culture, and what advice they would give us for living with social media? Which do you think is closer to the truth, and why?*" In order to answer that, they'd first need to, of course, supply an adequate summary of the relevant bits of Aristotle's and Wolf's theories of ethics and value. It's still a pretty fine assessment tool. But the important part is that the end-points of the analysis are up to them. They get to figure out what Aristotle would actually think of Instagram culture, which is a pretty hefty and substantial extension of what they learned in class. And they get to pick a side.

What's most important to me is the spirit of the question. First, the question conveys a sense of the flexibility of philosophy, and its ready applicability. Second, it gives students a sense that they have some intellectual agency in the matter. And third, I hope that the novelty of the questions, and the broadness of the topics, will inspire a sense of curiosity and excitement. It will, I hope, leave them with a sense that the philosophical theories we've learned are alive and flexible, and deeply applicable to their own interests.

I offer them lots of questions. Like, I'll offer them ten possible questions, from which they get to choose three. Again the point is to move away from the sense that the point of the exam is to catch them out and trap them for what they missed, and encourage, instead, a sense that the exam is letting them exercise their own curiosity and interest. They get to choose to write where their strengths are – they get to pick which topics jazz them up the most. (I also offer some very straightforward, traditional questions. The vast majority of the students prefer the novel questions, but a small number are afraid of them, and prefer straight-up regurgitation questions. I also tell them that the standards of precision are higher for regurgitation questions, and that I'm more forgiving for the creative questions. Students seem to accept this as fair.)

The goofy questions are actually surprisingly easy to assess. A student's critical thinking capacity is on clear display when they have to cope with a novel topic. And the more you leave room for students to be inventive, you might discover that your students can actually surprise the hell out of you. I am, in the grading process, occasionally entertained, and even inspired. But there is clearly at least one trade-off between fairness and openness. This kind of exam does not do as well as a traditional exam in assessing the completeness of a student's knowledge. A student who missed some of the lectures and never learned some of class material can certainly game the question set to hide the gaps in their knowledge. (Though, if you fix the range of theories attached to each question cleverly enough, then they can't get away with an excessive number of gaps.)

My questions vary in their style of novelty. Some are obvious variants of in-class examples, but with a bit of spin and silliness on them. ("*Suppose the Fox Network proposes a new reality show where they'll let felons fight to the death on live TV, but they promise to donate half the proceeds to anti-crime charities. What would philosophers X, Y, and Z think of this solution, and why?*") Some of the questions are genuinely and deeply weird. ("*Suppose genetic engineers propose to solve the problem of animal rights by creating a new species of cow that desperately wants to be eaten, and begs for it ... *") Some of the questions introduce some new subtlety to a case they know of. Some of the questions present radical political proposals that they haven't heard of before, but which they can apply what they learned in class to. (I typically steal these from applied and political policy. I particularly like to surprise them with Hugh LaFollette's argument that, based on the logic of driver's licenses and physician's licenses, we should also demand a license for parents. And then ask them to analyze the proposal using some philosophers we read.) And some are more practically minded—like asking them to apply some philosophy of technology we've read and propose new regulations to improve social media platforms.

The questions are meant to be a range of things. Some are goofy and weird, some are about pressing political issues. They are meant to present genuinely fascinating thickets and tangles—and to offer students an enjoyably wide choice space of different modes of intellectual interestingness. No question can do all these things. But the point is for an exam to present them with a menu of possibilities. Then, their experience of an exam, especially of a final exam, is not one of authority and fear, but of possibility and of choice. The final exam is supposed to be an opportunity for them to exercise their intellectual curiosity.

And the results are delightful. I get a steady stream of students coming up to me after the final exam, with a vague look of pleasant bewilderment on their faces, to confess to me that they had, against all expectation, enjoyed the exam. They tell me they found it interesting, that they had fun, that they found the questions exciting and thought-provoking. Sometimes they wanted to meet with me later to talk about the exam questions, just to find out more. I hear students in the hallways after the exam still working out what the answer should be. They leave excited, with their appetites whetted for more. And that seems pretty important to me.

And recently, I've been trying out this approach with their final papers. I was teaching a first-year "great books" seminar, doing the *Tao Te Ching*. During the class discussion, I asked my students to imagine what a truly Taoist school might be like. They said, there would be no central authority figure. There would be no grading. Students could pursue whatever paths interested them. There would just be resources available for them to explore, to play around with. I asked them why our educational system wasn't like that. They said, it must be because our educational system was more about evaluating them, getting them to fall into line, than about actually helping them grow and develop.

They were getting super excited. Then one of my students said, "Professor? Could we do that? Could we just do whatever final project we wanted?" The whole class was vibrating with enthusiasm. My syllabus had the usual final term paper programmed in, but the students were boiling over with other ideas. An animation student wanted to animate some of the poems we'd read; a women's studies student wanted to write a feminist updating of "The Wife of Bath's Tale."

And I froze. Because how the hell was I supposed to grade this stuff fairly? I didn't want to just point-blank refuse, but how in god's name could I issue meaningful grades to an animated movie, a critical paper, and a film script? We'd been extolling the virtues of creativity and open-mindedness, originality and adaptability, and here I was about to embody the bureaucratic authoritarian. I was about to tell them: "You cannot do this thing that you love and are excited by, that actually integrates with your life path and goals. Because *I could not grade you fairly*."

So I let them design their own final projects: whatever format they wanted, so long as it engaged with the class material in an interesting way. I had them pitch me their ideas, and we negotiated a project that would satisfy both of us. And what I got was completely amazing. About a third of the students did the standard term paper. The rest went wild. I got a short film, and a podcast about Homer's concept of heroism. A ceramicist tried using traditional Japanese ceramics methods that she'd never used before, and kept a diary, informed by Japanese aesthetics texts we'd read. The women's studies student gave me a (sharp, hysterical) screenplay updating the Wife of Bath, called *The Wife of Wall Street*.

The trade-off here is like the trade-off with the exams, but even more extreme. What the students gain is the ability to integrate what we were doing with their own career paths, their own animating values. They get to exercise their creativity and their intellectual autonomy in choosing the path of their projects. They got to listen to their sense of curiosity, or push the project in the direction that seemed to matter to them. But these projects are even harder to grade with anything like perfect fairness.

I don't always do projects like this. The original setting was a particularly good one since my classroom mandate was to encourage engagement and critical thinking, and not to cover material. Right now, I'm doing open-ended projects like this in my upper-division aesthetics and design class, but not in my introduction to philosophy class. (Though I have started to tell students that they can, if they want, pitch me some alternate project to the usual final paper.)

A lot depends on the goals of the class. There is certainly a trade-off between the value of fair evaluation and the value of these more open-ended approaches. And I'm certainly not saying that fair evaluation is entirely unimportant. But I think it is important to remember that fairness in assessment is but one of many possible goals in the classroom. We have choices in sculpting our exams and final projects. That choice involves making a complex set of trade-offs. In the past, I had unthinkingly gone all-in for fairness and left other pedagogical values on the wayside, in designing my assignments. But we have a choice—and sometimes that choice is really a choice between evaluating our students, and teaching them.

36

It's Not "Stephen's Final" Project

Stephen Bloch-Schulman

I am convinced a class has not really worked well any time I hear a student refer to the class as "Stephen's class" or the work as "Stephen's" (e.g., "I need to finish Stephen's paper," "I really like Stephen's final assignment"). To the extent that students think of the class or assignment or work as *mine* or *about me*, they remain distanced from the experience and the learning. They might do what is required, but their valuing of the work remains limited. (Note: relatedly, I don't describe classes as "mine" or "my class" but as "the class I teach" or something similarly recognizing of the work as a shared enterprise.) While allowing students to select their own topics for a paper, for example, might move in this direction, I find it moves the needle only little and often unhelpfully. In my experience, students often struggle to understand how to ask the kinds of questions that work well as the basis for a philosophy paper. And we rarely teach question-asking skills that would allow them to better understand how to do this well.

But even if they could well determine appropriate topics, scope, and questions for their work, I don't see that as sufficient because the work is still written for and submitted to me for my assessment. I want students to be excited and proud of their work, to do work that they really want to show off, that is meaningful to them and that they are excited to talk about with their classmates, certainly, but even more—with their friends, in their other classes, and with their parents and guardians.

I will add that I have been really impacted by a study done by Lee Shulman (no relation). He was, for many years, the head of the Carnegie

Foundation for the Advancement of Teaching. He was also a professor at Stanford worried about the paucity of learning in higher education. He and his colleagues did a study wherein they simply gave a group of Stanford graduate students (not a group disinclined to take classes and classroom learning seriously) their own college transcripts. Unsurprisingly, many spoke in great detail about many of their classes, faculty, and what they learned. There were many classes where the learning was quite hazy. But to me what was important—both stunning and totally recognizable—was that there were classes graduate students had taken that they literally did not remember having taken, at all. While Shulman admits rightly that that does not mean that these students didn't learn anything in those particular classes, it does ask us to question the standard model of teaching (Shulman 1999). To me, it speaks to the need for wildly innovative, creative, and (if nothing else) memorable classes. And it speaks to the gap between our hope for what students are learning and what their experience and learning really is. I always set out to teach in ways that are, at the very least, highly memorable.

Finally, I believe in backward design because of its commitment to students and student-learning. Typically, faculty design backwardsly by thinking of the skills or content they want students to learn and work backwards from those skills and that content to fill in the semester with activities that will help students acquire (or improve) those skills and that content knowledge. I typically do not do that. There are, in any class, a world of different skills and content that would, in my view, do students right. I often teach a political philosophy class and find it just as impactful to teach them close reading skills as it is to teach summarizing skills, and so on. I could name maybe ten skills I think could be the focus of such a class. And I think of the content (to whatever extent I do think of content), also, as incredibly wide-open: a class on Latin American philosophy of Liberation, a class on Black Power, a class on feminist theories of power, etc., all would be excellent and do students well.

So, I typically do not think that there is one skill (or skill set) or one content set that fits with any class type. I do not, therefore, backward design toward skills or content acquisition. Instead, I backward design by designing a series of events or a final outcome, a final project, in one way or another, something big and audacious and challenging that will anchor the class. And it sometimes doesn't work. But it is "dare-to-be-great" and, I believe, it is memorable.

For example, in the Rap, Race, Gender and Philosophy class I have taught, I often end the semester with a final event wherein students perform, in groups, original rap music (they can use already available instrumental background music, but they need to write the lyrics and perform them live) that summarizes the class themes. They also annotate, RapGenius style, their lyrics, offering hyperlinks and further details about the lyrics they have written. And I don't require that these final projects be performed in any but the standard forum for final presentations—in class, with only other students and me present. But students in the class want to share their work, the class vibe, and the experience with others. So, while I don't require it or even suggest it, students regularly ask if they can invite their friends to their final exam and their friends attend and love it. In one iteration, a student in the class who was a musical engineering major and worked the sound board at a local bar, on his own, reached out to the bar owner and got the bar space during our final exam period. Students thus performed their music on stage, to a rather large crowd of friends. It was a concert of their own making. The Rap class is, at its heart, a class about ownership—about who owns city space, who owns music, who owns the bodies of others, and who owns culture. And the songs they had written and crafted lovingly were about deindustrialization in the New York City of the early 1970s; about Black Capitalism in rap music; about whether white people should rap (or teach classes about rap!);[1] and about sampling and its ethics[2]; among other things, thinking through ideas from Tricia Rose, bell hooks, Michelle Alexander, John Locke, and Lewis Hyde alongside other philosophers like Malcolm X, Martin Luther King, Jr., Immortal Technique, Brother Ali, and Kendrick Lamar. And the performance was an enactment of them taking on, for themselves, responsibility for making the final something fun, profound, and highly memorable. It was their own statement about community and ownership, one that questioned the traditional boundaries of private and public, property and collaboration. I will add: it was a not a class where I dreaded, for a single moment, grading the final exams. (This too, I take as a sign of a class that has gone well and one I teach toward: final projects or exams or assignments that I look forward to reading or seeing.)

I have, in this class, now started a project with Graham Pelligrino, who was a Teaching and Learning Apprentice, and Jakman, a librarian.[3] The TLA was a musical engineer/philosophy major who had taken the rap class previously, and the librarian, Jakman, is part of the library staff and is overseeing an internal grant at Elon for the production of open access educational materials because of his concern about the exploitive business model of academic publishing.[4] We got a grant from the Student Government Association and reached out to colleagues at other institutions including Robin Zheng and Christina Hendricks to think through what such a project would mean. The idea is that, over several iterations of the class, students will, in small groups, write articles that will take the place of the other readings. This means that the quality of the work needs to be quite high (and to help students produce such high-quality work, significant scaffolding of the project is provided throughout the semester). The semester ends with a meeting of the students, who decide which of the essays they think should be part of the textbook, and an outside board consisting of other people knowledgeable about rap and philosophy. Together, the students and board decide on a few essays to include in the open access textbook. By producing something that will be used by others (rather than submitted, graded, and forgotten by both students and faculty), the work takes on a greater import. Additionally, the structure of an open access textbook calls into question material conditions of the lives of students in just the way the class is intended to show, and is a major theme of some (and often the most politically conscious) rap music. Thus, the more formal content goals of the class (to think about property and ownership and how it matters to rap—for example, in the ownership of samples) is furthered by engaging in questions of ownership; for example, which photographs can be used in an open access textbook and what the process for getting access to photos looks like (our initial answer: easy to do, it just costs $600 or $800 and a signature for a newspaper photo from 1976).

In this backward design process, I start with the thing I want students to *do* or *achieve* (rather than specific skills or content) and I work backward to ask myself: what do they need to know and know how to do to be successful in that project? And then I structure the classroom and homework activities so students can be successful meeting the challenge I have set for them.

This process is, for students, often daunting because I am asking them, from the beginning of the semester, to do something by the end that they do not know how to do. Or that they believe they are bad at. And the learning we do in class, therefore, has a real charge to it: they need to know it because they want their final project to be good, or at the very least, they don't want to have to show off work they don't believe in. The work is real, public (often), and becomes meaningful to them in a way that goes beyond the classroom. Often, they end up doing extra work on such projects (e.g., writing their own beats). It also means that the learning isn't directly focused on the content and skills of the class, but on using the content and skills toward something else that remains the focus of our attention throughout. I am not testing content knowledge and skills directly. I am giving them a task that they can only achieve by having already learned the content and skills and utilizing them in the service of a project they (and their friends and often family) and I think is worthy of them.

Like other pedagogies, this pedagogy doesn't always work. Interestingly, there is often a clear feeling, for me and anyone I co-teach with (I often co-teach with students and staff), of a "race against the clock." That is, this model of teaching increases in intensity as the demand for authentic engagement nears—as the final exam which will be at a local bar, sans adult beverages, where students will perform their exams as rap performances in front of their friends and other invited guests; as a monologue in the coffee shop on campus. Imagine the tension rising in the class I taught, a Senior Seminar centered on Shannon Sullivan's *Revealing Whiteness: The Unconscious Habits of Racial Privilege*, where I invited her both to offer a lecture for the department and to attend the student-conference where students presented papers about her work to the department faculty, to other students (both in the Senior Seminar and in our Methods of Philosophical Inquiry lower-level class) and to Sullivan herself; and sometimes ones critical of her work, to boot.

There is often a moment when the whole thing becomes clear to a student or to the class: "oh, he *actually* means that we are going to do that thing!" But sometimes, it is only while other students are presenting that a student sees they are too late to take real advantage of the opportunity that they have; and sometimes this occurs even later than that. Sometimes, students never see it. And when they aren't seeing it yet, there is a real gap between what I am asking them to do and how I am asking them to engage and what they think I am asking, or what they are willing to do to engage. When it doesn't really work, most often, it means the thing just fizzles: that they do it, but without it ever mattering to them.

One way this plays out is particularly interesting and important, in my view. Often, getting to an idea worth working on and sharing, a student (or the whole class) needs to try out some ideas and work with them a bit before it is clear that the ideas will not really work. And when students feel stuck, kind of knowing that their ideas don't work but unable, yet, to come up with a better one, or feeling like the time they put in was wasted or that they don't have enough time to do the required revisions, or they see me as trying to trick them, as if *I* really know what I want and have hidden it from them, and it can cause feelings of antagonism toward me. And sometimes they just really give up, at that point, no matter how much encouragement I offer. But more often than not, they do keep working, and when they do, they do come up with an idea that is unforeseen by me and them that they love and are really excited about. This is a moment of unimaginable magic; and it feels to them, they say in different words, like they are explorers who have finally come upon the treasure that was buried within themselves the whole time.

Notes

1. For more, see Stephen Bloch-Schulman, "When Privileged Teachers Set Out to Teach about Privilege to (mostly) Privileged Students," published with Arianne Payne's blog post "A student wonders who should be teaching a course called 'Rap, Race, Gender, and Philosophy.' Can a white male professor do the job? If so, how?" on *The Blog of the International Journal of Feminist Approaches to Bioethics*, July 16 and July 18, 2018, available at: http://www.ijfab.org/blog/2018/07/pedagogy-part-2-privileged-teachers-teach-about-privilege/.
2. I write this note on a bittersweet day: the very day that De La Soul's work finally!!! is able to be streamed, having been held up since 1989 because of copyright issues, having been the subject of a Teen Titans Go! Episode about these issues, and having just lost one of their members, David Jolicoeur (Trugoy the Dove, Plug Two) having died just about two weeks ago.
3. Unlike a teaching assistant or graduate assistant, who often enact a plan created beforehand by the professor they are working with, a Teaching and Learning Apprentice is a collaborative role for a student with the explicit goal of the TLA learning about philosophy pedagogy. TLAs often include a syllabus for their work focused on reading and research in relevant philosophy pedagogy research and, often, their own final project is creating their own syllabus. Graham Peligrino goes by the name of Graham Prichard to most people, and Jakman is known as Jesse Akman in most contexts.
4. Note: in the rap class, we only use rap names. I typically have no idea what students' given names are who take the class. I know them as H-Dot and MamaPayne, as EmC2 and Big Zo. And they know me as DadRock, a moniker I was given by my children because I am ride-or-die with the Beastie Boys.

References

Shulman, Lee (1999). "Taking Learning Seriously." *Change* 31(4): 10–17.

Sullivan, Shannon (1999). *Revealing Whiteness: The Unconscious Habits of Racial Privilege*. Bloomington, IN: Indiana University Press.

37

A Student's Reflections

Micah Williams

It is rough to be a philosopher right now. I've been preparing myself to accept this reality throughout my undergraduate journey, but as a postgraduate, I didn't expect reality to feel so unreal. Politicians and justices are currently overturning fundamental human rights (Chamberlain, O'Neill and Hicks 2022). The concurrent epidemics of Covid-19 and gun violence have left hundreds of thousands of people dead, and many more traumatized (Elamroussi, Yan and Andone 2022). The United States has become more of a carceral state[1] than ever—to our bodies, mind, history, and future. And as a student of philosophy whose concentration was in ethics, it is revolting to see people debate whether certain persons should exist. As an individual who intersects some of those marginalized identities being debated, the effects are debilitating. Mournful, even. I cannot fathom the repercussions that the nation's decisions have on women and those who give birth, Native Americans, and the trans community, among others.

The thing about being a young philosopher is that I wish I could turn my brain off sometimes. I wish I could fly away and escape beyond the reprieves I take from social media and the news. However, when you've been trained to think, and to think critically, you cannot help *but* to think, return to the discourse, and come back to Earth. You recognize that if you're a human in society, there is no true escape from the politics that shape said society. And you know that when you can think enough, you can at least reflect and get yourself together to effectively speak and do. Thanks to the privilege of academia, one avenue in which I can say something is through this keyboard.

I graduated from the University of Alabama at Birmingham (UAB) with a Bachelor's in English and Philosophy. I attend the University of Rochester as a doctoral student in English but still retain "philosopher" as an aspect of my scholarly identity. However, compared to literary analyses and my primary space of African American literature, philosophizing has always been something I've wrestled with.

Western philosophers, in particular, have not had the greatest takes concerning social justice. Thus, being a philosopher today means acknowledging that some of our "faves" are problematic. My Ethical Theory class taught me about how modern-day philosophers have reconsidered these ethical dilemmas well enough to make it worthwhile, but it nevertheless frustrated me to read the original theorists of deontology, consequentialism, and virtue ethics while knowing they weren't made for a Black person like me.

Take John Stuart Mill, for instance. His principles did not apply to children or "those backward states of society" who weren't as "civilized" as Western societies ([1859] 2017: 19). The famed philosopher Immanuel Kant defended scientific racism and detested "miscegenation," stating that Black people had no talents whatsoever compared to Whites—the only one of his four races with potential for perfection. Philosophers such as David Hume and G. W. F. Hegel also interweaved racist ideologies into their theories. I speak mainly on racism, but many of the philosophers of the past made no space for women, trans, and non-binary individuals (who certainly existed), or even those affected by poverty in the utopias they were envisioning (Baggini 2018).

Since that class, my views on philosophy have broadened. Western philosophy and I still have beef, but I've found other philosophers who've inserted themselves into the dialogue to challenge, recontextualize, and improve upon the classics. Feminism, Critical Race Theory, Queer Studies, and Social Justice literature are inherently philosophical, at least for me. But sometimes, I wonder if they share equal spaces in our canon.

For a moment, consider Philosophy Street: the Ancient Greeks—Plato, Socrates, and Aristotle—own the first house built here. Hume, Kant, Mill, among others built their houses along this street later. Over time, we built homes for more philosophers like Marx, Benjamin, Foucault, Rawls, Nozick, and Singer.

Then, we finally made (smaller) homes for Beauvoir, Wollstonecraft, Haslanger, Nussbaum, Card, and Butler, who were once crammed together in a house at an offshoot fork at the end of the road. The homes of DuBois, Hall, King, Shabazz (X), West, Yancy, Appiah, and Shelby are crammed together in that same offshoot now. Those who didn't fit in the house were kicked from the street and erased from the map. And as for the homes of

Davis, Spillers, Collins, Lorde, Hartman, hooks, Wynter, and Crenshaw? If any of them are on the street, they are hardly on the map at all, even with continual updates.

Let's not forget the philosophers we never allowed to consider moving onto the street, and also the distinctions between what is analytic and continental in the discipline. Those I've mentioned are only a sliver of the many philosophers across the world I still don't know about yet. Perhaps a few of the houses not mentioned are not there because they would challenge the existence of such a street. Though all these homes share foundations in creating a worldview that's as consistent as possible, it was philosophers challenging canonization that helped me gain appreciation and perspectives on a philosophy for the consideration and inclusion of all. We shouldn't keep our discourses contained on one street. Seeing how they placed themselves in dialogue inspires me to do the same—to involve myself with the canonical and the contemporary, and the blurring of those into discourse and dialogue.

Philosophy is cultivating a love for thinking (and articulating those thoughts) better. If I wanted to maneuver in the discipline, I had to develop and defend the views in my own mind rather than regurgitate someone else's thoughts for an exam. Be damned if it wasn't nuanced to some degree with counterarguments and understanding views other than my own. This conflicts with how we generally engage with fundamental issues now, where folks confuse philosophy with politics. Yes, philosophy can intertwine with politics for sure, hence the sector of Social and Political Philosophy. But in politics, where one is attempting to compromise both public and private spheres to solve all the issues in the world immediately or else, nuance means complication. Complexity in politics is usually defined as uncertainty, and uncertainty invokes fear. Thus, answers tend to be simplified into black and white, left or right, and maintaining stasis for a narrowed set of goals.

Politics expects to have an end, perhaps at the ballot or with a major legislative measure. The goal of philosophy is not to win, though. It's impossible to lose or win an ongoing dialogue. Dialogue is conversation. At times, it can be a debate, but it can also be compromise, innovation, or even a space of release.

Dialogue is engagement that's not just regulated in the classroom. Whenever I read philosophical literature, I am actively in dialogue with its authors. There's not an opportunity to take on the voice of the Other or to simply be a spectator because the voice in the back of my head is always talking—whether he's confused, inspired, or unconvinced. Philosophy allows me to become a voice in the Dialogue, and to engage in discussion with other philosophers. Most importantly, it is ongoing.

What I learned from philosophy is that engaging with Dialogue in a constructive way means constructive engagement with others as well as with oneself. Individually, philosophers attempt to alleviate their "cognitive dissonance" in this sort of internal struggle one goes through to make sure one's worldview and ethics align as much as possible. And then there's the external struggle of collaborating with others who think differently, and perhaps the polar opposite, of you. I learned the importance of both Dialogues at my time at UAB. It's important for philosophers to face their potential cognitive dissonance head-on with others, in hopes to be share views and explore truth through means of reason and reflection.

All of my courses helped to produce Dialogue through articulating our thoughts beforehand through short writing assignments or making notes on the material and then coming to class to discuss the material with each other. Not only is there a deeper connection between the students and professors in the roundtable environment, but it also makes students feel as if our contributions matter. It reminds us that our philosophy professors fight the same mental hurdles we do to pinpoint and resolve dissonance when it hits them. Just as much as we learn from them, our inputs are important enough for them to listen and respond to us as equals in the Dialogue (even when we're not equals professionally).

Engaging in this work of Dialogue takes enough willpower to cringe at our old selves and challenge our present selves. That requires a type of critique that many people fear now because we have associated having inconsistent views with being a corrupt and wrong person. Inconsistency is not evil, but it's in our best interests to reevaluate ourselves when learning new information and perspectives. Answering our past selves assists engagement with our dissonance to help resolve the philosophical cacophony of our worldview. When we don't evaluate ourselves in this manner, politics and social media capitalize on the cacophony to stir debate rather than Dialogue.

My frustrations with general discourse, then, stem from those who consider themselves detached from Dialogue. Or worse, they enter debates intending to undermine the political and philosophical engagement of those who want better for the present and future. If there's anything philosophy has taught me, it's that *nothing* is simply apolitical. I know plenty of people who have argued with me on this before, and even for those who take part in arguing, they reveal to themselves how political everything is.

The personal is philosophical, as it is political. Whether popularized by feminist Carol Hanisch, her editors Shulamith Firestone and Anne Koedt, or the "the millions of women in public and private conversations," this phrase has been recontextualized to mean what goes on in our most intimate, private lives shapes much of what we see in society. Philosophy courses taught me how to articulate what I always knew: there were no ways for me and my identities to transcend[2] the political and just pretend it didn't exist. I further learned that transcendence doesn't even work for even those with the most privilege. To feel as if current political trends don't affect you is still political, in that the current politics fits your personal well enough at the cost of others.

We are all people of multiple identities and lives, so we are inherently tied to the political system in a society. Thus, the decisions we make, and especially choose not to make, matter. Not so much as whether to make a PB&J now or wait for an Uncrustable[3] to thaw out, but of whether we choose or choose not to take critical, philosophical stances that affect entire groups of people, especially those most marginalized.

Many people I know do not want to involve themselves in Dialogue because they hate choosing the lesser of two evils. I empathize with that: side-taking in American politics, at times, feels like picking the left or right side of a Twix bar. But that's where nuance, engagement with others, resolving cognitive dissonance, critical thinking, and other values come in. I do not consider my opinions and values on the state of the world to be mere side-taking if I've done my part in trying to unravel these complicated issues. Rather, these political, philosophical stances interlock with my personal worldview, which can change and solidify based on the information I gather, the mistakes I make, and the views that I learn from others.

Last, I believe it's always been in philosophy's nature to expand and explore alternatives; I can agree or disagree with Hegel or Kant to craft another perspective that I can then share and discuss with others. This is what I must constantly remind myself of as an aspiring academic, or in general, a civilian who wants to make change in my community. This is the doing that gives me hope, and one of the key drivers of this hope is in philosophy and Dialogue. In Dialogue, we don't really have many enemies, but our greatest would most definitely be our own hubris, undergirded by our fear to resolve our dissonance—dissonance that makes it that much harder to listen to the philosophical currents that set the course for action.

Notes

1. By carceral state, I take from author Hari Ziyad's definition; America has consistently proven itself as a nation built upon *carceral logics*: "beliefs rooted in policing, punishing, and incarcerating the socially undesirable and in locking up those who don't fit neatly into this society's binary definitions of selfhood" (2021: 7).
2. My use of "transcend" comes from the philosopher George Yancy's idea of "transcendental norms:" the phenomena that privileged identities (particularly as whiteness) seem to abstract themselves from politics and society, and thus are seen as the ideal standard of humanity, rather than a category of humanity. Virginia Held's "Feminist Transformations of Moral Theory" assisted me in understanding this transcendence as it comes to gender and maleness.
3. A delicious invention of smooth peanut butter and honey/jelly-of-choice, filled into a white-bread shell. Can potentially chip a tooth if attempted to eat while frozen; any inquiries into my knowledge about this are closed.

References

Baggini, Julian (2018). "Why Sexist and Racist Philosophers Might Still Be Admirable." *Aeon*, November 7. https://aeon.co/ideas/why-sexist-and-racist-philosophers-might-still-be-admirable. Accessed March 1, 2023.

Chamberlain, Samuel, Natalie O'Neill, and Nolan Hicks (2022). "Clarence Thomas: Court 'Should Reconsider' Gay Marriage, Birth Control." *New York Post*, June 24. https://nypost.com/2022/06/24/court-should-reconsider-gay-marriage-birth-control-clarence-thomas/. Accessed March 9, 2023.

Elamroussi, Aya, Holly Yan, and Dakin Andone (2022). "What We Know and Don't Know in the Texas Massacre." *CNN*, June 3. https://www.cnn.com/2022/05/25/us/uvalde-texas-elementary-school-shooting-what-we-know/index.html. Accessed April 28, 2023.

Harper, Douglas (n.d.). "Etymology of Philosophy." *Online Etymology Dictionary*. https://www.etymonline.com/word/Philosophy. Accessed August 11, 2022.

Held, Virginia (1990). "Feminist Transformations of Moral Theory." *Philosophy and Phenomenological Research* 50: 321–44.

Mill, John Stuart (2017 [1859]). *On Liberty*. Auckland: The Floating Press.

Steiner, Mike (2017). "Cognitive Dissonance and Philosophy." *A Philosopher's Take*, April 5. https://aphilosopherstake.com/2017/04/05/cognitive-dissonance-and-philosophy/. Accessed January 21, 2023.

Yancy, George (2015). "Through the Crucible of Pain and Suffering: African American Philosophy as a Gift and the Countering of the Western Philosophical Metanarrative." *Educational Philosophy and Theory* 47(11): 1143–59.

Ziyad, Hari (2021). *Black Boy Out of Time*. New York: Little A.

Part IV

What Comes Next

38

The Why and How of Mentoring in Undergraduate Philosophy Teaching

Emma Prendergast

In what follows, I'll discuss strategies we can use to position ourselves to form good mentoring relationships with our students. These strategies are especially important for philosophy teachers, because the classes we teach often put us in a great position to get to know our students and establish the kind of trust that makes a mentoring relationship thrive. We facilitate class discussions on intimate subjects—how we should live, what we can hope for, and what we can believe. We learn how our students think and what they value. Students often leave philosophy classes with renewed understandings of themselves and the world they inhabit, and as their teachers, we may seem like sensible people to ask for guidance about how to move through that world. So, we ought to think carefully about how to be good mentors and why it's important.

Why Students Need Good Mentors

Mentoring relationships make a huge difference in the lives of college students even past graduation. In a Gallup-Purdue study, college graduates who "recalled having a professor who cared about them as a person and encouraged them to pursue their dreams" were twice as likely as others to be engaged at work and to thrive in other aspects of their well-being (Ray and

Marken 2014). Mentoring by college teachers has a positive impact on student persistence and academic achievement, especially among minority students (Crisp and Cruz 2009). Upward socio-economic mobility is restricted in many parts of the world—especially the United States—but research shows that upwardly mobile adults often have cultural guides, including teachers, who help them understand the workings of institutions, give advice, and intervene at critical moments (Lareau 2015). College students, especially underprepared and disadvantaged students, benefit immensely when they find a professor who is willing to serve as a mentor—someone who gives support, shares expertise and cultural knowledge, and guides the mentee through new and challenging circumstances.

A challenge is that college professors by and large come from highly privileged backgrounds, meaning they may have less in common with their less privileged students, meaning they are less likely to see these students as potential mentees. In *Lean In*, Sheryl Sandberg (2013) describes dreading the question "Are you my mentor?" from young women in the workplace, saying:

> If someone has to ask the question, the answer is probably no. When someone finds the right mentor, it is obvious ... Chasing or forcing that connection rarely works, and yet I see women attempt it all the time. When I give speeches or attend meetings, a startling number of women introduce themselves and, in the same breath, ask me to be their mentor ... The question is a total mood killer—the equivalent of turning to a pensive date and asking, "What are you thinking?"

This passage from Sandberg makes me cringe a little bit, imaging vulnerable women seeking help from a powerful figure who inspired them, only to be told they are looking for help in the wrong way. But there is some truth to the idea that effective mentoring relationships are those built on authenticity and that organic relationships take time, common interest, and personal investment to build. Add an unequal distribution of cultural capital to our tendency to form friendships, and mentoring relationships, with people who are like us (e.g., in the case of college professors, privileged), and you should start to see a problem. There are no easy solutions here, but what I'd argue is that we must situate ourselves and our students such that we can build relationships with students from a plurality of backgrounds—not just the students who find it easy to approach us.

Some professors may opt to get involved in student extra-curriculars, spend more time chatting with students before and after class, or aim to teach smaller-sized courses that enable them to get to know their students better. At the very least, professors who are unaccustomed to mentoring undergraduates must become psychologically at ease with the idea of mentoring students whose background experiences are alien to them. Two practical steps I encourage philosophy teachers to consider taking include (1) emphasize office hours and (2) prepare to provide references and letters of recommendation.

Strategy 1: Emphasize Office Hours

Authentic mentoring relationships can develop during office hours and one-on-one meetings. Often, the students who readily attend office hours already know how to get their needs met by the institution they attend. (I was not surprised one recent semester when the first student to show up to my office hours mentioned that one of her parents is a college professor.) Less advantaged students may not realize that office hours can be helpful, and they may be intimidated by the thought of a one-on-one conversation with a professor. Indeed, many disadvantaged students may even be unaware of the point of office hours.

In *The Privileged Poor*, Anthony Jack recounts testimony from a college administrator, who said, "I made a discovery two years ago ... that many of my [lower-income] students interpreted 'my office hours' to be just that, my hours to spend in my office alone, [where] I was not to be disturbed" (Jack 2019: 83–4). When professors are not clear with their students about what office hours *are* and do not encourage students to attend, students from disadvantaged backgrounds are placed at an even greater disadvantage. Asking for help and finding mentors help students gain access to resources and accommodations, but part of the hidden curriculum in higher education is that "students are expected to ask for help ... But not all students have had a chance to learn how to navigate mainstream institutions like colleges before they actually enter them" (Jack 2019: 126).

To help students understand this crucial role for office hours—and get them comfortable coming to you to ask for help—you can ask your students to show up to office hours early in the semester for a brief meet-and-greet and offer course credit for it. Students who meet with you early in the semester are more likely to come back, and students are much more likely to be engaged and ask questions once you've developed a one-on-one rapport.

Crucially, I find that when I require students to attend my office hours, they are more likely to talk to me when they're facing a barrier to their success, rather than simply dropping off the grid. The office hours requirement can also be built into your course assignments—I often require students to meet with me for a one-on-one conference about an upcoming essay. The result is that my students write better essays, I get to read better essays, and we have an opportunity to get to know each other. Students tell me that these meetings are helpful, and many return for future (not required) meetings. This strategy can help mitigate student fears that professors will be annoyed when students show up at office hours—by incentivizing office hours, we can make it clear that not only will we not be annoyed, we will reward them for it.[1]

Strategy 2: Prepare to Provide References

Suppose you emphasize your office hours and you develop some good relationships with your students. What may well happen next is that many of these students will feel that you've gotten to know them well enough to write them a letter of recommendation or to serve as a reference. This brings me to my second strategy for effective mentorship—we can do things to prepare ourselves to be good references and letter writers.

Harry Brighouse has a lovely blog post at *Crooked Timber* that explains some great strategies for references and letter writers, and I recommend reading it in full.[2] Importantly, Brighouse emphasizes conducting classes in a way that will help bring out job-relevant traits in students—like collaborative work—and encouraging students to discuss other things they do, like volunteering and interning, through which these traits will be revealed. This way you can speak to those things when your student is job seeking or applying to professional school or graduate school. In addition, here is a crucial excerpt from Brighouse (2016):

> Asking for a letter of recommendation is easy for some students but it's hard for others, and my anecdotal evidence is that this ease and difficulty are not unrelated to social class background. But even for students who are not inhibited by their undue deference, I have found that some are inhibited by the relationship—especially if I know them well, they do not want to make

the relationship seem instrumental (even though, to some extent, it is—they NEED a professor to know them well enough to write them a letter, and if I am that professor they shouldn't waste that opportunity). So sometimes, indeed increasingly often these days, I pre-empt the request by pointing out to a student that I am in a good position to write them a letter, and say that when the time comes I will be happy to do it. This is especially important, I think, for working class, and especially minority working class, students who find it difficult to ask, and are not necessarily being urged by their parents to build the relationships with professors that yield letters. It usually works. If a student does ask and seems embarrassed I always point out to them that (though I am entirely untrained) it is my job to write letters, but then add that I would be glad to do it even if it weren't my job.

We can be upfront with our students about our willingness to write them letters of recommendation and encourage them to tell us about this need early on so we can begin collecting ideas for a letter. I never forgot my high school history teacher who informed us on the first day of class that he will gladly write us letters of recommendation for college, but we should make sure to do great work in his class so he would have great things to say about us. As a very shy student, this early assurance that someone would be willing to vouch for me—and that I didn't need to feel weird to ask for it—made a big difference. I worked hard in that class, and the teacher wrote me a letter. An important part of preparing to serve as a reference for students involves preparing our students to ask us to do it.

Mentoring Strategies in Practice

Drawing from my experiences, here are just a few examples of putting mentorship methods into practice.

First, in a large lecture course of eighty students, I tested out the office hours assignment. For credit, students simply had to show up and say hello. In a large class such as this, there may be scheduling concerns with this type of assignment—some students may not be able to make it to the scheduled office hours. In this semester, most students were able to attend at the usual times, and I had very few students who needed to schedule a time to meet outside my usual office hours. It was easily doable. If there had been very many students who couldn't make it at the scheduled times, that would have been a challenge in terms of my workload. The potential problem could be mitigated by polling students early in the semester to see if the timing of office hours fits with most students' schedules, or rescheduling office hours in the event that very many students have scheduling conflicts. This assignment could be a challenge for overworked teachers, but it also presents an opportunity to investigate whether our office hour schedules are inclusive enough for our students.

Many students attending my office hours for credit took the opportunity to ask questions about the course or inform me about accommodations they needed. One of these office hours has stuck in my memory. Four students arrived at roughly the same time. I asked them if they had any questions. One student chimed in, "I don't have a question—it's more of a concern."

The student went on to tell me that he was concerned that I was teaching the class wrong! He was a business major taking the course to satisfy an ethics requirement for his program. He explained that his business professors in large lecture courses typically lectured for the full hour, while I was using quite a bit of class time for discussion activities. He explained, "This discussion stuff you're doing—that's really what a discussion section with a TA is for."

To be honest, the conversation stung me a bit. Two of the other students said that they agreed that it was too much discussion for a lecture course. The imposter syndrome I was already confronting as a woman graduate student teacher heightened at the thought my students thought I didn't know how to teach correctly in a lecture hall. If not for my office hours assignment, I wouldn't have even known. I tried not to feel defensive as I explained that discussion activities were an important way we're learning in the course. The students seemed skeptical.

Three of them parted ways, while the fourth, Isaac, who had been quiet, hung back. I asked Isaac if he had any questions and if he shared the worry the others had raised. "No, I don't have a problem with how you're teaching the class," Isaac said. "I was wondering about something else." To my great relief, he had a philosophical question for me: "Do you think people need to believe in God to be moral?"

I told him it was a great question and asked him what he thought about it. He had a lot to say. This kicked off a discussion that we sustained until my office hours ended. We talked about religion and morality, and also the ethics of doping in sports, drug legalization, and euthanasia. Near the end, he told me about what he wanted for his career. He told me his dreams differed from the dreams his father had for him.

This office hour meeting sticks out to me as an important one. First, it clued me in that my class would benefit from an intervention to clarify the point of the discussion-based methods I was using in the lecture hall. I hadn't yet realized that my students had a perception that the teaching and learning wasn't going well in class—some students thought there was too much discussion going on. These types of active learning activities are widely recognized as superior to passive learning methods such as the traditional lecture. However, students often *perceive* that lectures help them learn better compared to active learning activities. Deslauriers et al. (2019) attribute the mismatch between student perception of learning and actual learning to the sustained cognitive effort involved active learning. Active learning is *hard work* and makes students aware of their own confusions. It's both why it works so well and why students are often resistant to it, including the students who expressed their concerns in my office hours. In comparison, when students hear a teacher deliver a lecture with great fluency and command of the subject, students can be misled into feeling that they increased their own understanding, even though assessments show otherwise. Deslauriers et al. (2019) recommend coaching students early in the semester to address student misconceptions and persuade them that they benefit from active instruction. After realizing that my students held misconceptions about active learning, I started the next class with this kind of intervention. It resulted in substantially more buy-in during my discussion activities.

Second, I made an important connection with Isaac, who was capable and intellectually curious but struggled with his classes that semester. At some point Isaac stopped attending lecture. He was missing in-class assignments and losing points. Before I had the chance to reach out to him, he found his way back to my office hours. He told me flatly that he had not been going to class, and I said I had noticed and was worried. He elaborated, "It's not just your class. I've been skipping all my classes. I did this last semester, too."

He told me that at a certain point he gets so far behind that it doesn't seem worth it to start trying again. He failed a number of courses this way. But it wasn't too late to succeed in my class—he just needed to start showing up! I told him so. He told me he had never reached out to a professor in this situation before. He'd never been to any office hours but mine. Once he started failing a class, he thought it was game over. We came up with a plan for him to reach out to his other professors to figure out what he needed to do to get through the semester. Isaac was back in class the next meeting and every one after that. He passed the class.

Another example, in a small class of about twenty, I assigned one-on-one paper conference meetings with students. The meetings made their papers better, but they also allowed me to get to know the students really well, and even more so because of the types of questions we were discussing. The syllabus included units on love, friendship, marriage, and sexual consent. I learned a lot about what mattered to these students—many of them had registered for the class in the first place because the topics were important to them. One senior in the class explained, "I always said I was going to take classes in college that were *interesting* to me but I've been stuck taking classes for my major. This semester I'm finally doing it—I'm taking this class *just because it's interesting*."

I wrote letters of recommendation and served as a reference for several students in this group—for law school, medical school, seminary, and business internships. Many of them had not taken many—or any—classes where they had one-on-one contact with their professors, or in which they had the opportunity to showcase their thinking in the ways they did in our class discussions about love and relationships. It was easy for them to ask me to endorse them. In turn, it was easy for me to speak highly of their academic capabilities, soft skills, and personal qualities.

One student needed my help in another way. During a class period in which I was screening a film, Miranda approached me and asked me to step into the hallway. Once we exited the classroom, she broke down in tears. Over the weekend, she had been sexually assaulted. She had just discovered that a video of the assault had been posted to social media. Her immediate concern was getting the video taken down, so I sat with her and talked her through how to report the video to the website.[3] After Miranda filed the report, I helped her find her way to campus health services where she got additional support. She later told me the video was taken down. She also told me that I was the only adult on campus that she felt she could trust in that moment.[4]

Most universities have career centers, academic advisors, and crisis counselors. All of these resources can help a struggling student. But professors are the ones who have consistent, weekly, and (usually) in-person contact with students. We are often the first line of defense when a student needs help. We can do a better job providing it by positioning ourselves to form meaningful relationships with our students. Philosophy teachers in particular ought to do this with intention, because we are well positioned to form meaningful mentoring relationships with our students due to our intimate subject matter and the nature of our in-class engagement.

Notes

1. I am grateful to Brynn Welch for emphasizing this point.
2. https://crookedtimber.org/2016/11/29/letters-of-recommendation/.
3. I think a perfectly respectable response to this situation would have been to immediately send the student to health services—or campus safety—and have *them* help contact the website. Some student needs are better served by others, and we should know our limits. (But as a social media native I had the know-how, so I went ahead and helped how I could.)
4. Note that professors who situate themselves as mentors for their students could be more likely to receive this type of report and should familiarize themselves with mandatory reporting policies at their institutions.

References

Brighouse, Harry (2016). "Letters of Recommendation." *Crooked Timber*, November 29. https://crookedtimber.org/2016/11/29/letters-of-recommendation/. Accessed May 5, 2023.

Crisp, Gloria, and Irene Cruz (2009). "Mentoring College Students: A Critical Review of the Literature between 1990 and 2007." *Research in Higher Education* 50: 525–45.

Deslauriers, Louis, et al. (2019). "Measuring Actual Learning versus Feeling of Learning in Response to Being Actively Engaged in the Classroom." *Proceedings of the National Academy of Sciences* 116(39): 19251–7.

Jack, Anthony (2019). *The Privileged Poor: How Elite College Are Failing Disadvantaged Students*. Cambridge, MA: Harvard University Press.

Lareau, Annette (2015). "Cultural Knowledge and Social Inequality." *American Sociological Review* 80(1): 1–27.

Ray, Julie, and Stephanie Marken (2014). "Life in College Matters for Life after College." *Gallup*, May 6. https://news.gallup.com/poll/168848/life-college-matters-life-college.aspx. Accessed May 5, 2023.

Sandberg, Sheryl (2013). *Lean In: Women, Work, and the Will to Lead*. New York: Alfred A. Knopf.

39
Making Teaching Count

Britta Clark and Gina Schouten

We think teaching is an intrinsically important part of a philosophy teacher's job. With generational change and changing attitudes, the intrinsic importance of teaching is becoming better recognized within academic philosophy. But even as the profession is getting better at treating teaching as an important part of what we do, graduate students are still frequently advised against investing much time and energy into the work of becoming strong teachers. Sometimes, presumably, this advice reflects the advisor's (mistaken) judgments as to the relative intrinsic value of teaching and research. More often, we think, the advice reflects a strategic, professional calculation: Because *the profession* still does not value teaching as highly as it should, and because time spent developing one skill set can impose tradeoffs in terms of time spent developing another, well-intentioned mentors advise graduate students to deprioritize teaching in favor of research so as to enhance their prospects for success in a difficult job market.

We don't doubt that this can sometimes be sound advice. But on its own, it is not particularly *helpful* advice, because it leaves open *how much* to deprioritize teaching, relative to *what baseline*, and *what aspects* of teaching to focus on within these constraints. One way to make the advice more helpful would be to clarify those parameters. We suspect that many advisors would clarify those parameters in ways that have us deprioritizing teaching too much: that is, in ways that give inadequate weight to the interests of the students we teach in being taught well, and that overstate the tradeoffs between teaching well and our prospects for professional success. Even if the advice is only to postpone investment in teaching until one achieves professional security, this strategy comes at a high cost to the scores of students most of us will teach before we attain job security. It can also come at a cost to the graduate student herself, as graduate school can be a prime time to hone the skills needed to teach well: Our initial classroom experiences can be highly formative and generate path dependencies, and for many, graduate school affords relatively favorable access to teaching support and coaching. And of course, how much investment is needed to serve students well and what tradeoff that investment imposes with respect to professional success are matters that depend heavily on the person, her circumstances, and her professional aspirations.

For these reasons, we think the generic advice to "deprioritize teaching" is at best under-informative and at worst pernicious. But how *should* advisors guide graduate students in allocating scarce time to manage tradeoffs between pursuing research accomplishments and developing teaching skills?[1] We propose to shift the focus of our thinking about the importance of teaching in an incentive structure that still under-appreciates it. Ours is a model that focuses not on *deprioritizing teaching* but on *making teaching count*. Some graduate students might still rightly be advised to deprioritize teaching to some degree, relative to some baseline. But that context- and person-dependent advice will be more helpful, and more responsive to the claims of the students our graduate students teach, insofar as it is delivered within a framework that includes discussion of practices for making teaching count. And happily, to the degree that we can effectively make teaching count, we limit the need to deprioritize it.

In line with this shift in focus, we propose that graduate students invest in growing their teaching practice, and that their advisors support them in so investing, with a preference for strategies that meet four desiderata: The investments should aim at *genuine growth* in one's skill and confidence as a teacher; they should constitute a *good bargain* with respect to any tradeoffs they impose in terms of graduate students' prospects for future professional success; they should *show up* in the materials that prospective employers consult when evaluating job candidates; and they should work over time not to *reinforce* but to *disrupt* the professional incentives that impose the tradeoff between growing teaching skills on the one hand and prospects for professional success on the other. That is, we should look for ways to make teaching count professionally for individual graduate students on the way to making teaching count for more in the profession as a whole: on the way to making the profession value teaching for its own sake.

In the sections that follow, we explore and attempt to illustrate these desiderata. As we write, one of us is a graduate student and one of us advises graduate students, including with respect to their teaching. Our thinking on this issue is no doubt limited by our backgrounds and by the institutional context in which we teach and study. We acknowledge that "making teaching count" will look different in different contexts and that others face direr tradeoffs in this space than we do. We offer this chapter in an exploratory spirit, and we hope others will join the exploration and contribute their own perspectives.

1 Genuine Growth

Graduate students are often given blanket advice to limit the time they invest in teaching. But the advice typically stops there; in our experience, graduate students are rarely advised as to what exactly to *do* to improve their teaching, holding constant time constraints. Our first suggestion for making teaching count is that advisors take an active role in filling this educational void by encouraging graduate students to focus on improving the elements of their teaching that contribute most to student learning.

For instance, we have both heard or received the following advice: minimize the number of office hours and extra sessions you hold for students and spend this time on research instead. Yet office hour sessions are a remarkable opportunity for new teachers to hone their teaching skills in a low-stakes setting. A new teacher can toy with different ways of explaining the same material, explore which examples and explanations seem to stick with different kinds of learners, and practice facilitating a discussion where students take an active role. Importantly, research suggests that students learn more when they actively participate in well-facilitated classroom discussion, and so time invested in learning how to cultivate such discussions is time that is not merely invested in *teaching, broadly construed*, but time invested in becoming a genuinely *good* teacher (Deslauriers et al 2019). In contrast, time spent preparing line-by-line scripts for course lectures or regimented outlines for discussion sections is not, we believe, time invested in one's genuine growth as an educator, since the learning outcomes from heavily scripted, lecture-based courses and prescriptive, rigid discussions tend to be subpar.

Another example where time spent *teaching* may not be time spent becoming a *better* teacher is when new teachers provide extensive, in-depth comments on student work. Providing the kind of detailed feedback that is common in graduate seminars may overwhelm and confuse undergraduate students; pedagogical research suggests that clear and concise rubric-based grading is often better correlated with student comprehension (Wolf and Stevens 2007).

Our suspicion is that graduate students, and often the faculty that advise them, are inclined to think that teaching strategies that require *more work* are pedagogically superior, and resist alternative, less work-intensive models on this basis. But offering less-than-comprehensive feedback on student work and spending less time scripting lectures can be ways of investing in one's growth as an educator. Resisting long-held beliefs about the right way to teach in favor of pedagogically superior practices involves a different kind of labor than tediously grading and writing lecture notes, but it is work that aims at improving the experiences and learning outcomes of students. In sum, not all time spent doing teaching-related work is time spent being or becoming a better teacher, and advisors should aim to help graduate students understand the difference. This requires them to stay informed about best teaching practices. Without an understanding of what good teaching looks like, advisors will be unable to help guide students toward teaching strategies that aim at genuine growth.

2 Good Bargain

The previous section considered cases in which strategies that aim at genuine growth as an educator are in fact less time-intensive than available alternatives. These are situations in which advisors can guide graduate students in minimizing the tradeoff between good teaching and time spent on research. But tradeoffs cannot be entirely eliminated, nor should they be—even within an incentive structure in which teaching is appropriately valued, teaching and research will compete for time and attention. In light of this, we propose that part of the role of graduate advisors is to help graduate students navigate this tension within the incentive structure they inhabit. Doing this successfully might *sometimes* involve advising students to deprioritize teaching but should *always* involve thinking with students about which investments in teaching are a *good bargain* with respect to any tradeoffs they impose.

Consider a graduate student writing a dissertation on philosophy of science who has the opportunity to design and lead a course on a topic of her choosing. There is significant interest from the undergraduate student population in a course on Business Ethics, which is not taught by anyone else within the philosophy department, and the graduate student agrees that this content should be covered. But the graduate student judges that any gain in job market appeal she might derive from teaching such a class will be outweighed by foregone research accomplishments resulting from the time investment of creating the new course in an unfamiliar area. Assume she's right about that. We think that in this situation, while the time spent creating and teaching this course may well be an investment in genuine growth as an educator, it would *not* represent a good bargain when it comes to navigating the tension between teaching and research. Among other reasons, the graduate student can gain many of the benefits of curriculum design and independent teaching with a course topic closer to her areas of specialization.[2]

Importantly, what constitutes a good bargain depends on the institutional context and on the student's goals after graduate school. Navigating the tradeoffs between research and teaching may look very different for a student who hopes to teach at a teaching-focused school than for a student who hopes to teach at a research university, and different still for those who plan to leave academia. This means that graduate advisors cannot give good advice unless they understand their institutional context and check in regularly with students about their future goals.

Given the above heterogeneity, it's difficult to defend any specific principles for thinking about the tradeoffs between research and teaching over time. Instead, we propose that advisors have individualized conversations with students about navigating the tradeoffs between research and teaching. Students are asked to make a plan for writing their dissertation chapters, but rarely encouraged to make a teaching plan to ensure that they have enough experience for the kinds of careers they are interested in. Moreover, even more general blanket advice is often lacking: Students are rarely advised, for instance, to teach in areas that are relevant to their own research, nor encouraged to teach independently in one-off, low-stakes settings. We propose that part of making teaching count involves advisors and graduate students critically and iteratively reflecting together on how best to navigate the teaching-researching tradeoff.

3 Making It Show Up

Our third suggestion is to make teaching skills and growth in teaching skills show up. These days, most hirers do aim to evaluate candidates in part on the basis of teaching skill. But only when graduate students find ways to demonstrate their skill and investment in teaching can it be a professional benefit. In our view, most genuinely valuable investments in teaching can be made to show up in job market materials. In some cases, the how-to is straightforward. Perhaps it involves including a "teaching professional development" section on one's C.V. In other cases, getting teaching skill and growth to show up requires creativity, and it begins long before a graduate student starts to compose her job market materials.

Insofar as graduate instructors are skilled at facilitating student learning, they can raise the likelihood that qualitative course evaluations will attest to these successes by sharing with students just what kind of learning they aim to facilitate. Suppose we want students to reflect on the ways in which philosophical questions arise in their lives outside the classroom. If we tell them that we have this goal, and if we align our teaching in service of that goal, we not only raise the likelihood that students will attain it; we raise the likelihood that the attainment will be salient to them in their reflection about the course. This, in turn, raises the likelihood that they will mention it when qualitative evaluation questions prompt them to reflect on their learning. Now suppose the sample learning activities a graduate student submits as a part of their teaching portfolio clearly work to promote the learning goal in question. This begins to make manifest that a candidate is a reflective and conscientious teacher who successfully pursues her learning objectives through carefully crafted learning exercises.

We also think the teaching statement is an under-utilized vehicle for making teaching skills show up. Far from a collection of pedagogical platitudes, a teaching statement can be a sincere and illuminating record of one's developing thinking and growing practice. Advisors can support graduate students in developing such a statement by prompting them to think about their teaching goals and practice iteratively over several years. It is not uncommon now for graduate programs to include some pedagogy course, workshop, or orientation to support graduate students during their first teaching experiences. Advisors might invite participants to develop a "working hypothesis" about their learning objectives or priorities as a teacher. Course heads and advisors can prompt them subsequently to revisit their working hypotheses, asking themselves whether they still endorse it, how they would now revise it and in light of what kind of pedagogical insights, and how their practice aligns with the pursuit of whatever objectives they'd now endorse. Teaching statements will be more thoughtful, more honest, and more interesting insofar as graduate students have been prompted over the course of their graduate teaching years to be thoughtful and honest about what kind of teacher they want to be, what they want to help their students achieve, and how they're measuring up to their aspirations. Additionally, letters of recommendation will be more informative insofar as advisors are primed to observe and attend to graduate students' development as teachers and to their developing reflectiveness about teaching.

These ideas can seem crass. But if we're right that hirers want to hire thoughtful and skilled teachers, we should make sure that we develop practices for making thoughtful and skilled teaching show. We should also be careful to guard against insincerity. But in prompting graduate students to think about their teaching over time and in helping them think through the space in which they can find a way of teaching that feels authentic and meaningful, we can make more graduate students more thoughtful teachers even as we make thoughtful teaching show up.

4 Erode Pernicious Incentives

Thus far, we've focused on strategies that largely take for granted that graduate students should deprioritize teaching to some extent in response to the professional incentives that presently devalue it. But these incentive structures can be rebuilt and molded with conscious effort. We advise prioritizing teaching strategies that contribute to this effort.

We think that, for many of us, teaching is the most publicly valuable part of our work. For many of us, it can be deeply *personally* valuable as well, at least once we reach the point of experiencing it as the exercise of a skill. Insofar as philosophers are generally disposed to be reasons responsive, one way to change the professional incentive structure is to *make the case* for teaching as a personally and publicly valuable activity. This is a measure within the reach of those who advise graduate students and of graduate students themselves, and it is a measure we can pursue even as we invest in our teaching practice and even as we advise graduate students investing in theirs. For instance, we can expand our practices for recognizing teaching excellence and build language esteeming teaching into our recognition practices. We can also manifest our commitment to good teaching through our hiring practices. For example, asking candidates to do a teaching demonstration not only equips hiring departments better to assess candidates' teaching skills; it can expose graduate students to different teaching practices and signal the faculty's commitment to hiring skilled and reflective teachers. Departments that have yet to do so can institute pedagogy lunches, workshops, seminars, or peer advising practices, and where these measures are not forthcoming, graduate students can self-organize to support each other's development as teachers. A pedagogy peer-support measure can be as simple as organizing in pairs to watch each other teach and then meeting afterward to debrief. Done well, these practices can improve teaching in the short-term, and in the long-term help to erode pernicious professional incentives that are misaligned with the true value of teaching.

Beyond making the case for the value of teaching and normalizing practices in alignment with it, those of us with relative job security should work to offset the pernicious incentives directly within our own institutions. We can resist consciously or unconsciously under-investing in students with intense teaching interests. We can resist assuming that students with strong research skills are not interested in teaching focused jobs or that students who manifestly excel at teaching are *only* interested in teaching focused jobs. We can remind ourselves that teaching is both an art and a science, and that along both dimensions we can all grow and develop. This might mean attending and supporting APA programming on teaching, joining in when graduate students at our institutions self-organize for teacher observations, and attending teaching professional development events to raise their visibility and participate in generating a sustained demand for this kind of training and accreditation.

Finally, if hirers often *do* want to select in part on the basis of good teaching, then we should resist overstating the misalignment of professional incentives lest we perpetuate the very problem we're concerned to alleviate. Students who neglect teaching and who think it's professionally advantageous for them to do so should be disabused of what is often a strategic mistake. Meanwhile, they should be compelled during graduate school to have experiences that enable them to correct their *evaluative* mistake as well: experiences that enable them to appreciate the public value and the potential personal value of teaching.

5 Conclusion

Our discussion has focused on making teaching count within the constraints characteristic of professional philosophy, namely, the fact that teaching is often undervalued when it comes to obtaining secure employment in the field. In closing, we want to emphasize that teaching counts in ways and for purposes that are far less instrumental than our above discussion might suggest, both for the teacher and the student. Being a teacher is being part of a system, however flawed, that aims, and sometimes succeeds, at equipping the next generation with the skills to lead meaningful and flourishing lives. The practice of teaching has noninstrumental value for the teacher as well: Teachers reading this will likely be familiar with the joy of watching a student fall in love with philosophy, or the satisfaction of finally presenting an idea or argument in a way that resonates with and excites students. Finally, teaching can encourage reflection and change one's values and habits. Teachers are placed in situations where they must choose the content they deliver and the values they uphold, and the challenge of deciding how to share philosophy with students has for us often resulted in a better and altered sense of ourselves.[3]

Notes

1. We suspect that what we write about graduate students applies more broadly to those who experience professional precarity and for whom a secure position within the profession of academic philosophy is a goal. We do not intend to suggest that a secure position within academic philosophy *should* be a goal for all graduate students; many graduate students have other worthy career aspirations.
2. We do not mean to suggest that graduate students should *never* take "bad bargains." Perhaps very well-positioned graduate students are obligated to make some professional sacrifices for very worthy teaching causes. And of course, there will be situations in which teaching outside of one's area of specialization is *not* a bad bargain, because doing so would be particularly advantageous for a student's job market prospects.
3. Thanks to Brynn Welch, Harry Brighouse, and Josh DiPaolo for helpful discussion and feedback.

References

Deslauriers, Louis, Logan S. McCarty, Kelly Miller, Kristina Callaghan, and Greg Kestin (2019). "Measuring Actual Learning versus Feeling of Learning in Response to Being Actively Engaged in the Classroom." *Proceedings of the National Academy of Sciences* 116(39): 19251–7.

Wolf, Kenneth, and Ellen Stevens (2007). "The Role of Rubrics in Advancing and Assessing Student Learning." *The Journal of Effective Teaching* 7(1): 3–14.

Notes on Contributors

Karen Adkins is Professor of Philosophy at Regis University in Colorado. She teaches undergraduate courses from introductory philosophy and first-year writing, through seminars in nineteenth- and twentieth-century philosophy, feminist theory, and political and social philosophy. She was a finalist for the 2021 APA/AAPT Prize for Excellence in Teaching Philosophy and has won awards at Regis for outstanding teaching.

Zyaire Hadrian Agee grew up in a small, but culturally rich, community in Mississippi and later moved to Washington (state, not DC) before settling in Alabama. When he's not spending time with his wife (though they are both philosophically side-eyeing marriage as an institution) and his black cat who is affectionately named Bruce after his favorite superhero, Bruce Wayne (Batman), he's working (unfortunately), kickboxing, reading murder mystery novels, arguing trivial topics for the heck of it, or searching the internet for comic books to add to his growing collection! He also dabbles in provoking existential crises amongst his friends.

Rima Basu is Assistant Professor of Philosophy at Claremont McKenna College. The central theme of her research is that when it comes to what we should believe, morality is not voiceless. What we owe each other is not just a matter of what we do or what we say, but also what we believe. The central theme of her teaching is that philosophy is, at its heart, fun. When students are excited about a question, when they can see the stakes of a question, that excitement leads to engagement and to students finding their voice and realizing that philosophy isn't dead. These questions are live questions and they each have something to contribute in how the questions philosophers ask get answered.

Christopher Blake-Turner is Assistant Professor of Philosophy at Oklahoma State University. Before that, they worked for two years at the University of Alabama at Birmingham. They received their PhD from the UNC Chapel Hill. They work in epistemology, philosophy of action, and philosophy of logic. They have also served as the UNC Philosophy Department's Teaching Assistant Coordinator, and they are active in various ways with the AAPT.

Stephen Bloch-Schulman works at the intersection of political theory and philosophy pedagogy. He was the 2017 winner of the Prize for Excellence in Philosophy Teaching, awarded by the American Philosophical Association, American Association of Philosophy Teachers, and Teaching Philosophy Association. He has twice won the Lenssen Prize. He is the author, with Anthony Weston, of *Thinking Through Questions: A Concise Invitation to Critical, Expansive, and Philosophical Inquiry* (2020) and has a book forthcoming from Flip Learning which is a guide to the core skills needed for introductory philosophy students, *Philosophy for the Rest of Us*.

Harry Brighouse is Mildred Fish Harnack Professor of Philosophy of Education, Carol Dickson Bascom Professor of Humanities, Affiliate Professor of Education Policy Studies, and Director of the Center for Ethics and Education at the University of Wisconsin-Madison. His frequently-taught classes include a first-year seminar on Children, Marriage, and the Family, a large lecture applied ethics course and a case study-based class on ethics and education. His books include (with Adam Swift) *Family Values: The Ethics of Parent-Child Relationships* (2015), and (with Helen F Ladd, Susanna Loeb, and Adam Swift) *Educational Goods: Values and Evidence in Decision-making* (2018).

K. Lindsey Chambers is Assistant Professor at the University of Kentucky. Prior to this, she was a postdoctoral fellow at Harvard University and at Stanford University's Center for Ethics. She received her PhD from UCLA in 2016. Her primary research interests are normative ethics, bioethics, and social and political philosophy. She is especially interested in procreation and the family. Her main area of focus has been on the moral relationship between procreators and their offspring. In more recent work, she examines what obligations society has to procreators and parents.

Britta Clark is a PhD candidate in philosophy at Harvard University. Her research addresses a range of ethical and political questions raised by the climate crisis. In particular, she is interested in how new technologies such as solar geoengineering and carbon removal impact what climate justice demands of us. Prior to Harvard, she earned a master's in philosophy at the University of Otago in New Zealand on a Fulbright Fellowship and a bachelor's degree at Bates College in Maine.

Notes on Contributors

David W. Concepción is Professor of Philosophy at Ball State University [BSU] where he teaches feminist ethics, environmental ethics, and *Stance: An International Undergraduate Philosophy Journal* <stancephilosophy.com>. BSU Awards include Outstanding Diversity Advocate and Outstanding Faculty Service, and all four of BSU's university-wide teaching awards. National recognitions include the American Association of Philosophy Teachers' [AAPT] Lenssen Prize for research about teaching philosophy and the American Philosophical Association's [APA] Prize for Excellence and Innovation in Philosophy Programs. He is co-designer of the AAPT teacher training program, leader of inclusive pedagogy workshops, and editor-in-chief of *AAPT Studies in Pedagogy*.

Joshua DiPaolo is Associate Professor in the Philosophy Department at California State University, Fullerton. His philosophical research addresses extremism, evidence, and social epistemology. He is a first-generation college graduate committed to helping other first-generation students succeed. He has taught courses on a wide range of philosophical topics to a diverse body of students across four US public universities. He has received awards, fellowships, and grants for teaching projects and achievements. He has participated as a speaker in APA Teaching Hub sessions, and in 2021, he organized the Teaching Hub Session on "Challenges in Teaching Philosophy of Gender and Race."

Barrett Emerick is Associate Professor of Philosophy at St. Mary's College of Maryland. His research is in social and feminist philosophy, moral psychology, and normative ethics. He was a 2020 finalist for the American Philosophical Association Prize for Excellence in Philosophy Teaching and has received multiple additional awards for teaching and contributing to student life.

Karen S. Emmerman is Education Director of the Philosophy Learning and Teaching Organization (PLATO), part-time faculty at the University of Washington in Philosophy, and Philosopher-in-Residence at John Muir Elementary School. She is also Associate Editor of the journal *Pre-College Philosophy and Public Practice*. Karen researches and writes on ecofeminist animal ethics as well as pre-college philosophy (KarenSEmmerman.com).

Jimmy Goodrich is Assistant Professor of Philosophy at the University of Wisconsin-Madison. He specializes in normative ethics, political philosophy, and the ethics of technology.

Maralee Harrell is Teaching Professor with a joint appointment in the Department of Philosophy and the School of Public Health at the University of California, San Diego. Her research focuses on developing tools and curricula to teach critical thinking. She is the author of *What Is the Argument? An Introduction to Philosophical Argument and Analysis*.

Ramona Ilea is Professor of Philosophy in the Philosophy Department at Pacific University Oregon. Her research focuses on demonstrating that philosophical work can contribute to public debates and social issues. She developed EngagedPhilosophy.com with Monica Janzen and Susan Hawthorne and co-edited (with Julinna Oxley) *Experiential Learning in Philosophy*. She is passionate about the role of civic engagement in philosophy classes. Her publications on this topic include "Beyond Service Learning: Civic Engagement in Ethics Classes" (with Susan Hawthorne) and "Be the Change: Student Activism" (with Monica Janzen). She won Pacific University's President's Award for Excellence in Undergraduate Teaching.

Monica "Mo" Janzen is Instructor and Chair of the Philosophy and Humanities Department at Anoka-Ramsey Community College and a recipient of the Prize for Excellence in Philosophy Teaching awarded by the American Philosophical Association (APA), the American Association of Philosophy Teachers (AAPT), and the Teaching Philosophy Association (TPA). She has worked on faculty development at ARCC and within the Minnesota State Colleges system. She developed the website EngagedPhilosophy.com with Ramona Ilea and Susan Hawthorne and her research and writing focus on civic engagement and the scholarship of teaching and learning (SOTL).

Claire Katz is Professor and Head of Teaching, Learning, and Culture in the School of Education and Human Development at Texas A&M University where she holds the Claude H. Everett, Jr. '47 Endowed Chair in Education. She is Founding Director of P4C Texas and the Aggie School of Athens Philosophy Summer Camp for Teens and Tweens. She is the author of *Levinas, Judaism, and the Feminine: The Silent Footsteps of Rebecca*, *Levinas and the Crisis of Humanism*, *An Introduction to Modern Jewish Philosophy* and editor of *Growing up with Philosophy Camp: How Thinking Develops Friendship, Community and a Sense of Self*, *Everything you wanted to Know about Starting, Organizing, and Running a Philosophy Camp*. She teaches and conducts research at the intersection of philosophy, Judaism, gender, and education.

Susan Kennedy is Assistant Professor of Philosophy at Santa Clara University. Prior to this, she was a postdoctoral fellow in Harvard's Embedded EthiCS program where she worked with an interdisciplinary team to incorporate ethics into the computer science curriculum. She received her PhD from Boston University and a certificate in bioethics from Yale's Interdisciplinary Center for Bioethics summer program. Her research focuses on the ethical, social, and political impacts of emerging technologies.

W. John Koolage is Professor of Philosophy and Director of General Education at Eastern Michigan University. Teaching has always been near and dear to his heart. His research displays his fondness for teaching, as well as his care for general and feminist philosophy of science.

Greta LaFore is Assistant Professor of Philosophy at Gonzaga University. She is an advocate and architect of trauma-informed, Gameful and role-playing pedagogies that empower students to take ownership of their own learning with enthusiasm. With a vibrant group of student peer educators and interdisciplinary collaborators, she has held workshops in innovative pedagogies for faculty and students across disciplines. At Gonzaga, she teaches philosophy in the University Core and Honors programs.

Alida Liberman is Associate Professor of Philosophy at Southern Methodist University. Her research interests are in theoretical ethics, practical ethics, and the space in between. Her work on pedagogy has been published in *Teaching Philosophy* and *AAPT Studies in Pedagogy*. Alida received the 2022 APA Prize for Excellence in Philosophy Teaching and the SMU Altshuler Distinguished Teaching Professor Award. She is co-chair of the APA/AAPT Teaching Hub at the 2023 and 2024 Central APA conferences, a regular facilitator of Teaching and Learning Workshops for the AAPT, and a member of the AAPT Board of Directors for 2023–5.

Dustin Locke is Professor of Philosophy at Claremont McKenna College. He works primarily at the intersection of epistemology and ethics, with a special interest in moral debunking arguments and moral/pragmatic constraints on rational belief. He has published in such journals as *Philosophy and Phenomenological Research*, *Synthese*, *American Philosophical Quarterly*, *Inquiry*, *Thought*, and *Philosophical Studies*. He is also the author of "The Levels System: An Application of Mastery Learning to Teaching Philosophical Writing" (forthcoming in *Teaching Philosophy*).

Russell Marcus is Professor and Chair of Philosophy at Hamilton College, specializing in philosophy of mathematics and philosophical pedagogy. He is President of the American Association of Philosophy Teachers; the founder and director of the Hamilton College Summer Program in Philosophy, a two-week laboratory for pedagogical innovation; and a co-recipient of the 2020 APA/AAPT Prize for Excellence in Philosophy Teaching. He has published a monograph, *Autonomy Platonism and the Indispensability Argument*; a co-edited reader, *An Historical Introduction to the Philosophy of Mathematics*; and a logic textbook, *Introduction to Formal Logic with Philosophical Applications*.

Alessandro Moscarítolo Palacio is the Truax Postdoctoral Fellow in Philosophy at Hamilton College. A native of Caracas, Venezuela, Moscarítolo Palacio received his Ph.D. in philosophy from the University of Illinois, Chicago. His current research lies at the intersection of the philosophy of education, the philosophy of race, Afro-Caribbean and Latin American and philosophy, Latina feminist philosophy, the Indigenous philosophy of the Americas, and environmental philosophy.

C. Thi Nguyen was a food writer before becoming Philosophy Professor at University of Utah. Nguyen's first book is *Games: Agency as Art*. It was awarded the American Philosophical Association's 2021 Book Prize. It's about how games are the art form that work in the medium of agency. A game designer doesn't just create a world—they create who we are in that world. Games shape temporary agencies for artistic purposes. And games turn out to be our way of writing down and communicating modes of agency; by playing them, we can try out different forms of agency.

David O'Brien is Assistant Professor of Philosophy at Tulane University, with a joint appointment in the political economy program in Tulane's Murphy Institute. In 2022–3 he was a Fellow-in-Residence at the Edmond & Lily Safra Center for Ethics at Harvard University, and in 2021–2 he was Interim Director of the Center for Ethics and Public Affairs at the Murphy Institute. He has written on issues in moral philosophy (in particular, issues concerning egalitarianism and the ethics of distribution), political philosophy, metaethics, and the philosophy of education.

Heather Anne Phillips is Lecturer and Coordinator of Graduate Teaching (CGT) at Georgia State University. As CGT she leads a nationally recognized teaching training program, teaching and overseeing over forty master's students as they learn how to teach in their first year and then teach their own core course in their second year. Heather has a Ph.D. in philosophy from Rice University, master's degrees in philosophy and bioethics, and a BA in journalism from Northwestern University. Beyond pedagogy and philosophy course design, her interests lie in applied ethics, epistemology, free will, and philosophy of race and gender.

Kristopher G. Phillips is Assistant Professor of Philosophy at Eastern Michigan University. He serves as editor-in-chief of the journal *Precollege Philosophy and Public Practice*, and is co-founder of the Iowa and Utah Lyceum pre-college philosophy summer camp programs. A trained modernist, he has published broadly on Descartes, Cavendish, philosophy of mind, pre-college philosophy, the philosophy of education, interdisciplinary pedagogy, and popular culture and philosophy. An award-winning instructor, he was also a finalist for the 2021 and 2022 APA/AAPT Prize for Excellence in Philosophy Teaching.

Emma Prendergast is Assistant Professor of Philosophy at Utah Tech University. She received her Ph.D. in philosophy at the University of Wisconsin-Madison in 2023. Her research and teaching interests include political philosophy, ethics, feminist philosophy, philosophy of sex and love, and philosophy of education.

Corey Reed is Assistant Professor of Philosophy and affiliate faculty member in the Race, Gender, and Sexuality Studies (RGSS) program at Butler University. He earned his BA in English and Philosophy from Morehouse College, his MA in Humanities from the University of Louisville, and his Ph.D. in Philosophy from the University of Memphis. His specializations are in Africana Philosophy and the Critical Philosophy of Race and Racism. His work involves projects of Social and Political Philosophy, Twentieth Century French Continental Philosophy (specifically in Existentialism and Phenomenology), Black Feminism/Black-Male Theory, and Black Aesthetics.

Gina Schouten is Professor of Philosophy at Harvard University. She writes on issues of justice and legitimacy, gender, and education. Her 2019 book, *Liberalism, Neutrality, and the Gendered Division of Labor*, assesses the adequacy of a neutrality framework of political legitimacy and considers its capacity to approve political intervention aimed at eroding the gendered division of labor. Her forthcoming book, *The Anatomy of Justice*, develops a pluralist approach to theorizing liberal egalitarian justice and argues that that approach supports compelling resolutions to long-standing disputes and difficulties internal to egalitarianism, and compelling defenses of liberalism against egalitarian critics.

Rebecca G. Scott is Associate Professor of Philosophy at Harper College. She received her Ph.D. from Loyola University Chicago in 2017. Her current research focuses on the philosophy of teaching, inclusive pedagogies, and the use of play and creativity in the classroom.

John R. Torrey is Assistant Professor of Philosophy and a contributing professor in the Africana Studies unit at SUNY Buffalo State. As a public philosopher, his primary research interest is the interconnection between moral arguments for reparations for Black people and their political limits in America. He has also done work in applied ethics, philosophy of education, and pre-college philosophy. More about his work can be found at jtorreyphd.com.

Anna Ulrey is currently a medical student at UAB Heersink School of Medicine. Anna's research interests lie mainly in applied ethics and narrative medicine, and this is rooted in her desire to reintroduce the human experience that she feels is missing in much of philosophical and ethical study. Her research paper, titled "Your Patient Is a Person: A Narrative Medical Approach to Weight Discrimination in Medicine," was recently published in *Clinical Ethics*.

Meg Wallace is Associate Professor and Chair of the Philosophy Department at the University of Kentucky. Her primary areas of research are metaphysics, mind, and language. Her teaching interests include getting students to love philosophy any way she can—especially through the spectacular art of circus.

Brynn F. Welch is Associate Professor of Philosophy at the University of Alabama at Birmingham. Her research focuses on the intersection of the family with other social institutions and explores whether and when broad social justice considerations constrain what individuals may do for their family members. In 2016, she received the Excellence in Teaching Award from Emory & Henry College and the Washington County Teacher of the Year Award. In 2021, she received the Dean's Award for Excellence in Teaching at the University of Alabama at Birmingham. In 2022, she received the Disability Support Services Outstanding Faculty Award.

Micah Williams is currently a Ph.D. student studying English at the University of Rochester in Rochester, NY. Since graduating from the University of Alabama at Birmingham (UAB) with a B.A. in English and Philosophy, Micah's research interests center on exploring and highlighting the ways African American literature, media, and philosophy contribute to social justice efforts—especially along the lines of race, gender, and sexuality. In 2022, Micah received the President's Diversity Champion Award, the Outstanding Student Award in the Philosophy Department, and the Dean's Outstanding Undergraduate Student Award.

Index

active learning 82–3, 131–4. *See also* jigsaw lesson; learner-centered
activism 31–3
activity. *See also* jigsaw lesson; playfulness
   civic engagement 209–16
   floating chair 132
   prisoner's dilemma 261–6
   think aloud 125
   think/pair/share 125
   and underrepresented philosophers 273–8
Adkins, Karen 4, 13–21, 342
advising 333–9. *See also* mentor(ship)
Agee, Zyaire Hadrian 5, 91–4, 342
agency 211. *See also* autonomy
agents of change 85–90. *See also* empower
argument diagram
   for collaboration 230 (*see also* partnership; trust)
   for reading 229–30 (*see also* skills)
   for review 231–2
   for revision 232
   for writing 231 (*see also* skills)
argument mapping. *See under* games
assessment
   design 7–8
   of dispositional growth 190–4 (*see also* dispositions)
   fairness 298–303 (*see also* deadlines)
   self-assessment 122, 221–4 (*see also* discussion)
   virtues 197–206, 211–15, 298

assignment 15–19, 41–6. *See also* assessment; deadlines; games; grading; feedback; relativism
autonomy 130–6. *See also* agency; empower; expertise

backward design 82–3, 306–9
Basu, Rima 4, 41–8, 342
Blake-Turner, Christopher 4, 7, 49–56, 217–26, 342–3
Bloch-Schulman, Stephen 6–8, 167–71, 253–60, 305–11, 343
Brighouse, Harry 6, 8, 139–44, 269–72, 326–7, 343

canon 25–7, 33, 200. *See also* dialogue; freedom; syllabus; texts; underrepresented
Chambers, K. Lindsey 4–5, 69–75, 343
circus 57–68
civic engagement. *See under* project
Clark, Britta 9, 333–41, 343
Collaboration. *See under* argument diagram
Community. *See also* circus; gratitude; trust
   building 45–6
   epistemic 116–17
   of knowers 106–7 (*see also* diversity)
   of philosophical inquiry (CPI) 162 (*see also* philosophy for children/P4C)
Concepción, David W. 7, 140, 189–96, 344
content selection 4–5. *See also* texts

cooperative learning. *See* jigsaw lesson
core curriculum 69–73
creativity 302–3. *See also* circus; dispositions; playfulness; spectacle
Critical Race Theory (CRT) 31, 86
critical thinking. *See under* skills
curiosity 192–3, 196 n. 1, 300–3. *See also* dispositions

deadlines 49–55
de-center(ing) 13–19, 132, 162. *See also* empower
de-colonize. *See under* syllabus
dialogue 23–37, 168–9, 197–205, 314–17
DiPaolo, Joshua 7–8, 261–8, 344
Disadvantaged 136, 324–5
discussion
    assessment 221–4
    -based learning 183–5
    moves 149, 151 n. 6, 219–21 (*see also* playfulness)
dispositions. *See also* assessment; virtue(s)
    charity 178–9
    cultivating 6–8
    growth 189–95
    humility 161–2, 173–81
diversify. *See under* syllabus
diversity 37–8 n. 2, 106–7, 200. *See also* syllabus
Dotson, Kristie 25–6
Dungeons & Dragons (D&D). *See under* games
dynamics
    gender 139–44, 154
    power 102–3

embodied 58
Emerick, Barrett 6, 111–18, 344
Emmerman, Karen S. 6, 161–6, 344
empower 129–36. *See also* agents of change; autonomy; partnership
engaging students. *See* dialogue

evaluations 338. *See also* advising
exam(s) 297–303. *See also* assessment; project(s)
expertise
    faculty 130–6
    student 15 (*see also* jigsaw lesson)

failure 62–3, 148–9, 287. *See also* empower
fairness 52–3, 298–303. *See also* assessment; deadlines; exam(s); project(s)
feedback 203–5, 281–2, 335–6. *See also* grading
Fink, L.D. 102, 108, 209
floating chair. *See under* activity
freedom
    anchoring 23–37
    student 45–6 (*see also* exam(s); project(s))
Freire, Paulo 6, 13, 24–5, 102, 111–17, 290

gameful learning 153–7. *See also* games
games
    argument mapping 148–9
    Dungeons & Dragons (D&D) 41–8, 259 n. 1
    role-playing 41–8, 148–9, 154–7
gender. *See under* dynamics
general education. *See* core curriculum
goal-centered learning 77–83
Goodrich, Jimmy 6, 97–100, 344
GradeCraft 156
grading 43–5, 155–6, 286. *See also* assessment; exam(s); fairness; feedback; project(s)
gratitude 167–70. *See also* shout out
growth mindset 121–2

Harrell, Maralee 7, 227–34, 345
hooks, bell 24–5, 28, 92, 103, 108, 307
humility. *See under* dispositions

Ilea, Ramona 7, 209–16, 345
introductory course 14–19, 23, 70, 135. *See also* general education; texts

Janzen, Monica "Mo" 7, 209–16, 345
jigsaw lesson 235–43
job security 18–19, 31, 89

Katz, Claire 8, 289–95, 345
Kennedy, Susan 8, 273–9, 346
Koolage, W. John 6, 101–9, 346

LaFore, Greta 6, 153–9, 346
learner-centered 49–55, 101–4. *See also* empower
learning
    environment(s) 126, 145–52, 183–5
    goal(s) 120–5
    lab 147, 150 n. 1
    objective(s) 189–95, 201
lecture 97–100, 113–14, 328–9, 335–6. *See also* trust
letters of recommendation 326–7, 339
Liberman, Alida 6, 119–28, 346
Locke, Dustin 8, 281–8, 346
logic 235–43

Marcus, Russell 6, 7, 129–38, 235–43, 347
marginalized
    faculty 150
    philosophers 37–8 n. 2 (*see also* underrepresented)
    students 33–5, 219 (*see also* disadvantaged)
mastery learning 282–8
mentor(ship) 323–30. *See also* advising
Moscarítolo Palacio, Alessandro 6, 129–38, 347
motivation 120–5, 127 n. 7, 154–6, 249–50

Nguyen, C. Thi 8, 62, 145, 255, 297–303, 347
nonideal pedagogy 49–55

O'Brien, David 7, 245–52, 347
office hours 325–8, 335. *See also* advising; mentor(ship)

participation 154, 167–71, 173–79, 217–19. *See also* assignment; discussion; grading
partnership 104–5
peer review. *See under* argument map(ping)
Perusall 124
Phillips, Heather Anne 5, 77–83, 347–8
Phillips, Kristopher G. 7, 197–207, 348
philosophy for children/P4C 161–5
playfulness 66–7, 145–52. *See also* games
positionality 85–90
power. *See under* dynamics
Prendergast, Emma 8–9, 323–31, 348
presentation 64–5, 292–4, 307–9. *See also* exam(s); project(s)
prisoner's dilemma. *See under* activity
procrastination 50–1
project(s)
    civic engagement 209–15
    final 7–8, 64–5, 290–4, 302–3, 305–10 (*see also* circus; presentation; social media)
    journal 176–7
    sample 213–14 (*see also* jigsaw lesson)
puzzle 245–52. *See also* activity

race 23–39, 106, 261–5
racism 28–9, 87–9, 103, 314–15
reading. *See under* skills
Reed, Corey 4, 23–39, 348
relativism 253–9
role-playing. *See under* games
rubric(s) 192–3, 335–6

scaffold(ing) 51–3, 124–5, 210–15
Schouten, Gina 9, 333–41, 348–9
Scott, Rebecca 6, 145–52, 259 n. 1, 349
self-assessment. *See under* assessment
sexism 28–9, 103

shout out 118. *See also* gratitude
skills
    critical thinking 80–1 (*see also* argument diagram; exams; projects)
    discussion 217–25 (*see also* assessment; grading)
    reading 14–17, 119–27 (*see also* argument diagram; assignment; texts)
    writing 212–14, 281–8 (*see also* argument diagram; assessment; feedback)
social justice 29–39
social media 291–4. *See also* project(s)
spectacle 57–68
syllabus
    de-coloniz(ing) 23–39
    design 4–5, 41–8
    diversify(ing) 14–19, 23–6, 37–8 n. 2, 87, 273–8
symbolic logic. *See logic*

table-top roleplaying games (TTRPG). *See* games
teaching statement 338–9
Team Discussion and Analysis Assignment (TDAA) 15–19. *See also* discussion; skills

text(s) 77–83; 121; 273–8. *See also* argument diagram; assignment; canon; skills; syllabus; trust
think aloud. *See under* activity
think/pair/share. *See under* activity
Torrey, John 5, 85–90, 349
transformational learning 211–14. *See also* project(s)
trust 5–6, 63–7, 111–18, 323–30

Ulrey, Anna 6, 183–5, 349
underrepresented
    philosophers 273–8 (*see also* marginalized)
    students 33–4 (*see also* disadvantaged; marginalized)
unlearn(ing) 145–7

virtue. *See under* assessment

Wallace, Meg 4, 57–68, 349
warm-calling 141–2
warm-up 164
Welch, Brynn F. 1–9, 173–81, 349–50
Williams, Micah 8, 313–19, 350
Writing. *See under* skills